THE GREAT DIVING ADVENTURE

Horace Dobbs

The Oxford Illustrated Press

© Horace E. Dobbs, 1986

Printed in England by J.H. Haynes & Co. Limited

ISBN 0 946609 314

The Oxford Illustrated Press, Sparkford, Nr Yeovil, Somerset, England

Published in North America by Haynes Publications Inc., 861 Lawrence Drive, Newbury Park, California 91320, USA.

British Library Cataloguing in Publication Data
Dobbs, Horace E.
 The great diving adventure.—
 (The Great adventure series)
 1. Diving, Submarine
 I. Title II. Series
 797.2'3'0924 GV840.S78
 ISBN 0-946609-23-3

Library of Congress Catalog Card Number
86-80183

DEDICATION

To beautiful Rebecca

Other books by Horace Dobbs

Camera Underwater, Focal Press.

Underwater Swimming, Collins (Nutshell Series).

Snorkelling and Skindiving — an Introduction, The Oxford Illustrated Press.

Follow a Wild Dolphin, Souvenir Press and Fontana/Collins.

Save the Dolphins, Souvenir Press.

Dolphin Spotters Handbook (co-authors: R.J. Harrison, D.A. McBrearty & E. Orr), International Dolphin Watch Publications.

Follow the Wild Dolphins, St. Martin's Press, New York.

The Magic of Dolphins, Lutterworth Press.

Acknowledgements

Firstly I feel I should thank my lucky stars for being in a position to write a book such as this. It would have been a completely different story if my family had not been so understanding and tolerant, and accepted me for being the increasingly restless, wandering, free spirit I am. I thank them all, especially my wife Wendy, for supporting all my endeavours.

The events described in this book have brought me into contact with an enormous number of people, all of whom have contributed to the intricate tapestry of a life which has taken me from Buckingham Palace to a Wali's house in Musandam and a thatched hut in the Philippines. After completing the manuscript I realise what an incredibly fortunate person I have been to spend time with such a wide variety of people who have influenced, directly and indirectly, how I think, how I feel and how I act. It is they who have shaped the course of my life leading to the events described in this book, for I have never had a really long-term plan, and enjoy waking up not knowing what each day has in store. There are many who will never know the role they played. But there are numerous others, not mentioned by name in the text, who I hope will now be able to identify themselves and will recognise their involvement in my chequered life and therefore the influence they have had on the unfolding story. I thank that un-named multitude most sincerely.

There are, however, four people I must select for special mention because without their direct contributions I would not have been given the opportunity to experience the moments of magic, the moments of disaster and the moments of triumph which I store like treasures in my memory, and which I have called upon for this book. They are Bruce and Hedda Lyons of Twickenham Travel, along with my son Ashley (who worked with them for a time and now runs his own holiday/travel business) who organised the travel arrangements for journeys that have taken me, and the diving groups who accompanied me, to unusual and often remote destinations around the world. That leaves Chris Goosen, co-founder of Dobbs Goosen Films, with whom I made a television series called 'Wonders of the Underwater World' which is still being shown in an ever-increasing number of countries throughout the world.

Finally, now I have completed another manuscript, I express my appreciation once again to my long-suffering, part-time secretary Kerry Davis. She accepted with a smile and her usual grace the huge pile of scraps of paper upon which I scribbled in deplorable longhand the chapters for this book and transformed them into an immaculate and respectable typescript.

H.E.D.
1 August 1985

CONTENTS

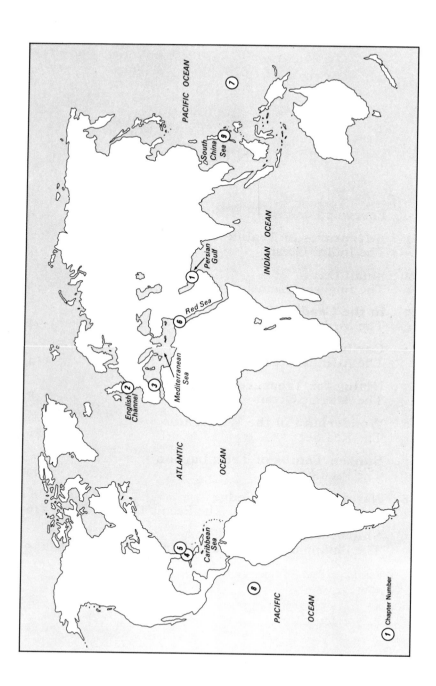

PACIFIC OCEAN

South China Sea

Persian Gulf

Red Sea

Mediterranean Sea

INDIAN OCEAN

English Channel

ATLANTIC OCEAN

Caribbean Sea

PACIFIC OCEAN

1 Chapter Number

Foreword

If anyone had said to me in the 1950s that one day I would sail on an Arab dhow out of Dubai, dive into the crystal waters of a cave in the middle of an island in the Bahamas, find a gold ring on the sea bed in the Mediterranean, explore the Great Barrier Reef, swim with sealions in the Galapagos Islands, investigate an undersea graveyard for ships in Micronesia, spend more time swimming with wild dolphins in the sea than anyone else in the world, make my own series of underwater films for television and be shipwrecked on a remote island in the Philippines, I would have suggested they had a quiet word with a friendly psychiatrist.

Yet for me all those things have now happened.

A number of people have said to me I was lucky because I took up diving when it was still in its infancy in Britain. Although I agree, I do not think that alone accounts for my success (if you can call it that) as an undersea explorer and film maker. To do what I have done all you need is a bit of luck plus a modicum of initiative backed up with what I call resolution and others call stubbornness.

I suppose I would describe myself as a realistic dreamer with a lucky streak. I dream about what I would like to do. When I do that, sooner or later an opportunity inevitably pushes itself into my life. Then I take the initiative and make it happen.

I will give you an example of how things work out for me. For some time now I have dreamed of writing a book about my diving adventures. I wanted to do so because when I write I relive in my mind the events I am describing in words. Thus I enjoy them all over again. So for me writing such a book would be a pleasant self-indulgent trip along memory lane. But apart from a handful of fiction writers all authors know that publishers do not come hammering on your door for manuscripts. So the dream rested in my mind until a short time ago when I read in *The Traveller* a review of Martyn Farr's book *The Great Caving Adventure*. That was my opportunity, because it was published by The Oxford Illustrated Press for whom I had already written a book entitled *Snorkelling & Skindiving — an Introduction* for which HRH Prince Charles kindly wrote a foreword. Although my book was out of print, I wrote to the young lady who had edited it at OIP — that was the initiative ingredient. My luck was in. When the reply came it was apparent that Jane Marshall had been elevated to the status of Editorial Director and was interested in my proposal. At a meeting with her in a pub in snow-bound Sparkford in Somerset on 10 January 1985, we discussed the synopsis I had sent her, and agreed a contract.

Now all I have to do is make it happen and that means getting down to writing 80-100,000 words. So I've started by writing this foreword.

But the writing of the book will not have to interfere with my adventuring. For although some of it will be written at home, much of it will be scribbled whilst sitting in trains, on aircraft, on cliff tops, in hotel rooms and in the cabins of boats, because I am still as nomadic as ever and looking forward to the next adventure which will inevitably befall me.

I know what I shall get from writing this book. But what, I ask myself, would a reader get for his or her investment in it?

Naturally, I hope you will enjoy, through me, the thrills of exploring the part of our planet which until recent times was as alien to humans as outer space. I hope also that I will be able to pass on to you my neverending sense of wonder at the beauty and diversity of the natural world and my concern for what can happen to it if we are not sensitive and sensible enough to preserve it for future generations to enjoy. I trust I will also be able to convey to you the idea that although one must behave responsibly, diving is fun, and like life, shouldn't be taken too seriously.

However I hope above all else that I will pass on to you the thought that if dreams can come true for me they can also come true for you . . . and that they may arise out of a catastrophe. For when I was in full-time employment in medical research ten years ago and I was called into the Medical Director's office to be told 'You are redundant', I thought at the time it was a disaster. What I did not know then, but I do now, is that he was launching me into a new life-style (I cannot call it a career) that I would not swap with anyone else in the world.

H.E.D.
North Ferriby
14 January 1985.

> Let us roll all our strength, and all
> Our sweetness, up into one ball.
> And tear our pleasures with rough strife
> Through the iron gates of life;
> Thus, though we cannot make our sun
> Stand still, yet we will make him run.

> Andrew Marvell

I

Adventures in Arabia

THE INDIAN OCEAN

In 1974, in his house off the Kings Road in Chelsea, I met a bearded, charismatic Italian, with flowing unruly hair, who was outlandishly unconventional in his clothing and his behaviour. As he transfixed me with his glittering eyes and told me tales of his exploits on board his Arab dhow, he enthralled me — even more than readings of Coleridge's *Ancient Mariner* had done when I was a schoolboy.

The name of my storyteller was Lorenzo Ricciardi. Lorenzo had a dream which started in Kenya where he had a villa on the coast and watched the dhows, or *sambuks* as they are also called, sail past. For centuries large numbers of these vessels, loaded with dates, would set out in the winter months from Iraq and Iran. They would sail in long convoys, through the Gulf and out into the Indian Ocean where the north-east trade winds would blow them to destinations as far away as Zanzibar in East Africa. Many of them finished their journeys in Mombasa in Kenya where they would remain until the winds changed direction. Then, reloaded with spices, ivory and slaves the flotillas would retrace their passages propelled by the monsoons that reached their peak in mid-summer.

When oil was discovered in the Gulf, the days of the dhows were numbered. The wooden sailing ships were gradually superseded by oil-driven, metal-hulled boats that were independent of the seasonal winds. Each year the numbers of dhows sailing the traditional route dwindled, and by the beginning of the 1970s only a handful of vessels still followed the age-old annual passage to Africa and back.

Lorenzo's dream was to own a dhow and sail with these remnants of a romantic bygone era before, like the dodo, they became extinct.

When I met him Lorenzo had already fulfilled part of his dream — he had acquired a dhow. The tales he told me of the incredible adventures he had getting as far as Dubai were as colourful as those of the Sinbads who had sailed the

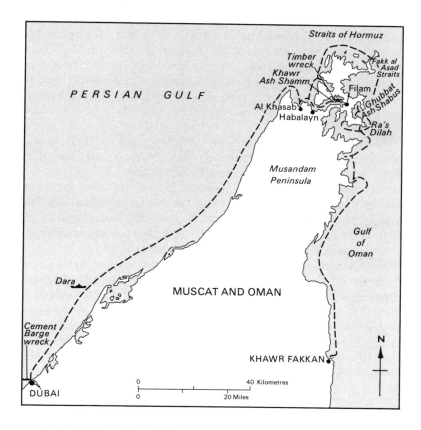

sambuks before him. Now, with his boat in Dubai, he had flown to London to for the next stage in the saga which was to sail round the mighty Musandam Peninsula at the throat of the Persian Gulf, out into the Indian Ocean, and thence onwards to Mombasa.

However, instead of just sailing through the Straits of Hormuz, Lorenzo wanted to explore the desolate fiords that

5

cut deep into the rock formations of the Musandam which stand like a gargantuan sentinel guarding the passageway into and out of the Gulf. But his plans didn't stop there. He wanted to combine sailing his dhow into this inhospitable region with his other passions — underwater hunting and fishing. Furthermore, a television film was being made of his epic voyage. Lorenzo had done some reconnaissance and had already formulated a host of ideas for possible underwater sequences for inclusion in the film. Which brings me to the reason for my presence in his house in Chelsea in January 1974 — he asked me if I would like to join the dhow in Dubai and shoot the underwater footage. But time was short. If I accepted I would have to leave in a few days.

At the time I was in full-time employment in medical and veterinary research. Fortunately for me, however, the offer came when I was due for some holiday leave. Lorenzo was a totally uncaged spirit who soared like a swallow between reality and the fantasy world of his vivid imagination. He had a roguish sense of humour; the angels were smiling on him. The dhow, he told me, was waiting for me in Dubai. There was no way I could resist his offer.

As soon as I accepted, Lorenzo had me registered in Panama as a seaman — which enabled me to obtain a cheaper air fare as a registered seaman joining his ship. A few days later, preceded by Lorenzo, I was on my way to Dubai on an adventure that was to have a very profound influence on me, changing my outlook on life thereafter.

Before I set off, however, I had a feeling that life on the dhow I was going to sail on would be somewhat different to life on an Arab dhow used purely as a trading vessel. And I was right. This became apparent shortly after I stepped into the terminal at London's Heathrow airport where I had been told I would meet a Frenchman and his companion.

Heathrow was crowded, as Heathrow always seems to be crowded, but I recognised the people I was looking for in an instant by their baggage which consisted of diving holdalls lashed to which were a slalom water ski and an armoury of spearguns.

The baggage was accompanied by a man with a face that

could only be French. It was a face chiselled out of light brown stone capped with a mass of tousled black hair. His name was Bob Zagury. Two of the few facts I was later able to find out about Bob were that he had directed films and that one of his previous girlfriends had been Brigitte Bardot.

His taste in female companions had not faltered, for beside him stood a very tall girl of exquisite proportions. Golden hair hanging down to her shoulders framed an open face of clear white skin tanned to a gentle amber. Cathie Sherrif, a beautiful model, was also an accomplished skin diver.

At 7.45 pm we were jet-lifted out of a black February evening and carried south-east. Some people find plane travel boring. I have always enjoyed it. That night I looked down as we passed over Kent and saw towns with illuminated roads radiating from their centres like the delicate legs of fairylight brittle starfish. I gazed into the clear night sky and pondered on the wonders of outer space and tried to relate it to the vast liquid space of the oceans. Down below people were going to bed and making love. I was floating four miles above them, encapsulated in a silver tube with wings. I dozed a little when the lights of the aircraft were dimmed. A few hours later I looked down and saw great orange-yellow flames leaping out of the black ground below. We were flying over the desert. The flames were of burning gas venting from one of the world's biggest natural fuel bunkers.

We landed at Bahrain and through the window I saw for the first time one of the low multi-arched buildings that characterise Arab grand architecture. It was still dark. The new illuminated airport building was like a palace, built not for a sheik, but for the new nomads of the world — the air travellers.

Our stop was short. As we climbed into the sky again a pale line started to rise from the horizon. The sensitive light of a new day was gradually spreading across the desert.

The sun had risen by the time we reached Dubai. I looked down onto a grey-yellow landscape dotted with rectangular houses and brown-green palm trees. The sea was yellow-blue. It did not look clear. Much to my surprise there were numerous puddles in the compacted sand alongside the runway.

We were met by a smiling Lorenzo, in a khaki coat, who oiled our way through customs with the minimum of arm waving. We piled our enormous heap of baggage into a taxi that had red fur covering the dashboard and oriental music blaring from the car radio. As we drove off, Lorenzo described a recent storm which had nearly caused him to send a cable cancelling the trip. We stopped to collect a strut for the diving ladder from a blacksmith and proceeded towards the waterfront. Five minutes later we clambered out of the taxi. A haggle ensued over the payment for the extra baggage with Lorenzo getting the better of the taxi driver who stormed off in a huff.

As we stood looking at the dhow which lay heeled over in very shallow water just a few yards off shore, we were spotted by the two black Kenyans on board. They rushed ashore to greet Lorenzo whom they were obviously delighted to see. They also welcomed Bob warmly — greeting him with broad ivory grins — although one had only a three-quarter smile as he had lost a tooth.

Still dressed in the suit I had worn to a business meeting in London prior to departure, I paddled through a few inches of water and swung up a rope ladder hanging down past the freshly varnished hull. The deck was at a steep angle as the boat had been careened and was resting on the sea bed. I slithered on the caulking and tallow on the inclined deck and was quickly informed that bare feet were the order of the day if I wished to remain upright. Jobs were immediately allocated in order that we could dive the next day. Cathie cleaned languidly. Bob went off to find the missing part for the compressor and I checked the diving gear. The dhow slowly started to right itself as the tide rose.

Gradually the day warmed to the gentle heat of a sunny day early in an English summer. As it did so the activity in the port increased, for we were on the edge of a fleet of trading dhows which was busy with a continuous flow of people and goods.

The name of our *sambuk* was the *Mir-el-lah* — a romanticised Arabic version of Lorenzo's wife's name

8

Mirella. She and their daughter Marina were due to arrive the following evening. As soon as they did so we planned to set sail for the Musandam Peninsula. In the meantime there was much to be done.

At high water, by dint of much heaving on a line anchored in deeper water, we managed to pull the dhow free of the bottom. While we were doing this, Lorenzo rushed hither and thither, frequently consulting a book containing addresses and telephone numbers. One problem that had to be resolved was that of a crew. Lorenzo consulted his book and an hour after telephoning one of his contacts, a boat arrived alongside with two Indian sailors. They leapt aboard the *Mir-el-lah* and a one day trial period was mutually agreed.

One of the subjects that Lorenzo had described in vivid detail when we met in London was a dive he had made on the wreck of the *Dara* that lay about twenty miles north along the coast from Dubai. Lorenzo explained how a large number of huge fish traps, constructed like open-work wicker and wire igloos, had become hooked into the wreckage of the vessel. The Arab fishermen were unable to retrieve them. Fish swam into them and remained trapped. When the trapped fish became weak they attracted more fish — which in turn became prisoners. Consequently the pots were permanently filled with fish until the traps decayed, or were broken-up in a storm. He said he had never seen such an intense concentration of fish in one place. Lorenzo wanted me to film him swimming amongst the wreckage and examining the traps. In one of the final sequences he wanted to open one of the cages and watch the fish swim away to freedom. We had just one day in which to complete the project, for by the following evening we had to be back in Dubai to pick up Lorenzo's family and another passenger — Roberto.

Having made our plans Lorenzo rushed off to invite another of his inexhaustible supply of friends and contacts to join us on the trip to the *Dara*. This particular acquaintance worked with the international diving company of Comex. He was French and his name was Jean Pierre.

At eight o'clock the next morning Jean Pierre stood on the

9

quayside — immediately recognisable by the coupled twin yellow aqualung cylinders standing on their rubber bases beside him. He was the epitome of the dapper French sporting gentleman. He wore a nautical cap and his fashionable flared jeans were immaculately creased. He had short black hair and his eyes smiled behind silver-framed, pebble glasses; he spoke good English.

With Jean Pierre and his diving equipment safely installed in the *sambuk* we set sail for the *Dara*. Several times during the outward journey I peered into the water that was scurrying past our hull. It did not have the quality that I associated with the good clarity essential for the success of our filming mission. I was concerned that conditions on the *Dara* would not be good. But I kept the thoughts to myself in the hope that I would be proved wrong.

The *Dara* lay about a mile from the shore and as it was a hazard to shipping, a buoy had been placed seaward of the wreck. Thus approaching ships steamed seaward of the buoy and thereby avoided hitting the wreck.

After we had been cruising for about $2^1/2$ hours the black spike of the buoy broke the line of the horizon formed between the flat deep blue sea and the pale blue cloudless sky. A thousand feet starboard of the buoy was a scattering of polystyrene floats indicating exactly the scene described to me by Lorenzo at our first meeting in London. Bob, Lorenzo and Jean Pierre — fully kitted in wetsuits — set off in one of the inflatables to locate the best diving site.

The dhow wallowed in the swell and for an hour Cathie and I watched the inflatable moving amongst the fishing boats also assembled on the site. From a long way off we saw the black figure of Bob, complete with aqualung, topple backwards into the water. Diving had begun. Ten minutes later his head reappeared, like that of a seal, on the surface. After a further delay the Zodiac planed across the sea and came to an abrupt stop alongside the dhow. We leaned over the gunwale and looked down on three disappointed faces. I realised immediately that my misgivings concerning the underwater visibility had some foundation. Bob had pulled himself down one of the float lines and could not see the end of his speargun at a depth of 65 feet. His demand valve was leaking badly and he had to drink a lot of the water flooding into his mouth. They had not been able to locate the wreck. Photography was out of the question.

I had tossed my fins and mask into the Zodiac inflatable when Lorenzo said he would have another go at locating the wreck by trawling with an anchor. We motored out to the floats, put the grapnel anchor on twenty feet of line and began to trawl. Within ten minutes the anchor snagged. We cut the engine. A strong current was running and the inflatable was immediately swung into the line of flow of the water. The anchor rope was taut and snatched at the Zodiac with the passage of each small wave.

I put on my mask and fins, slid overboard, and pulled myself down the line. In the milky water I discerned the metal structure of the wreck and a few small fish before bursting back to the surface completely out of breath. The visibility was less than three feet. We were definitely on the wreck but the previous judgement that photography would be hopeless was right. Nevertheless, I decided to have a look round and put on the aqualung that Bob had used previously. Jean Pierre and I rolled backwards into the sea from opposite sides of the inflatable. Jean Pierre reached the anchor rope first and disappeared beneath me.

I wondered about the problems of sharks in such waters as I hung on to the anchor rope to prevent myself from being swept away. Water flooded into my mouth as the tubes from my twin hose regulator oscillated in the strong current. The metal corpse of the wreck loomed out of the bright milky luminescence that surrounded me. I clung to a metal strut and tried to clear the tubes of water, but each time I did so more water flooded in. The sea that trickled into my wetsuit reached my fresh vaccination blister and it started to sting. Jean Pierre was nowhere to be seen — nor were his bubbles.

This certainly was not the ideal diving I had been hoping for, the visibility was extremely poor. I was in shark-infested waters, the tide was running so fast over the wreck that I certainly could not swim against it; I couldn't see my partner, and to cap it all I was getting a mouthful of water every time I inhaled. The common sense thing to do was wash out. So I spluttered back to the surface and dejectedly climbed into the inflatable.

The surface of the sea was regularly disturbed by a burst of bubbles from Jean Pierre who was somewhere in the wreckage. Twenty yards away two manta rays leapt out of the water; I momentarily glimpsed the tips of their wings curled upwards and inwards like wrought iron scrolls. At last Jean Pierre surfaced; he had been trying unsuccessfully to remove a porthole as a souvenir from the wreck. We skimmed back towards the waiting dhow and a huge turtle poked its head out of the water. We swung round for a closer look but it dived quickly out of sight into the opalescent sea. Could I really hope that conditions would be vastly improved round Muscat and Oman? I just did not know what to expect.

The prospects for our proposed film diminished further when we arrived back in Dubai to learn that Lorenzo's wife Mirella and his daughter Marina had not arrived on their scheduled flight. As we could not start the trip without them, we would have to wait.

We spent the night in Dubai in the very heart of the world of the dhows and the dhow people. I awoke early the following morning to find that we were moored alongside another dhow, about the same size as the *Mir-el-lah*. Our neighbour was carrying a cargo of bamboo matting that solidly filled the entire vessel from the keel to just above the side rails. The crew lived their lives entirely upon the top of a springy mattress, which was ten feet thick and composed of layer upon layer of woven bamboo matting. Merely by standing on the deck of our *sambuk* I was able to witness life aboard a dhow as if it were enacted on a stage — for there was absolutely nowhere below where the sailors could hide.

When I first walked on deck the men were all asleep under blankets. As the sun rose they stirred and the cook started to prepare a meal in a tiny cupboard-like structure containing a fire of brushwood in front of which he squatted on his haunches. He spent thirty minutes slowly repairing the pottery base of a broken hookah pipe with a lashing of wet rope. Having got the base airtight — an essential operation if the smoke from the tin pot on the top is to be sucked through the water — he had a quiet puff before the rest of the crew joined him for their 'early morning switch-on' as Cathie called the ritual smoke.

There were about ten crew members in all and they sat in a circle smoking the hookah. I started filming from our dhow. As they did not object, and indeed they seemed to be as curious about us as I was about them, I gradually moved in closer until I was photographing them in close-up in both still and cine. They were very cheerful and friendly. Each face was completely different; a mixture of Arab, Indian and African. I was invited to join them for a glass of tea that was clear yellow and extremely sweet. We exchanged messages in sign language (which comes easy to a diver) as they could speak no English and the only Arabic I could muster was 'Salaam alegra' which I understood to be a friendly greeting.

I was so enthralled and captivated by my new surroundings that the disappointments of the previous day faded, and I was further cheered by the arrival of Mirella and Marina who suddenly presented themselves, bubbling with gaiety, on the quay. They had caught a later plane and had spent the night at the house of my diving partner Jean Pierre. Roberto, another friend of Lorenzo, also turned up. Now our human cargo was complete. Whoopee! We could leave as soon as we had taken on provisions and obtained the necessary official clearances.

The two sailors on probation, who had proved themselves to be competent seamen on our brief excursion to the *Dara* the previous day, decided that they did not wish to come on the rest of the trip. Amidst all the other negotiations Lorenzo had to recruit two replacements, and so he took on two of the stateless people who drift like flotsam along the waterfront at Dubai. Tolerated because they provide a cheap labour force, each one knowing that they can be deported at any time, they work for minute wages. The two we hired came aboard carrying their lives in plastic bags. They were disliked by almost everyone, including the two black Kenyans on board our dhow. Our two recruits were Pakistanis. We did not have time to give them a trial and were to find out later that their qualifications for the title of sailor were nil — neither of them could even row a boat.

At the end of a day when all on board bent their backs to the enormous number of tasks essential for our onward journey, we adjourned to Jean Pierre's beautiful home on the edge of the desert. And there, in simple and extraordinarily elegant fashion, his wife Françoise cooked and served an impeccable Chinese meal. Half-way through the main course, Lorenzo began to shiver and went to bed. Mirella said it was malaria and it would be several days before Lorenzo would be fit enough to take the dhow to sea. However, the food and wine dulled our disappointment and enhanced the camaraderie that was developing between us; despite the setback we decided to enjoy ourselves. In a short time our spirits were restored and we were again engrossed in multi-lingual discussions ranging from the effect of the Watergate scandal on America, to the Pope and the pill.

An hour after his retirement Lorenzo silently and somewhat shakily reappeared. To an incredulous company he declared that we would set sail immediately.

It was as if he had set light to a box of fireworks. Mirella, Cathie and Françoise burst into a vivid and violent display of verbal sparks to illuminate the utter stupidity of the decision. Bob, dreaming of giant fish lurking in deep caves just waiting to be speared, supported Lorenzo. Roberto and I agreed that as Lorenzo was Captain, it was his decision. Mirella held both hands in the air as if calling on the Almighty for support — and then swept them downwards and outwards, with the fingers outstretched and flared, in a final appeal to his sanity. But to no avail. The fireworks went out as quickly as they had begun. There was no simmering hostility. The matter was settled. Lorenzo was quite mad. But we were going.

Within a few moments we were driving past the gaudy neon-lit cinemas of Dubai to the waterfront. We set sail at one o'clock in the morning.

The following days unfolded like the acts of a play. At the end of each day, often when I was absolutely exhausted, I would write up my diary and this forms the basis of the following account of our expedition. To reduce confusion I have listed the characters at random, neither in order of appearance nor importance, but just as they came into my head.

CAST

Mir-el-lah The dhow. It is like a gypsy caravan that follows sea routes instead of the roads. It has a broad stern that slopes backwards over the sea and has a slight resemblance to the elaborate superstructure of a Spanish galleon. It is not a lovely boat but it is loveable.

Lorenzo The Italian owner of the dhow.

Mirella Lorenzo's wife. Born of French and Italian parents she considers herself Afro-Franco-Italian. Traveller, photographer and author of the book *Vanishing Africa* in which she vividly portrays life in the wilds of Africa.

Kimuyu Black African from the Macamba tribe. A delightfully quiet and modest man who speaks no English. He is the ship's cook.

Matheka A Kenyan also from the Macamba tribe. An apparently self-assured man who speaks English and has been trained in marine engineering. He is Lorenzo's willing handyman and acts as the dhow's engineer.

Rani One of the Pakistanis we picked up as crew in Dubai. He speaks English — Peter Sellers' style.

Rangi The other Pakistani crew member. He does not speak English.

Roberto A charming quiet international businessman from an Italian family famous for its interests in the wine trade.

Bob A French-Moroccan businessman from Paris.

Cathie Canadian-born model whose assignments have taken her to many parts of the world.

Marina Thirteen-year-old daughter of Lorenzo and Mirella. At school in England which has given her a slightly 'cut glass' English accent.

15

Our metaphorical play opens aboard the *Mir-el-lah* as she sets out on a journey to explore the sea that has eaten into the massive rocky region that forms the Musandam Peninsula of Muscat and Oman. It is pitch dark. The sky is speckled with stars. The engine throbs. Everyone has gone to bed. Lorenzo and I are alone on the deck. Lorenzo holds the wheel. He looks tired but says he is O.K. I offer to take the next watch. Lorenzo agrees but I feel he does not expect me to.

I went to bed at 2.00 am and got up again at 5.00 am to find Rani at the wheel and Lorenzo standing on the starboard deck, binoculars hanging round his neck. He was peering into the blackness ahead. We plotted our course on the chart and Lorenzo went below for some sleep. I set a north-east course, 45° on the compass and stood on the deck, five paces away from the wheel checking the lights on the shore through the binoculars. I let the glasses hang loosely round my neck and absorbed the scene; this is how I recorded it in my diary:

'The stars are brilliant specks in the inky velvet night sky. The north star hangs over our starboard quarter. The lights on the coast move by, very, very slowly. Engine throbbing. Sensational feeling of being alone in the world. We pass the *Dara* buoy and move into the endless night and the sea. Another dhow, with no lights showing, slips swiftly by on our port bow. Why is she carrying no lights? Is she a smuggler? Everything on the deck is saturated with dew. Cartons everywhere. The new refrigerator I wired up last night is making its first ice cubes. Rangi seems to have mastered the steering, but I check the compass course regularly with my torch.

'A pale light creeps across the horizon as dawn breaks. I am cold and wet with the dew and go below to get a sweater. I am away for no more than two minutes, but in that time the steersman has completely lost his confidence and we are 180° off course when I check the compass. I take the wheel and tell Rangi to get some sleep. He understands and lies on the deck just behind me covered in a blanket.

'The stars fade like magic as the sky becomes pale blue. The huge dark mass of the Musandam Peninsula solidifies on our starboard bow. Standing alone at the wheel I feel supremely happy. It is not the feeling of outside joy that comes from scoring the winning goal; it comes from inside like a subterranean spring and floods in every corner of my body. It is the joy of aloneness. It is a joy that comes of having confidence in myself and it is a joy I keep to myself. With Marina fast asleep on the bunk that spans the stern of the dhow and the Pakistani shrouded in a blanket with just his black head showing, I steer the gently throbbing boat into the dawn. In the rising light I look over my shoulder at our wake. It is arrow straight.

'All of a sudden the ship comes to life. Marina wakes first.

"Hello Nelson," she says in her precise voice.

Kimuyu appears next and soon presents me with a welcome cup of tea. Within minutes the deck is buzzing with activity. I am still enjoying the pleasure of controlling the dhow from the wheel, but the moment of pure magic has passed. The sun-warmed air dissolves the dew. At nine o'clock I ask Bob to take the wheel and yawning, I go below for a brief reviving sleep.'

When I next came up on deck I looked over the side and saw a sea snake twisting its way sinuously through the water. The sea was deep grey-green in colour which indicated that the underwater visibility was poor. We were close to shore and the land mass, volcanic and dun-brown, thrust itself out of the sea.

In mid-afternoon we entered one of the fiords that cut into the tortured rocks. At the far end of the inlet was the tiny village of Al Khasab. We anchored the *Mir-el-lah* in the bay and Matheka took us almost to the water's edge in one of the inflatables. We waded the last few feet to the black sandy beach. Just above the high water line was a collection of tiny, primitive, stone box houses — but no signs of their occupants. We made our way along the beach towards a fort that looked as if it was stage scenery from *The Desert Song* except that it was garrisoned, not by singing actors, but by Arab soldiers armed with rifles and garlanded with belts of live bullets. We ambled into the forecourt, our motley group no doubt looking stranger to the Arabs than they did to us. One collection of men, squatting in a circle on the dusty ground, were noisily engaged in a game that looked like five-stones. Others propped themselves against the walls of the garrison like rolls of carpet — not moving — but eyeing us suspiciously. We said nothing to them and they said nothing to us.

Our presence had not gone unobserved by the Wali of the Sultan of Muscat who resided in the fort. We were invited to tea at the Sheikh's house which was about a mile away from the shore. As I walked up a wadi I saw a few small bundles of black cloth, almost pyramidal in shape, moving between stone hovels set amongst the date palms. They were women of the desert, completely shielded from view, peering into the world through slits in black masks. I felt as if I had slipped back centuries in time.

We removed our shoes as we entered the Wali's house and were led into a large bare room where we were introduced to a dignified man who bade us be seated. There were several other men seated around the edge of the room. Then one of the first pairs of female Arab legs I had seen toddled into the room. They belonged to the Wali's delightful two-year-old daughter who crossed the room, sat on her father's lap and cuddled up to him, peeping at us intermittently with her large brown eyes. Heavy circular gold earrings hung from her pierced ears. She was the only female Arab in the room.

The Wali was proud of his children and he introduced us formally to a slender boy, about ten years old, who ceremoniously served coffee. He carried a tray bearing a silver coffee pot and four small cups. He slowly circled the room, filling the cups and giving them out. Each person took a few sips and handed the cup back to the boy who refilled it and handed it to the next person on the circuit. The boy performed his duty with dignity whilst the Wali engaged us in conversation. There were a thousand questions I would have liked to have asked, and I could tell that Mirella also wished to stay longer, but Lorenzo was anxious to continue our journey.

That night, as we lay anchored in a flat calm bay buried in the mountains, from out of nowhere came a single Arab fisherman. He rowed alongside and we welcomed him aboard. Without saying a word he knelt on the deck and remained there for fifteen minutes, his head bowed in silent prayer. As he prayed I looked over the side at his small craft, lying quietly alongside; there appeared to be no metal in it at all. On the duckboards lay a few small fish; the fisherman and his boat were like biblical characters.

We invited the fisherman to join us for our evening meal and he accepted. After the meal Bob and the Arab had an ardent conversation, liberally spiced with gestures, about fishing and before he left Bob arranged to see him again the following morning.

Later, when everyone was asleep, I went up on deck and savoured the night. Silence hung over the scene like an eiderdown. The boat was absolutely still. The enormous rocks all around looked like walls of coal joined by a jagged line to the navy-blue sky. The water was liquid jet. The majesty, beauty, peace and silence of that first night on the Musandam Peninsula I shall never forget; on the chart it is marked as Khawr Ash Shamm.

Early next morning our Arab fisherman appeared as arranged. We lowered one of the inflatables into the water and set off with our guide on a voyage of reconnaissance. Bob was looking for a place where he might find some big fish; Lorenzo and I were looking for a location that would provide some good film material. The water was green in colour indicating the presence of phyto-plankton. This was the cause of some concern to me because a concentration of plankton sufficient to give the water a distinct green colour would reduce the underwater visibility and I would be unable to get the spectacular shots of scenery I was hoping for. As I looked down into the turbid green water a magnificent leopard ray winged its way three feet under the boat — the slow powerful beats of its fins in some ways resembling the flight of a swan. The sunlight, refracted from the waves above, produced a pattern of light that briefly danced across its broad body with its characteristic light spots. It was a majestic, handsome fish. I was itching to go overboard.

After a thirty-minute run we returned to the dhow, hoisted our two anchors, and with Roberto at the wheel we went slowly ahead along the fiord. We decided to make our first dive off a small island which looked as if it had been used for military purposes during the Second World War for it had a number of derelict reinforced buildings on it.

Bob and Cathie quickly donned their wetsuits and disappeared with the Arab fisherman in one inflatable. Lorenzo and I set off in the other to investigate the sea bed closer inshore. Having been deprived of our film on the *Dara* the underwater camera was still loaded and Lorenzo was anxious to see if we could find an alternative wreck; he hoped to find the remains of an old dhow. I thought the chances of finding such a wreck were hundreds to one against but I refrained from voicing my opinion.

We dropped over the side into twenty feet of water onto an area of white sand scattered with broken staghorn coral. The light intensity was very bright with a visibility of about thirty feet. Here and there were small outcrops of living coral interspaced with larger masses of dead coral. There were few fish about. Those that were, were small. If there is not much life to be seen over a coral reef, then the place to look for it is under the stands of coral. I sank onto the seabed and started to peer into the shadows.

My first encounter was with a medium-size moray eel. It had an evil-looking face. The moray eel adopts two alternative and opposite attitudes to the approach of a diver. One, which is annoying if you are after pictures, is to slither slowly backwards into the dark recess of its lair and disappear completely. The other reaction, which is more intimidating, is to come towards the diver with its mouth open, revealing an ugly set of teeth. My moray adopted the latter tactic. As it advanced towards me it left the dark shadow beneath the coral and emerged into bright sunlight. As I watched it through the view-finder of the camera I observed that the eel had a dark brown head. Immediately behind the head the colour changed abruptly to a greenish-yellow. It slithered towards me with its mouth open, as deliberately and menacingly as a hissing snake. Six inches from the front of the camera it stopped its advance. I shot my film, backed quietly away and continued my hunt for more subjects.

I looked around for Lorenzo and he waved me over excitedly. He had spotted a lobster and wanted it for the cooking pot. He hurried up to the surface and Matheka handed him a small speargun. Within a few minutes he was back down with me. I had filmed the lobster's antennae protruding from the coral and waited for Lorenzo to go into the attack. He pointed the spear into the hole and fired just as I started to shoot film. Clouds of sand emerged from the hole as if the lobster was putting up a good fight. Lorenzo pulled on the cord and withdrew the shiny metal spear — but there was no lobster on the end. I had filmed the entire sequence. That was one shot that would end up in the waste bin at the editing stage. However, Allah had willed that Lorenzo should have the lobster and after the next shot the ill-fated lobster was dragged protesting from its home by a triumphant Lorenzo — whilst I was rewinding the camera.

When two and a half minutes of film had run through the camera and it was time to change rolls, I continued to peer under the corals out of interest, but my impression of the site was that it was poor from a filming viewpoint and so when my air supply ran low I returned to the Zodiac inflatable.

Lorenzo stayed in the water with Matheka in the Zodiac following his bubbles and collecting the lobsters that were brought to the surface. Despite the fact that I had worn a full wetsuit, my hour in the water had chilled me and I was happy to sit in the boat and let the sun restore my lost warmth as we idly followed Lorenzo to a new area where there was a large outcrop of rocks extending from the shore. From its colour the water appeared to be deeper. I was happily daydreaming when Lorenzo suddenly surfaced. Matheka had the inflatable beside him in seconds.

'I've found a dhow. Man I've found a dhow!' he cried

triumphantly. . . . I couldn't believe it.

Back on board the *Mir-el-lah* Lorenzo explained that he had found what appeared to be the keel of an old dhow in a gully between the rocks. We agreed that it would make a good sequence in our film of the dhows, and decided to attempt to raise it. I located a small, home-made lifting bag I had brought from England. Lorenzo went below decks and emerged with a huge commercial lifting bag made by Technisub. We were in the salvage business.

Bob and Cathie returned with their Arab guide; they had not seen any big fish.

They said farewell to their lonely Arab fisherman friend and watched him row away into the distance and then disappear into the hazy heat of the mid-afternoon sun. Where he came from and how he lived we did not know. We never saw him again.

The camera was reloaded with film and after a brief lunch, during which we recharged the air cylinders, we were ready for action again. Clutching the camera tightly in one hand, and holding loosely onto the anchor line with the other, I exhaled and allowed gravity to pull me gently, feet first, towards the sea bed. My ears, which are invariably slow to clear, were slightly painful, but not excessively so. I made periodic pauses until the pain eased indicating that it was safe to continue my descent.

I found the anchor in about thirty feet of water. As it was to be a reference point for our diving operations I jammed it firmly into a crevice in the rocks and set off to locate the wreckage. Lorenzo had described its location with his usual detailed precision and I found it without difficulty. It was lying in the bottom of a gully and was the home territory of three Moorish idols; the delicate elongated tips of their dorsal fins trailed like bunting as they unhurriedly twisted and turned, suspended over the large piece of timber.

I swam gently along the length of the valley in the rocks trying not to disturb the silt that swirled up when I swam near the bottom. It certainly was quite an impressive piece of wreckage, apparently composed of solid wood with some heavily encrusted metal bolts projecting through it. Nearby I found a smaller piece of wreckage, also with a metal bolt through it. I surfaced and after a brief conference with Lorenzo we decided to lift the smaller baulk of timber with my mini lifting bag as a practice run.

I filmed the entire sequence and all went smoothly. It was time to try the big lift.

The large pieces of wreckage lay at a depth of about twenty-five feet and I filmed an establishing tracking shot in which I swam along the length of the timber with the camera running. As I filmed the sequence to establish the location for the subsequent lifting shots the Moorish idols drifted delightfully across my field of view. Filming prospects were looking up.

Having completed the first of the shots Lorenzo and I had agreed during our pre-dive plan, I waited patiently for him to appear on our film set. It seemed an age before he did so and I started to shiver. At last down through the blue-green light came the figure of a diver towing behind him the large lifting bag. He held it by the top and it trailed through the water in the slight current like a heavy canvas sail. He descended to the timber we were about to raise and disturbed silt swirled in a cloud about him. He unravelled the hitching rope and managed to tie it to one of the bolts conveniently protruding from the wreckage. This operation took much longer than it would have done on land. Above water a rope stays where you put it. Under water as you untangle one knot the rope has a habit of floating away and twisting itself into further tangles.

Having secured the buoyancy bag and put a small quantity of air into it from his mouthpiece, Lorenzo returned to the surface to collect another air cylinder from the inflatable that was being manned by Roberto. Lorenzo soon returned, inserted the valve of the cylinder into the neck of the buoyancy bag and opened the stopcock. The rising air, trapped inside the bag, displaced the water and as the bag rose it expanded into the shape of a hot air balloon. The pull on the rope attaching the bag to the huge baulk of wreckage was enormous. Little did I know that the baulk of timber lying innocently on the sea bed was shortly to cost me very dearly in terms of personal distress. And two days later it could have cost the lives of all aboard the *Mir-el-lah.*

This disastrous chain of events started when, after Lorenzo had swum back to the surface, I swam back to the lifting bag. How much more buoyancy would we need to lift the wreckage I wondered? I splayed my legs and put one foot on each side of the gully in which the beam was jammed. Holding on to the cine camera with my left hand I grabbed the rope attached to the lifting bag with my right hand and gently heaved on it to see if the wreckage would budge. To my consternation the extra pull I applied was sufficient to raise the timber. And it did not sink back down again when I released the rope, for the bag had risen in the water and the air trapped inside had expanded sufficiently to give the extra buoyancy necessary to counterbalance the weight of the keel. Once the bag had gone past that equilibrium point nothing could have stopped it continuing its journey to the surface. The air, trapped inside the partially full buoyancy bag, continued to expand as it rose higher in the water, giving more and more buoyancy.

I chased up to the surface only to discover that I and the bag, although only a few yards from the inflatable, were being carried away from it in the current. I dived, grasped the rope and desperately tried to tow the balloon with its heavy cargo towards the boat. But to no avail. I could make no progress against the current.

Lorenzo was blazing with rage in true Latin, uninhibited style as I climbed aboard and he started the outboard. We moved forward and then stopped; we tried tugging at the anchor rope from all directions but it was hopeless — the anchor I had carefully jammed in the rocks stayed where it was — thirty feet below. Whilst this was going on our prize was drifting away from us. When it reached the end of the island we saw it pick up speed as it became caught in the strong current that was running round the headland. By now, my embarrassment was acute.

The sound of strange voices distracted Lorenzo. We followed the sound, and round the headland appeared two Arab fishing boats with six oarsmen in each, making straight for our balloon which was by now drifting into the channel between the island and the coast several miles away. The prospect of having his prize pirated electrified Lorenzo.

Standing up in the inflatable and waving his arms he screamed, 'No! No!' at the top of his voice. Fortunately the Arabs interpreted his message correctly, eased up their rowing and veered away from our floating treasure. Temporary peace was restored.

I realised that if we did not soon recover both the balloon and the keel suspended from it, the chances were high that we would lose them both, and so I offered to go down and free the anchor. Throwing on my aqualung, I dropped over the side and pulled myself as rapidly as I could hand over hand down the taut anchor line until I could see the anchor ten feet below me. Then — BANG! It was if somebody had fired a gun in my head.

I knew immediately what had happened. I had burst an eardrum. I instantly recalled that this was likely to cause vertigo and so I clung tightly to the rope, shut my eyes and waited for the world to spin round. But it didn't. I felt no pain. Instead I could feel a trickle of cold water inside my head. It stopped. When nothing happened I continued downwards to free the anchor. That accomplished, I hung onto it and Roberto pulled me to the surface. Back aboard the inflatable, I mentioned my burst eardrum to Lorenzo, but as there was nothing we could do about it, we set about recovering our lost wreckage.

With the powerful outboard at full throttle we planed effortlessly over to the white blob that had turned golden in the setting sun. But luck was still against us for as we trailed the newly recovered anchor under the lifting bag we snagged one of the ropes. With the engine at full power we could just make headway diagonally against the current with the inflatable veering madly from side to side; the stresses on the bag must have been colossal.

It soon became obvious that it would be impossible to tow the buoy and the wreckage to its original site and so we decided instead to trail it into the lee of the island and leave it grounded on a sandy bed about ten feet down where we could recover it easily.

Whilst depositing our recovered trophy we were joined by Bob and Cathie in the other inflatable, with Matheka at the helm. Bob dived and unhitched the lifting bag, leaving a small marker buoy in its place, ready for us the next day. It was almost dark by the time we got back to the *Mir-el-lah*.

A perforated eardrum is not usually a serious condition, unless it becomes infected. The tympanum heals spontaneously if it is kept dry and is not subjected to pressure stresses and so, to a diver, this means staying out of the water for a minimum of two weeks. Deafness results if the eardrum does not mend itself.

An air of gloom settled on the *Mir-el-lah*. One of the major objectives of the expedition was to make an underwater film. I was the only cameraman on board and I would not be able to dive for the remainder of the voyage; there were only ten days left.

Lorenzo's anger at the keel episode quickly subsided and was replaced by concern for the film, and then, more importantly, for my health. When my ear started to ache I was given the last remaining glass of whisky on board, and when it started to discharge profusely, I took some antibiotic tablets as prophylaxis against infection.

After our meal the pain in my ear became unbearable. I was utterly miserable — not so much because of the pain itself — but what it represented. Here I was enjoying a diving opportunity of a lifetime and it had been smashed to smithereens by my stupidity. I tried to tell myself that such as accident could happen to anyone, that in the excitement of the moment I had just not felt the signs that should have warned me that I was diving too fast. But I hadn't felt the signs and I had burst my eardrum. That was the fact of the matter and my diving on this trip was finished.

I hated myself and the sympathy everyone so openly showed.

I took two Codis tablets, which rapidly muted the pain, retired to my bunk and thankfully fell into a deep sleep. I was told the next day that during the night Cathie and Mirella, who were both extremely concerned about my condition, visited me to make sure I was all right and although I dismissed their sympathy, almost with brusqueness, inside I felt quite moved that they should be so concerned.

At 8.00 am an inflatable bearing Lorenzo and Roberto

came roaring across the calm water towards the *Mir-el-lah*. They had been after big kingfish but had not had a single bite. They left the inflatable tied alongside and after a hasty breakfast Lorenzo zoomed round the headland to where we had deposited the ill-fated piece of wreckage. He quickly returned with the news that the tide had dropped exposing a large number of beautiful corals surrounded by clear blue sea. We decided to take the dhow round the headland and attempt to raise the wreckage.

Bob and Cathie joined in the operation and worked from the inflatable. Bob dived and attached a heavy hawser to the sunken keel but the hawser was not long enough to reach the dhow. The obvious answer was to take the *Mir-el-lah* closer in to the shore but the area was bristling with coral heads and Lorenzo was afraid of holing her. At this point Lorenzo wanted to give up the entire project — but I protested. I was not to be cheated of a prize that had cost me so dear.

Having decided that we could not get in close enough to do a straight lift over the side of the dhow, I suggested we took the *Mir-el-lah* in to the shore bows first. Lorenzo, in a nervous state nosed the dhow slowly forward. We attached the hawser to our anchor rope and then put the dhow into reverse. The keel, one end of which was secured to the hawser, slowly trailed out along a sandy gully into deeper water where the *Mir-el-lah* was safe.

Once he knew his boat was safe Lorenzo relaxed and every man aboard gave a hand at heaving the huge water-logged timber out of the water. When at last it thumped onto the deck I was able to examine it in detail. I discovered it consisted of several large pieces of teak bolted together and was heavily encrusted with very large barnacles. As soon as I had filmed it being raised Bob wanted to throw it back overboard — and in the light of later events it would have been better if we had done so. But I had another idea. I pointed to the barren rocks all around us.

'Tell me, where do you see any trees?' I asked.

As there was no vegetation to be seen anywhere Bob had to agree that he couldn't see any trees.

'Yet wood is an essential ingredient of life in these parts is it not?' I continued. 'So it must be valuable. We will barter it with some fishermen and it will make a good sequence in the film.'

Bob conceded the point reluctantly, warning us that the sharp barnacles on the pieces of teak would puncture the inflatables if we were not careful. As maintenance of the inflatables and the compressor were his responsibility, I sympathised with his view and countered his argument by saying that we could stow the boats on one side of the dhow and my smelly piece of wreckage on the other.

Lorenzo wasn't too happy about my idea of bartering the wood either, but agreed it could stay. As always he was anxious to move on, so we hauled the inflatables aboard, lashed them down, and set sail on a route that was to take us deeper into the heart of the mountains. In my diary I wrote:

'We are sailing into the most spectacular seascape I have ever encountered. It is like the Grand Canyon flooded one third of the way up. Striated rocks climb out of a blue ink sea. Cliffs tower all around. This place has a very humbling effect on me. We are on the sea in the heart of a mountain range in the desert. There can be few such majestic places on earth.'

At dusk we reached the village of Habalayn. Nobody rowed out to meet us. The village looked deserted and sombre in the fast-fading light. It was a sinister place not helped by its description in *Persian Gulf Pilot* which said that it was advisable to be armed in this area because of bandits. We pulled up anchor after breakfast and still without meeting anyone, we sailed away again. Even in daylight it was not an attractive place.

What happened next was recorded in my diary as follows:

'After a short time we see two boats with about 10 men in each, rowing steadily. I put it to Lorenzo that such a group may be interested in our keel and could provide the sequence I am looking for. Could we do a deal with them?

'As they draw alongside, I notice that their boats are

very primitive. Pairs of what look like bulls horns are lashed to the prows of the boats giving them the appearance of a Viking longboat. A man standing in the stern of one of the boats appears to be their chief. Lorenzo invites him to climb aboard. He is dark skinned and his face is partially hidden by his turban. We stop the engine.

'Like a hoard of pirates the other men scramble aboard the dhow and swarm into every corner. They are an uncouth crowd of ruffians. Bob is getting very agitated. We spread out in order to keep an eye on our belongings. The invaders flow over the deck; some go below. Bob appears to be unable to make the leader and his companion understand what we want. Lorenzo is also getting excited and the Arabs start to pocket things. They are so numerous we cannot keep an eye on them all at once and they are swarming everywhere. Lorenzo and Bob order them off the dhow. They take no notice, some reach for their knives. Lorenzo dives below into his cabin and calls me down. He takes a book from the shelf and opens it. It has a false centre and is full of bullets. He calmly loads a Beretta and hands it to me. He takes its shotgun out of its leather case and inserts two cartridges. The situation is boiling up like a saucepan of milk. Lorenzo is astonishingly calm. He walks up to the wheel and calls, "Matheka, start the engine". The engine immediately comes to life. "Slow ahead." The two Arab fishing boats tied alongside bump against the side of the dhow as we start to move ahead.

'The Arabs realise that if they do not leave immediately they are likely to lose their boats. In an instant they swarm over the side and as the last man jumps aboard they cast off.

"Full ahead," orders Lorenzo.

'Like a saucepan taken off the gas ring just as the milk boils to the top, so the tension on the dhow subsides. I realise that for the first time in my life I am holding a loaded gun in my hand. Bob is still very distraught. "Do you realise that they were migratory fishermen — probably bandits?" he asks.

"On this boat they have probably seen more riches than they have ever seen in their lives before."

"If they had been properly armed they could have killed us, sunk the dhow and disappeared."

"Who knows we are here?" he asks rhetorically. "Nobody," he exclaims, holding both of his hands in the air in a typically French gesture.

"I tell you those men are very dangerous. I know these people, they are not nice." Bob continues emphatically. "Even now they could be planning to collect their guns and return if we stay here."

'Lorenzo agrees and we sail north away from Habalayn.

'It seems that the keel of the wrecked dhow that has already cost me an ear could have cost us all our lives. Even I have to agree that it is high time we got rid of it. When we are moored at lunchtime we again lift it with block and tackle onto the gunwale. It perches there precariously as we disconnect the rope. With a heave we topple it into the sea. I watch it slide rapidly down, like a great black fish, into the deep blue depths beneath us.'

Ever since we had discovered and raised the keel of the wrecked dhow we had been dogged by bad incidents. It was as if raising it from the sea bed had disturbed an evil spirit that would not leave us until its earthly manifestation was again resting peacefully five or more fathoms beneath the sea. Casting the encrusted timber back into the sea was like an exorcism. Nobody said so, but they were all glad to see it go. Rangi swept the barnacle shells, that had been dislodged and crushed during its manoeuvres, over the side, and washed down the deck. It was gone and so too was our bad luck.

We headed out of Khawr Ash Shamm into the open sea.

I joined Lorenzo at the wheel and we checked the charts and the *Admiralty Persian Gulf Pilot* before we entered the Strait of Fakk al Asad — an inner passage in the Straits of Hormuz which are the gateway to the Persian Gulf as the

Straits of Gibraltar are the gateway to the Mediterranean. Going through that narrow passage was a moment of great achievement for Lorenzo. He had a dream to sail a dhow from one end of a trade route to the other and with almost no knowledge of ships or navigation he was living his dream. For as we passed through Fakk al Asad we were passing from the Arabian Gulf into the Arabian Sea — and the Indian Ocean. He was halfway home to Kenya.

We were approaching the next fiord for our explorations — Ghubbat ash Shabus — when Lorenzo made one of his instant decisions. He ordered the two Pakistanis, who were enjoying a brief moment of idleness, to hoist the sail. I took the wheel as Lorenzo went forward, sorted the ropes, and organised the haul. As soon as the sail was set, Matheka cut the engine. With the wind behind us I steered the dhow into the quiet waters of the inland sea of Ghubbat ash Shabus. Despite the fact that we were again in mountain-encircled water there was some swell, and the dhow rocked gently when we anchored.

As the evening closed we slowly dispersed from the stern deck and made our ways to our various sleeping quarters. I said goodnight and prepared to depart. As I did so Marina's crystal voice rose up the companionway from the stern cabin.

'Daddy, you have got a hairy bum.'

Then all was silent.

The next morning Bob was keen to start diving again, so the aqualungs were charged and all of the divers except myself got kitted-up in their wetsuits. Bob carefully studied the shore line. About a mile from the dhow was a headland. On the inside of the headland the sea was calm. Bob decided that would be the best place to try his hunting skill. The inflatables were lowered over the side and the gear was lowered into them.

I was extremely anxious to get some underwater film and had considered each member of the party in turn as a potential underwater cameraman. Could, or would any of them take the bulky 16-mm camera down with them, if I first set it up? The most obvious choice was Bob. He was by far the most competent diver in the group, but although I felt he could have managed to take some film his heart was really set on hunting. For him the objective of the expedition was to enjoy diving and spearfishing with Cathie.

To use the heavy cine camera safely one really had to be sufficiently proficient at diving to concentrate one's entire attention on the camera. Although I felt the kindly Roberto would be willing to try shooting some film I felt his diving experience was insufficient for him to do so without putting him at risk. I therefore decided not to ask him.

That left only Lorenzo. Lorenzo was very keen to make the film, but he had numerous other responsibilities, and he too was an addicted hunter. I dithered about asking him, but in the end decided to for the sake of the film and he reluctantly agreed to try. As I explained the various controls on the camera to him I realised it was optimistic to try turning a diver into an underwater photographer in five minutes — or even fifteen minutes — which was about the longest time Lorenzo kept his mind on any one subject, and it was unlikely to be a successful experiment. Nevertheless it was worth a try.

I handed the heavy camera housing down to Matheka in the inflatable before climbing down into it myself and joining the other divers. Lorenzo pulled the starter rope and we headed straight for the line of rocks jutting into the sea before slowing down into the lee of the headland. All of the divers put on their aqualungs, grabbed a speargun and disappeared over the side, including Lorenzo.

Matheka kept the engine running and attempted to keep his eyes on all of the sets of bubbles that rapidly diverged. Within five minutes Bob was back on the surface with a thirty-pound fish. Matheka took hold of the spear and heaved the flapping fish into the boat. He withdrew the stainless steel shaft that had passed right through the body and handed it back to Bob before delivering the final *coup de grâce* to the fish with a bludgeon he kept in the Zodiac especially for the purpose. When he had reloaded the gun Bob disappeared with scarcely a ripple. Only the bubbles that periodically burst on the surface gave an indication of the drama fifty feet beneath us.

Forty minutes later all of the divers were back in the Zodiac and we sped back across the bumpy sea towards the *Mir-el-lah*. I carefully guarded my wet, slightly bloody and fish-scale-spattered camera. Not a single foot of film had been exposed underwater. As soon as we were back on board Bob started the compressor, which made a considerable clatter. The suits were hung up to dry and Cathie recounted how she had become very cold, despite the fact that she wore two wetsuits, one on top of the other. The highlight of her dive had been an encounter with a turtle forty feet down.

'I went round a corner' she said, 'and there he was, looking at me.'

I could endure the prospect of losing so much marvellous film material no longer. There had to be a way. There just had to be.

The idea then crossed my mind that I might attempt to do at least some of the filming from the surface. I could lie on the surface wearing a face-mask and snorkel, and with good ear protection I should be able to film some shallow water action from that position. I announced my intention when the rest of the party were preparing for the afternoon dive and joined them in their preparations. I plugged my ear with cotton wool soaked in antiseptic cream and Mirella stuck a large piece of adhesive tape over my entire external ear before finally putting on a close-fitting rubber hood over the top. As I was doing this I noticed Cathie donning not two but *three* wetsuits, one on top of the other, in an attempt to keep warm. To counterbalance the effect of the extra one Bob added two more bright yellow weights from the large quantity he bought in Dubai just before we departed.

We were soon all ready to depart. When we assembled in the Zodiac I too was wearing a full wetsuit. The sky was cloudless and the mid-afternoon sun had a heat that was comfortably bearable, but made it a pleasant relief to get into the water.

By the time we arrived at the diving site, the sun, which was still high in the sky, was moving behind the mountain casting long pools of sombre shadow down the face of the cliff. Under water the difference between light and shade was intensely dramatic. I lay on the surface peering down. In the shadowy recesses of the cliff the sea was a deep Oxford blue. In the directly illuminated sea beyond, the water was a pale Cambridge blue. The demarcation between the two zones was as clear as the sea and the land on a map.

I lay on the surface gently rising and falling in the waves, spellbound by the exquisite beauty of the seascape beneath me. It was unlike anything I had seen before. The jagged, slightly sloping line of the rocks passed through the interface of air and water without change and slowly disappeared into the blue haze of the depths. All of the varied features of the spectacular rocks exposed above the surface were surprisingly still present underwater. There were crags, crannies, overhangs and gullies. The shallow submerged rocks were pale grey in colour and dappled with dancing areas of yellow where the sun's rays were concentrated by the ever-moving pattern of waves overhead. Under overhangs in the brightly lit area, the sea darkened into mysterious shadows — ideal lairs for large territorial fish. In the open shadow-cast areas close inshore the rock surface was a variegated grey.

Although the contours of the surface of the rocks had a similarity above and below water, the likeness ended there. Above the sea the rocks were barren and apparently devoid of any plants or animals. Yet a few feet below the surface life was profligate. The contrast was stunning. I looked down on one of Nature's tables set for a feast.

Shoals of brightly coloured fish swarmed over the rocks. Close inshore they rose and fell with the movements of the waves as if mesmerised — rhythmically rocked in the cradle of the sea. A scattering of sergeant major fish chased to and fro as skittishly as a large family of kittens. In addition to the shoals were the odd individual fish — the loners — who weaved their way up and down the rock face, periodically darting forward and nibbling at unseen morsels on the surface.

The richness of life, freely swimming in the water, was supplemented by the most beautiful soft corals I have ever seen. At the end of each branch were clusters of tiny delicate spheres vibrant with colour. The entire corals, including the main stems, were coloured — some brilliant pink — others orange.

Further down the slope I could see the intense neon blue of another soft coral — the sea whip. The branches of the sea whips also had an arboreal appearance, but were less divided than those of the soft corals. Their overall shape was similar to a poplar tree except that their branches were the same thickness along their entire length. They had the delicate appearance of a deer's horns in velvet. I could see none of the hard corals, such as the staghorn, that I had seen when we were diving at Khwar Ash Shamm.

I filmed Lorenzo as he dropped like a hawk beneath me. His bubbles streamed up behind him and boiled round the camera. He returned to the surface a few minutes later and took the camera from me. It was fully wound and all set to run. Holding the viewfinder to his eyes I watched him swim down towards the corals. As he swam past them they swayed like trees when a bus sweeps by. Much to my surprise he was back on the surface again in two minutes.

'It's not working,' he said.

'Look.' He rotated the shutter release knob and neither of us could hear the characteristic whirring sound of the running camera. I could not accept that even now we were being dogged by the bad spirit of the wrecked dhow. We weren't. I handed the camera back to Lorenzo.

'You've forgotten to wind it up,' I said.

Lorenzo shrugged his rubber-clad shoulders and descended again. I lay on the surface and watched him sink. He quickly shot the remainder of the 100 feet of film in the camera and returned the housing to the boat.

I had taken a still camera with me and snorkelled gently down to take a picture of some clown fish. As I did so they all darted into an anemone for protection. They moved into the safety zone in unison as swiftly as if they had been attached to the anemone with elastic. As soon as I rose to the surface they emerged again as cheeky as schoolboys. I didn't get the picture I wanted.

Bob was delighted with the hunt and the quarry he had successfully killed. He said the biggest fish he shot was called a *carangue* in French. Lorenzo informed me that the

35

African name for the fish was *cambazi*. Bob cooked one of his fish and served it with beans and a delicious sauce. Kimuyu prepared a dessert of pancakes served with sugar and fresh lime juice. At the conclusion of the meal Roberto complimented the two cooks and told them their meal was superb.

'Better than dining at Maxim's,' was how he described it.

Eating was one of Roberto's great pleasures and that night he really enjoyed himself.

Everyone on board the *Mir-el-lah* was happy. But the happiest person of all was me. I had got back into the water. The plaster I had put over my ear had not kept the water out but for some reason it didn't matter. I was back in business. I had Lorenzo as an understudy and some cine film had been taken. Just being alive on the dhow was tremendous. Tomorrow I would dive again with an aqualung.

Early next morning the *Mir-el-lah* pushed her way steadily through the silent waters of Ghubbat ash Shabus towards the open sea and the awakening day. A beautiful hawk-like bird swooped down to the sea and returned to its eyrie high on the cliffs.

'It's a sea eagle,' said Lorenzo.

My diary records the day's events:

'Off the headland of Ra's Dilah a lonely island rises majestically out of the sea. It is hundreds of feet high and in most places the rocks drop sheer into the pellucid water. We circle the island and in a small bay, surrounded by vertical cliffs, there appears to be a group of turtles just beneath the surface. We do not approach too close with the dhow for fear of disturbing them. I am keen to get into the water immediately.

'Under the hood of my diving suit my ear is plugged with cotton wool smothered in a cortico-steroid cream. Lorenzo and I have agreed that I will dive very, very slowly in order that I can equalise the pressure on my ears. He is keen to do a sequence where he searches for pearl-bearing oysters. There should be plenty round the island. He takes a net shopping bag and slips over the side. Matheka helps me on with my aqualung and

36

when all of the adjustments are made I fall backwards off the Zodiac into the water. Matheka lifts the heavy cine camera housing, and gives it to me in the water. There is no sign of the turtles.

'Lorenzo is thirty feet below me rummaging amongst the rocks looking for oysters. I sink very slowly down towards him. I am aware of the water running into my ear, but it is not uncomfortable. The water is fantastically clear and I settle onto a rocky ledge about eight feet down. There is no sign of the turtles or large fish but the water is alive with small ones. Lorenzo is using a hammer to remove a large oyster he has found and is totally engrossed.

'Lorenzo swims up to another oyster he has located on the rocks. At the same time I swim down towards it with the camera running. The sequence goes well and Lorenzo immediately disappears in search of more oysters. Once he gets a bee in his bonnet he acts immediately. Today Lorenzo is hunting for oysters in the hope of finding a pearl. Nothing is going to stop him pursuing that objective. I film him disappearing round an underwater headland. A few seconds later a shark, about three feet long, swims quickly by in the same direction. Bob and Roberto are nowhere to be seen. I am alone in an underwater wonderland.

'My fluid environment has the colour and clarity of blue zircon. The rock face is bustling with life and colour — like Montmartre on a Sunday morning. I can identify a few of the numerous species of fish that swarm over the rocks. Roberto appears far below. I happily film the fish and the beautiful orange soft corals. The two and a half minutes' filming time I have is soon used up in such photogenic surroundings.

'I rise slowly to the surface. There is no sign of the boat, or any of the divers. I inflate my lifejacket slightly from its integral air cylinder and wait, happily passing my time studying the bustle of piscatorial activity beneath me.

'Matheka has just helped Bob land a big fish and is back on patrol again. He takes my camera from me and

I haul myself onto the rubber tube. As soon as I am aboard Matheka moves off to pick up Roberto.

'Before long we are all back on board and decide to explore the seaward side of the island. There is a slight swell and the sea periodically swirls up the rocks in sheets of white foam. Bob slips into the water and Matheka hands him a speargun. Roberto and Lorenzo follow suit, also with guns. I prefer to shoot with a camera, not a gun. Holding one still camera in my hands and slinging another round my neck, I take to the water once more.

'The sea must be very fierce at times in this region for the rocks are bare. There are none of the soft corals I saw in the bay of the disappearing turtle-fish.

'Lorenzo and Roberto stay a few yards off the shore line and I follow Bob into deeper water until the seabed disappears in depths well in excess of one hundred feet. Beneath are a circling mass of tunny-like game fish, swimming fast. Bob takes a deep breath and streaks vertically down towards them, his speargun ready in his right hand. At a depth of fifty or sixty feet he stops and attains a horizontal position with his feet slightly lower than his head. He raises his left hand over his mask as if using it to shade his eyes and brings the gun up to a sighting position. The dark shapes, indefinable from the surface are still circling in the water. Sixty feet below Bob is holding his breath, waiting for the moment to pull the trigger. From above I see a flash of silver as the spear leaves the gun followed by the white trace of the line. One of the black shapes stops circling. It twists and turns flashing silver.'

At that very same moment two sharks, each seven to eight feet long, appeared from nowhere. One went straight for the wounded fish. The other projected itself towards Bob with the speed and straightness of direction of a rocket. They both hit their targets at the same instant.

I recalled a gruesome account I had read in a diving journal of a shark attack on another Bob.

'The shark came the opposite way and went straight under me, about 8 ft. down' said Warner, 'It came out of the blue like a rocket and grabbed Bob. It moved so fast that by the time I looked back it had Bob in its mouth and was shaking him like a leaf. I dived straight down. It was then more or less directly below me. I put a spear in the top of its head right where the brain should have been, but it didn't seem to affect it. Shaking Bob like a dog with a slipper, it broke him in half and rose up at me with his legs and flippers sticking from his mouth . . . His upper half just floated away.'

But that attack was by a great white shark in Jurian Bay, Western Australia. I did not expect to see great whites in these waters.

As I watched, the sharks veered away and disappeared into the blue. At the moment this action took place I could not tell if the sharks had attacked and wounded Bob or his fish. I strained to see if there were any signs of damage to the black-suited figure suspended in the blue haze sixty feet below me. To my relief he appeared to be unharmed and started to swim towards the surface, still clutching his gun. The white line attached to his gun was jerking and flashing from side to side as the impaled fish threshed in a frenzy of death and fear.

It seemed an eternity since Bob had gulped his last breath of air and glided into the depths. How much longer could he hold his breath and still fight the fish? I expected to see him reach for the knife and cut the line. But he did not. He was only ten feet away and rising rapidly. I could see him looking up towards the surface. I could sense the resolution of a man who was going to make it to the surface with his fish, or die in the attempt.

He broke surface a few feet away from me. I heard him suck in some thankful breaths in quick succession before he reeled in the fish. It was a magnificent specimen weighing forty to fifty pounds. It was a fish of the open seas, a fighting fish, a fish that would feed all on board the *Mir-el-lah*.

For a long time I have openly opposed spearfishing — mainly on the grounds that intensive spearfishing, and more importantly organised spearfishing competitions, can completely denude an area of fish. When this happens in popular diving areas I feel that a large number of people are deprived of the joy of seeing wildlife in its natural surroundings for the benefit of a few moments of pleasure by extrovert killers. However, life has taught me not to be too dogmatic about anything. There are justifiable exceptions to every rule and I felt Bob was the exception to my rule on spearfishing. He was not shooting territorial fish that stay in caves and are sitting targets. He challenged a game fish in its own territory — the open sea — to a joust. He won because he was fit, strong, skilful and resolute. It was a contest in the best sporting traditions. Some might argue that it was a very one-sided contest, but the speed with which the two unheralded sharks came into the arena could have signalled a very different end.

One thing the shark incident clarified in my mind was the fact that when a fish is wounded it must let out a signal that travels extremely fast like a sound wave. The sharks seemed to appear only a fraction of a second after the spear hit the fish. The time interval was far too short for blood to diffuse into the water to attract them. Also they were out of visual range, yet they homed in on the wounded fish without hesitation.

If a speared or wounded fish does emit a signal that can travel some distance underwater, does it act as a danger signal for other fish? I think it does. For I have noticed that when a fish is speared the number of fishes one sees diminishes rapidly. This applies to all species, not just the species that has been shot. I conclude, therefore, that most fish, like all successful animals, have built-in survival mechanisms which say 'take cover' when a fish cry is heard. If the fish death cry is associated with man — the reaction will be 'take cover' whenever man appears.

The shark incident with Bob happened so quickly and so far away that I was not able to take any pictures. I had been thwarted. Once Bob had recovered I discussed the possibility of getting shark pictures with him and Lorenzo who had joined us. Neither of them was enthusiastic about my proposal, but eventually they yielded to my entreaties and agreed to attempt to attract a shark exclusively for my benefit.

Lorenzo dived and I kept my camera trained on him from the surface. He aimed at a fish and missed. His next shot was successful and I watched the fish through my viewfinder waiting to press the shutter the instant the sharks appeared. But they didn't. Lorenzo returned to the surface and we dangled the wounded fish beneath us. We all lay on the surface watching it swim back and forth beneath us, its blood streaming into the water. After five minutes the fish was nearly dead, but still no sharks appeared, and I was sorry I had suggested the experiment.

Whilst we were shark baiting we allowed the current to carry us gently towards a major headland of the island. When we arrived at the headland the water was astonishingly clear and contained the biggest concentration of large fish I have ever seen. We regretted that we had used up all our air. The rock formations below us were so massive and the water so clear that to snorkel down thirty feet, which I was not prepared to try, would have been merely to dip into the top of the spectacle. Well over a hundred feet below me I watched a grouper, that must have weighed one hundred and fifty pounds or more, move from one overhang and to another with powerful deliberate motion of a bulldozer.

Bob was spellbound. He left his speargun in the boat. He said he had never seen such a high concentration of large fish before. When I asked him if he had any inclination to go down with his gun he said, 'No, I love spearfishing, but I will shoot only enough for us to eat.'

As we rounded the headland I realised that we had completed a circuit of the entire island for we were back again in the bay, with the vertical cliff walls, where we first thought we saw the turtles.

Lorenzo emptied his bag of oysters on the deck and immediately started to open them with his diving knife watched by an excited Mirella. Lorenzo said the shells alone would fetch one pound sterling each in Kenya. But that was small beer compared with the possible jackpot prize of a good pearl. Leaving Lorenzo to work on his dreams I washed my still cameras and was changing the film in the cine camera when an excited cry from Lorenzo and Mirella caused me to rush over to them. Lorenzo had discovered a pearl. He scraped it gently free from the flesh of the oyster and exposed a dark pearl the shape and size of a small grain of rice. Although it did not fire *me* with dreams of eternal wealth, for Lorenzo it was the catalyst needed to prolong his interest in pearl diving — which was just one of his many ventures for making money.

As we were moored in a convenient spot and Lorenzo wanted an underwater shot of the anchor dropping into the water, I decided to have another dive under the dhow during the afternoon. It was a brilliantly sunny, windless, lazy day and we lay at anchor in a sheltered bay. Fully kitted-up, I climbed down the ladder and stepped backwards into the sea. Matheka put a rope through the handles of my camera housing and lowered it gently down to me over the side of the dhow.

The water had a slightly green tint. When I looked up I could see Matheka's face looking over the side. His face was circular, oval, pear-shaped and moon-shaped as the water surface, ruffled by the bubbles of my exhaust air, constantly changed the image, like a hall of mirrors at a fun fair. The underside of the dhow was completely clear of any growths due to the application of an anti-fouling mixture of sharks' fat and lime that had been applied before we left Dubai. I could see the keel from one end to the other and watched my bubbles rise and flow over the hull like silver pools of mercury. I was taking a series of sequences holding the camera in front of me and pointing upwards towards the hull, when I saw plumes of bubbles periodically bursting into the water on one side of the dhow. They were accompanied by an obnoxious brown stain that diffused into the very area I was filming. A slightly unpleasant taste permeated the water surrounding the mouthpiece of my regulator. I surfaced immediately and was disgusted to see the black hose from the bilge pump projecting over the side of the vessel. Every few seconds bouts of vile grey-brown water gushed out of the pipe; a very fine oil slick was spreading out over the surface of the sea. I was angry and yelled out for Matheka. His black face appeared over the side and I let him have a broadside of invective that knocked him backwards — the bilge pump was turned off immediately.

That evening, after a superbly cooked meal of fish, we were all enjoying a rare moment of talk and idleness on the poop deck when Marina went below and came back with a guitar. She begged her father to play and sing. Lorenzo was reluctant but he tuned the guitar and started to hum and sing songs in English and Italian. His music was enchanting. Marina, who adored her father, listened with pleasure and so did we all.

In the late evening, when everyone else was thinking of going to bed, I started work on an underwater lighting unit I had brought with me from England. Although I was very tired, I was determined to use it. It was a perfectly still, warm night. There was no moon. The sea was as black as ink. It was an ideal night for underwater filming. When I announced my intention to go diving nobody volunteered to accompany me. Indeed, our two Kenyans thought I was insane and were convinced they would never see me again — unless they caught the shark that would certainly eat me.

Roberto agreed to act as a surface cover for my diving activities. He rowed me to the rocky cliffs about fifty yards away. I put on my aqualung with difficulty in the dark. I checked all my equipment with extra care before sitting on the tube wall of the Zodiac and rolling into the water. I switched on my hand torch and somehow managed to hold both the torch and the cumbersome camera plus lighting unit in front of me as I sank slowly into the quiet sea.

When I had been preparing the lighting equipment Bob had reminded me that sharks never sleep. If they stop swimming forward they sink to the sea bed and die. This thought was in my mind as I drifted downwards, turning continuously and probing the darkness with the powerful beam of my torch. I tried not to sink too quickly. My adrenalin level was in the red zone.

I shone my light onto the sand and several pairs of pink lights were switched on and off as the beam of my light passed by. In one area my light picked up a dozen pairs of pink glowing beads. I moved towards the nearest pair of lights and when I got close they resolved themselves into the eyes of a prawn. The body of the prawn was transparent but its eyes were afire with reflected light. The sandy seabed between the coral heads was thickly populated with his brothers, sisters, aunts, uncles and cousins, all out on their nightly scavenge, eating particles that I could not see.

I became so engrossed in the play of my light on the nocturnal inhabitants of the sea bed that all thoughts of sharks faded from my mind. A black crinoid starfish, its numerous legs like black, curved, feathers, slid like a snail over a coral head. During the day these delicate creatures curl into balls and remain hidden in recesses in the coral. At night they emerge like nocturnal flowers.

Sweeping my torch through the Cimmerian darkness gave spectacular results for when the beam fell upon any form of life the colours were even more intense than they appeared during the day. When the much more powerful filming light was switched on the effect was even more stunning. The animals in its path glowed with colour as if they were illuminated internally. Turning both lights off simultaneously was like being dropped head-first into an inkwell: instantaneous and terrifying blackness.

The light from my hand torch was as reassuring as gold to a Swiss banker. As I prodded the recesses of the coral clumps with its stick-like beam, I spotted many of the fish I had seen during the day now huddled in the backs of holes. They were invariably sideways on to the beam so that their one illuminated eye would stare into the light. I felt like a policeman on night patrol, shining a torch onto a sleeping tramp. But I would leave them in peace for filming them with my cumbersome equipment was not possible.

A lobster was out on the prowl, like a cat, between the coral alleys. It took little notice when the floodlight was switched on and just waved its long antennae towards the lens. I moved forward and it reversed away from me on its stilt-like legs along a sandy gully before quickly backing into a cave in the coral. I followed the sandy path down the gentle slope.

The most spectacular of all the forms of life I encountered were the soft corals whose colours were dazzling. When the floodlight was on I noticed many bright specks in the beam. These were the plankton upon which the corals were feeding, trapping the tiny organisms in numerous polyps.

When I eventually surfaced the kindly and patient Roberto rowed over to me and lifted the cumbersome camera and lighting unit into the boat. As I sat in the Zodiac excitedly telling him of my underwater encounters I looked at my watch. I had been in the water for the unbelievable time of forty minutes. We tied up alongside the silent dhow. Roberto wished me goodnight and left me alone on the deck of the ghost ship to peel off my wet rubber suit and hang it over the boom to dry. It had been a long and very eventful day.

I had many more exciting experiences before I flew back to Heathrow airport. Amongst them was a dive on a wreck off Dubai which the local divers called 'The Cement Barge Wreck'. On that dive I collected a sack full of oysters which only produced one microscopic pearl but were consumed with relish at a memorable party.

Lorenzo Ricciardi sailed on and eventually reached Mombasa.* He later told me that the journey round the Musandam was the most exciting part of the entire voyage. A film of this voyage was shown on commercial television but none of my footage was included on the grounds that a diving sequence in such a film was inappropriate — perhaps, more significantly, I did not have a union ticket as a cameraman at the time.

The gamble of continuing to dive with a perforated eardrum paid off. The eardrum never became infected. It eventually healed over and my hearing was not detectably affected. However I was a changed person.

Never before had I mixed with a group of people who were so forthright and uninhibited in expressing their views and emotions. Their freedom of thought and self-found values left no room for status symbols, hypocrisy, or for

---

*The complete story is told in his book *The Voyage of the Mir-el-lah* published by William Collins.

following stultifying codes of behaviour. I didn't envy them their life-style, but by becoming aware of it I realised how much broader the horizons of my own life might perhaps have been, or indeed could be in the future.

Then, by one of those strokes of good luck with which I seem to be blessed, I had an opportunity to put the thoughts gestating in my mind into practice. Eight months after my return from Dubai I was made redundant. The obvious sensible and expected thing for a person with my qualifications and responsibilities to do was to look for another full-time job. But the events in Arabia had opened my mind to the possibility that the safest and most sensible solution to unemployment or any other problem was not necessarily the most rewarding, fulfilling or satisfying. It was better to follow the instinctive force that came from inside. And inside me I had a feeling that I needed more freedom and more time to explore the wonders of the underwater world than commitment to full-time employment would allow. Also, one of the few Arabic expressions I learnt kept coming into my mind. It was '*Allah akbar*' which Lorenzo told me meant 'If Allah wills, it is written in the stars.' So with the support of my family I opted for a totally new way of life the foundations for which were laid, unbeknown to me, when I took up underwater swimming as a hobby in the 1950s.

2

Salad Days

THE ENGLISH CHANNEL

My obsession with diving began with an object for which I still have a love-hate relationship — the television set. In the mid 1950s I didn't own one but I did have an affluent friend who occasionally invited me to peer at his proudly displayed status symbol. One evening I saw slightly fuzzy black and white images of Hans and Lotte Hass swimming into a fascinating new world of sharks and shipwrecks. Of such worlds young men's dreams are made. From that moment on I was hooked. For the first time in my life I was free to indulge my fancy as I had no more exams to swot for. So in the autumn of 1957 I joined the newly formed branch of the British Sub Aqua Club at Oxford to find out how it was done.

My tutor was an ex-naval frogman — John Littlemore — a gentle, slightly shy, modest, but strongly built man, who would occasionally regale me with stories of his exploits during the Second World War. The club met one evening a week. Starting with fins, mask and snorkel provided by the club, I learned how to snorkel dive in the public swimming pool at Oxford. After the pool session we reassembled in a pub and learned the theory behind the practice of diving. During the winter months I trained and passed the various tests necessary before progressing to the use of the aqualung.

I soon combined learning to dive with my other passion — photography. I started by designing and building waterproof housings for my cameras. Each week I would add an experimental photography session to my training in the pool. By the following May I was proficient with the aqualung and longing to go on my first dive in the sea and to

47

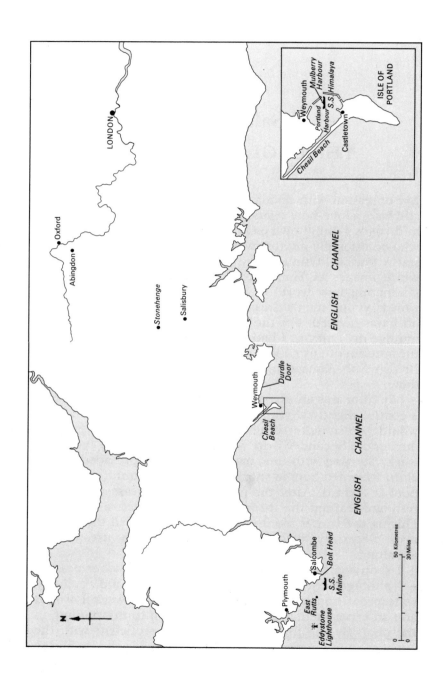

take my camera in its underwater housing with me.

At last the great day of the first club outing to the sea arrived. Early Sunday morning I anxiously awaited the arrival of the coach outside our house in Abingdon. The coach had already toured Oxford, collecting knots of divers at appointed corners and pre-arranged pick-up points. I was one of the last to board and passed along the gangway between the rows of happy young faces, to one of the few empty seats. It was a brilliant, sunny day; our destination was Durdle Door in Dorset.

After disembarking we gathered around the luggage boot at the back of the vehicle, and our precious cargo of charged aqualung cylinders was carefully unloaded. I was allocated an aqualung and strapped it on my back. Gathering up the bags which contained my other possessions, including my camera, I joined the crocodile of divers who were stretched along the narrow path that led to the cliffs. With their packs and bags of various kinds they looked more like an expedition setting off to climb a mountain.

A beautiful sight unveiled itself as we reached the top of the cliffs. A huge pillar of white rock stood defiantly out of the sea and curved in a graceful arch to connect with a continuous line of white cliffs. I placed my heavy camera bag on the ground and rested for a few moments absorbing the view that lay before me. Beneath the arch a flat calm sea sparkled in the mid-day sun and stretched like a sheet of blue glass to the horizon. Joining the sea to the shore was a thin line of white foam that pulsed gently and regularly as it advanced and receded over quietly rumbling amber pebbles. From my vantage point I could easily see the sea bed close to the shore. For the first time I looked at the sea with eyes of a diver. What was it like down there between the dark green patches of seaweed and the clear bright yellow areas of sand? Would all the weeks of training and experimenting be worthwhile? I picked up my bags and clambered down the path to the beach.

A pressure gauge was attached to one of the cylinders and it recorded well above the working pressure of 120 atmospheres due to the heat of the sun. John explained that with an internal pressure of nearly one ton per square inch the energy packed inside one cylinder was sufficient to cause a violent explosion. To cool them off we hurriedly placed the cylinders at the edge of the sea where they stood like a row of grey bombs.

To prepare ourselves for the dive we undressed, put on our bathing trunks and then got dressed again in old clothes. I put on a blue sweater and corduroy trousers, the idea being that they would help to protect me to some extent from the chill of the water.

We were divided into pairs. As I was carrying my precious underwater camera housing, which was a two-handed operation, my partner was given an inner tube with a length of rope attached to it. We flopped like a pair of ungainly and untidy penguins down the pebble beach to the sea. With a heavy aqualung on my back, a belt loaded with lead weights round my middle, and at the same time clutching my camera with both hands my progress was unsteady on land. In the water my balance became precarious. I found walking forwards through the water almost impossible due to the water resistance on my floppy fins which curled up under my feet and did their best to trip me up. I felt embarrassed that spectators on the beach should see me staggering like a drunkard in the sea with the waves swirling round my legs. Of even more concern to me was the possibility that I might fall and damage my camera.

I looked towards Tony, my partner. He was walking backwards into the water so that his fins trailed in the water and did not trip him. I turned my back to the sea and did likewise. It instantly solved my instability problem.

The cold water saturated my dark corduroy trousers and spread its icy fingers up my legs and torso. When it was nearly chest high I turned round and fell forward into a swimming position. The cold swept up my body and hit the back of my neck like a blow from a boxing glove, leaving a dull ache. I lay floating on the surface breathing through my snorkel tube catching my breath, and watching the pebbles beneath me move back and forth as the waves wafted me gently to and fro. Tony, who was a large lad weighing about fifteen stones, floated alongside me. He wore only swimming trunks and a tight teeshirt, his subcutaneous fat providing a convenient layer of built-in insulation. His weightbelt, which was loose, hung like a necklace threaded with lead beads about his generous waist. He towed behind him the buoyancy ring, one function of which was to indicate our whereabouts, when we were submerged, to our instructor on the shore. We were accompanied by a diver wearing just fins, mask and snorkel. He was called a snorkel cover and his job was to provide immediate assistance should it be needed.

About fifty yards from the shore we came across the first signs of marine life — a patch of dark green seaweed. It was time to dive.

I gave Tony the OK sign with my free right hand. I removed the snorkel from my lips and replaced it with the mouthpiece of my demand valve. I rolled on to my right side, so that any water in the corrugated rubber hose would run into the exhaust tube, and exhaled hard. It was a procedure I had practised a dozen times in the swimming pool to clear water from the breathing tubes. I inhaled cautiously. The air flowing through the demand valve made the 'ssschwark' sound of water running out of a bath as it passed from the high pressure cylinder on my back into the breathing tube and thence into my lungs. I breathed out through the exhaust tube and continued to exhale until I felt myself sinking gently towards the sea bed. I breathed in again as easily as if I had been breathing air on the surface. Tony and I again exchanged OK signals and propelled ourselves towards deeper water. A few silver fish, which I identified as mullet, swam nervously away from us and disappeared into the blue limit of visibility about thirty feet away.

A sense of elation suffused my body as I became acclimatised to the water and the sensation of cold completely dispersed. I breathed out and sat on the sandy sea bed twenty feet down. The controls of my camera were operated via a rubber glove. I tried to insert my hand but the rubber was sticky and I found it difficult to introduce my fingers into the collapsed rubber sockets. I had to be careful not to use too much force for fear of splitting the rubber and flooding my Agfa Isolette camera. Tony hovered patiently nearby. At last I managed to insert my fingers sufficiently to operate the camera controls. I held the external viewfinder up to my mask and took my first ever underwater photograph in the sea. I cocked the shutter again and we progressed to a clump of olive green kelp in which a pair of divers were rummaging, heads down. Frequent bursts of silver bubbles from their regulators indicated their whereabouts as boldly as a waving banner. One diver emerged triumphantly bearing a spider crab in his hands and looked for his partner to show off his prize. I noticed there were no signs of the fish we had seen when we were quietly snorkelling out earlier.

Our snorkel cover, about whom we had completely forgotten, swam down and hovered briefly in front of us. He returned to the surface at full speed when the urge to breathe could be suppressed no longer. We breathed easily from our aqualungs, free to wander in the fringe of the ocean off Dorset, breathing air from Oxford. Free from gravity we could hover, rise and plunge with the ease of humming birds.

We continued our journey away from the shore until the height of water above us was about thirty feet, at which depth the pressure of water was forcing the rubber glove well inside the housing making operating the camera controls difficult. We had been in the water about fifteen minutes and had become oblivious of the cold. But there are few sports more calorie-consuming than diving and all of the time the sea had been insidiously drawing the heat from our bodies. Suddenly I felt cold and started to shiver; I looked round and signalled to Tony that we should head back towards the shallower water.

Tony's teeshirt looked brilliantly white against the dark blue backdrop of the sea. As he exhaled a cloud of bubbles appeared above him and then chased one another to the surface, oscillating, expanding and dividing in the process. The sea was much brighter over the shallow sand and the underwater visibility appeared to increase. The water became perceptibly warmer. Everything appeared bright and clear. It was as if the underwater world was illuminated from within itself.

In the shallow water we again encountered a shoal of fish. This time they were sand eels. A glistening mass of tinsel strings streamed past our field of vision. A sudden movement on our part would cause those immediately in front of us to break formation and accelerate out of the danger zone. I streaked after them holding the camera in front of me, but as I did so I found my camera pointing at a hole in the curtain of fish. No matter how fast I swam, the eels could outswim me. Initially the passage of the entire shoal had been leisurely and only those immediately in front of me had shown any apprehension. After my burst of speed the entire shoal became nervous, quickened their pace and soon left me facing an empty sea. I was learning by experience. Fish-watching and photography require a very quiet, careful approach.

I clambered out of the sea with water streaming from my clothes. When I stripped them off I found I was not only blue with the cold, I was also blue from the dye that had bleached out of the sweater and trousers I had been wearing. Most of the divers wore old clothing to reduce heat loss. However, my own impression was that the little thermal protection afforded was outweighed by the encumbrance of the clothes both in and out of the water.

Having stripped off the soggy clothes and spread them over the rocks to dry, I vigorously rubbed my skinny blue and white body with a towel in a vain attempt to get warm and to rub off dye. I spread my towel on the beach intending to lie on it, but I was too excited and made my way to Tony. We chatted together communicating the experiences we had shared and not shared. When divers are under the sea they can pass only the simplest of messages via hand signals. They have to bottle up their experiences during the dive. I have often observed since that after a dive divers froth over with conversation like uncorked bottles of champagne. Indeed, the analogy with champagne can be carried even further: on the long ride back to Oxford the atmosphere in the coach could not have been merrier if we had all drunk a bottle of wine.

During the summer of 1958 we made other visits to the coast and I tried different techniques, different films and different filters in an effort to improve upon the mediocre results I was getting with my camera. At the same time the club were looking for waters closer to home to explore in order to avoid the long trek to Dorset.

* * *

In Oxford there was a small complex of open air swimming pools at Hinksey. Beyond the pools, away from the road, was a large lake. Behind the lake ran the York to Reading railway line. The lake was very deep; figures well in excess of 100 feet were commonly quoted. It was reported to be fed by a spring and the water was therefore extremely cold. Monster pike were known to be lurking in the depths; they patrolled the lake, snapping up any weak fish or ducklings. It was rumoured that any swimmers who invaded the lake were likely to be attacked by the jack pike with the ferocity of Alsatian guard dogs. The edge of the lake was lined with reeds and beyond that water-weed grew in great profusion, a further hazard to any person foolish enough to venture into the water. Around the lake were notices announcing the dangers and forbidding entry.

Amongst the many objects known by the locals to be in the lake was a German aircraft that had been shot down during the Second World War. And it was the prospect of finding this that prompted the club to approach the authorities for permission to search the perilous depths. They granted it but emphasised it was to be entirely at our own risk.

On Sunday morning a group of divers led by John Littlemore, assembled beside the lake with an impressive array of ropes, air cylinders, weight belts, knives and other miscellaneous equipment. Elaborate safety plans were made and these included maintaining an inflatable boat over the divers. The yellow inflatable air-sea rescue dinghy was unpacked and the laborious job of inflating it with a small hand pump began. It was a glowering morning, dark with expected rain, the reflections from thunder clouds giving the mirror-smooth surface of the lake a shine like wet black ink. The water looked evil and impenetrable.

John, who had spent the latter part of the war removing mines from canals in France was accustomed to diving in dangerous situations. Despite his outward calm I wondered what thoughts and memories were passing through his mind as he adjusted the straps of his harness, for he was not with a team of expert divers under the command of an experienced officer now. Instead he was in command of a group of apprehensive and inexperienced amateurs. I admired his courage.

The safety cover dinghy was launched. John stood briefly on the muddy bank giving last instructions before pulling his mask into position and wading out into the unknown. I noticed him feel for, and check the position of, his diving knife. It was the type worn by professional divers and had a black handle; the brass scabbard glowed dull-gold.

A few yards from the shore the water was up to his chest. He put the rubber mouthpiece connecting the breathing hoses into his mouth and inhaled. The valve issued its characteristic hiss and John, now head downwards, propelled himself into the sinister depths. His efforts were successful. In a few moments there was no sign of his presence apart from the bubbles that periodically boiled up from below and momentarily broke the surface. The rope attached to John's aqualung harness passed through his right hand and then to the shore. One of the club's more experienced divers stood on the edge of the lake and maintained a slight tension on the rope. At intervals the rope moved tighter and jerked rapidly backwards and forwards as the two men exchanged signals. One short sharp pull was the signal for 'Are you O.K?' to which John replied also with a short sharp pull which signalled 'Yes I am O.K.'

I watched the coil of rope play out as John headed deeper and deeper into the middle of the lake. The other divers stood alongside the tender maintaining an unnatural silence as they watched the rope slide like an endless snake into the water. By now we could not see the bubbles surfacing and could only judge John's location by the position of the yellow dinghy which was following him slowly across the lake. Then the dinghy made a sharp change in direction and started to move up the lake parallel to the shore.

The tender was having difficulty interpreting the signals on the now very extended rope. The signal for emergency was a series of sharp pulls on the rope. He pulled once hard on the rope and in return the rope gave a series of spasms and went slack. Was John in trouble? He pulled on the rope again but the path it took into the water did not line up with the yellow dinghy which was now in the middle of the lake and well away to our right.

The tender holding the rope yelled across to the man paddling the dinghy. 'Are bubbles still coming up?'

The man in the dinghy didn't understand the message and cupped a hand to his ear.

'What's that?' he shouted back.

'I am not getting the OK signal on the rope. Is he still breathing?' screamed the tender, now clearly getting very worried.

'Yes' came the laconic reply.

'Thank God for that' he said still pulling gently on the line and getting no positive response to any of his signals.

The possibility that John was now in real trouble in the middle of the lake but still breathing was uppermost in everybody's mind. The man in the dinghy stood up unsteadily, cupped his hands to form a megaphone, and directed his voice towards the tender.

'The rope has snagged — let it go slack.'

Then to the relief of all concerned a masked head surfaced alongside the dinghy; John held on to the side while he discussed the problem and two minutes later he submerged again with a flurry of splashing fins. The tender pulled gently on the rope and coiled it in a neat pile at his feet. Then suddenly the rope gave a short sharp pull — the OK sign. The tender repeated the signal and it came back again strong and clear. The crisis was over.

Eventually, all the rope was coiled up at the tender's feet and John emerged from the water with a piece of green pond weed dangling from his facemask.

'What's it like?' 'How deep is it?' 'Did you see anything?' were just a few of the questions the tender fired at him before he had clambered free of the water.

'You can see for yourself' was John's eventual retort as he

climbed up to the bank. 'You're in next with Horace.'

A dozen reasons, some real, some fictitious, as to why I should not venture into the water immediately came to mind. I hadn't got a suit; I had never dived very deep before; I had had a cold two months ago; I couldn't clear my ears; my wife was pregnant . . . I was pregnant. But they were snuffed out in an instant by a trait of character that I admit to, yet cannot overrule — pride. Within a few minutes I was stripped down to my swimming trunks and was heaving the webbing harness straps of an aqualung onto my bare shoulders.

John came over and checked that the equipment was correctly assembled. He pulled on the harness buckle and the jock strap bit painfully into my crutch. 'Steady,' I winced, 'I want to be intact when I die'. John smiled, but was still keeping silent on what he had seen on the bottom of the lake. The mystery heightened when he told us that he had decided that we should abandon the safety line and stay strictly in pairs.

Drops of heavy warm summer rain started to fall, shattering the flat surface of the lake and covering it with a thousand tiny short-lived craters.

'Remember, stay in pairs and if you get into any trouble come up' were the last instructions we received as we made our way to the water's edge, a few yards away. He made it sound so easy — but you can't just 'pop up' from 100 feet down. At least I didn't think you could. I had never been that deep before.

My fins behaved like suction pads as I stood on the muddy bed at the edge of the lake. I looked down at the black opaque water swirling round my white legs. The temperature of the water was very much kinder than I had anticipated; it felt pleasantly warm. I struggled forward through the weed until the water was about 4 feet deep and then dropped forward into a snorkelling position. With my face just submerged all I could see was a very pale glimmer of brown light through the water that had swirled around me. The underwater visibility was even worse than I had imagined; it was no greater than twelve inches at the most.

I remembered the training I had received for such diving

in the swimming pool when I had swum two lengths underwater with my face mask blacked out. Such diving requires a certain discipline that I enjoyed applying to myself. But as I felt my way along the glazed tiles on the bottom of the swimming pool I was secure in the knowledge that there was a relatively short escape route, upwards through clear water, to the surface. The situation in which I now found myself required a far tighter hold on my self control. Suppose I became entangled in a submerged tree? How could I see to find my way out in the thick brown mud?

I momentarily questioned the sanity of John Littlemore and his instructions about surfacing if I lost contact with my partner. In the all-engulfing brown turbidity I could not see the end of my arm, let alone my partner. With my adrenalin at full flood my respiration rate increased and I hungrily sucked at the mouthpiece. Plumes of bubbles were sent pulsing through the few feet of water above me to the surface. If someone had tapped me on the shoulder I would have left the water like a Polaris missile. But nothing of the sort happened and I pressed forward in what I hoped was the direction of the centre of the lake.

One yard ahead the water suddenly cleared as I passed through a mass of black sediment I had disturbed from the bed of the lake. It was as if somebody had suddenly removed a blindfold from my eyes. I emerged from the brown cloud into a soft yellow-green light. I could see at least 10 feet and my diving partner was swimming gently forward on my left. In front of me lay a fairytale landscape; a gentle panorama of delicate green plants suffused with a warm yellow-green stage light. The abruptness of the change was startling. I paused briefly to absorb the spectacle of the new environment that I had entered before following my partner who was finning slowly ahead.

A few small perch, almost transparent, apart from patchy black markings, darted away into the underwater jungle. The depth of the water was still only about six feet and overhead the surface of the lake looked like hammered silver with the rain. The inside world of the lake had a strange atmosphere of its own; it was almost as if it was dry — with the surface of the lake acting as an umbrella protecting us from the unfriendly grey world outside. Our sub-surface world had a warm, yellow-green inner glow. An eel, with its head projecting from the weeds and its pectoral fins splayed like two stubby arms, eyed us briefly and decided that discretion was the better part of valour. With a slight sinuous movement it slithered backwards into the green undergrowth and disappeared from view.

Another eel, caught off guard completely in the open, decided to depart from our path, and hurtled headlong into the sanctuary of a weed bank at full speed. The disturbance it created caused the plants in its track to shake and start a minute slow-motion cascade of yellow particles from the upper surface of the leaves. The movement of the weeds also unsettled a tiny spider. Coloured red, and no bigger than a sweet pea seed, it paddled past my field of vision with all its legs going like flails. It added to the strange unaquatic feel of the weightless environment. I mused on the strange quirk of evolution that had caused a creature like this to take to the depths. Why was it bright red in colour? Was it to alert its predators that it was poisonous?

The questions remained unanswered for my partner had disappeared ahead of me. It was imperative that I should catch up with him before he dived into the deep part of the lake. I didn't have far to go before I encountered him in the middle of a black cloud, swirling up into the clear water. His waving fins sent bits of weed and silt spinning into whirls as he grappled with some object or animal which I could not see because his head and shoulders were completely enveloped. In a few seconds he emerged triumphant and clutching a completely intact bicycle. When he attempted to sit astride the cross bar and pedal it, the whole situation took on the appearance of a bizarre underwater circus act with my partner taking the role of the clown, myself the sole spectator, and the lake surface providing our big top. When the novelty of a subaquatic velocipede ride had worn off we inspected the bicycle in detail. But our examination showed it had been in the water for some time and was not worth a salvage attempt. So we let it sink back again eight feet down into its pond-weed covered grave.

The scenery remained unchanged as we progressed and I

could sense none of the changes that indicated we were moving into deeper water. I looked at my depth gauge — it indicated a depth of ten feet — just slightly deeper than the deep end of the swimming pool. Were we not swimming into the middle of the lake? I swam over to my partner, touched his arm and having secured his attention I pointed towards the surface. He understood immediately and we both surfaced to find we were near the far side of the lake from our entry point. We had swum right across the centre of the lake where the abysmal depths were said to exist.

We took a different route back to our starting base, straight down the middle of the roughly rectangular lake. During the trip we encountered a few largish roach that took flight when we approached and numerous small fish that were less timid. Near the edge we found several pieces of junk tossed into the lake over the years. We saw no sign of an aircraft. The maximum depth of the water was fifteen feet.

One of the several lessons I learnt on that dive, was that non-divers have no concept of the real depth of waters. I have been told by one diver that he publicised a proposed search for a coach and team of horses that were reputed to have disappeared without trace into a deep lake. He was not amused when the newspaper men who assembled to record his fearless exploits fell over with laughter when he stood up in the centre of the lake with the water waist high.

It is perhaps a shame that such romantic myths are exploded by underwater adventures, but such adventures have more than redressed the balance by creating myths of their own. After all who, but other divers, can verify the tales told by divers.

★   ★   ★

My interest in underwater photography ran unabated during the winter of 1958 and the spring of 1959 — but the results I was getting did not please me. One of the major problems seemed to be lack of clarity of the water. Even the water in the indoor swimming pool at Oxford was far from clear except during the brief period around Christmas time when the pool was less crowded than usual. My experiments triggered a train of interest and people turned up at the pool with cameras enclosed in a variety of home-made housings. At about this time I felt that the club was losing too many of its members once they had been trained to dive, firstly, because of the lack of some more advanced diving and secondly, because of the lack of some other interests to which they could link their newly acquired sub-aquatic skills.

Having voiced this view in the club, the inevitable happened. I was charged with the job of organising dives to fulfil the need I had said existed. The grand-sounding post of Scientific and Photographic Officer was created and there being no other candidates, I was duly elected. I was therefore faced with resolving a problem I had created for myself.

Wrecks have a fascination for most people and the closest I had come to one thus far in my diving career was when I discovered the remains of an old pram in Hinksey Lake. I felt a dive on a wrecked ship would provide the new dimension needed in the club and should yield good material for photography. That raised an immediate question: where could I find a wreck that was within the diving capabilities and limited resources of the club? The problem of locating a suitable site was resolved when I met Frank Brooker, who had lived in Dorset, and knew of a number of good diving sites. He said the wreck of the *S.S. Himalaya* at Portland would suit our purposes admirably.

I had heard of other divers using their air fruitlessly looking for wrecks and I was concerned that we should not do likewise. 'You can't miss it,' said Frank. 'It's conveniently situated between the breakwater and the Mulberry harbour — Wilkie knows where it is.'

'Who's Wilkie?' I asked.

'He's your boatman. His real name is Bill Wilkinson but everyone calls him Wilkie.' Frank gave me Wilkie's address and continued rhetorically: 'Have you seen the Dunlop film *Horizons Below*? Wilkie is the one with the blue boat that took the divers to Durdle Door.' As it happened I had not seen the film, but Frank's next comment 'He's a real character', was one that I was later able to endorse.

'You can all stay at "The Sally Ann," said Frank.
'Is it a pub?' I enquired in all innocence.
'No,' said Frank. 'It's a Salvation Army Hostel.'
I continued my questioning. 'What sort of place is it?'
'Well, it's not exactly a four star hotel,' replied Frank.
That fact I was also later able to verify.
'Where is it?' I continued.
'Right on the quay at Castletown in Portland.'
'Can Wilkie take his boat in to the quay?'
'Yes.'

Frank's proposal seemed ideal in every way — a wreck we couldn't miss, cheap accommodation, and a boatman who was used to divers.

The proposed dive was greeted with enthusiasm at the next club meeting and preparations for the expedition were immediately put in hand. It was to be limited to eight of the most experienced divers in the club.

We decided that it would be best if we all travelled in one vehicle and after much hunting we managed to locate a car hire firm that was prepared to let us have a Bedford Dormobile for the weekend. When Friday evening came I assembled my equipment, including cameras, spare nuts and bolts, jars and preservatives for specimens, and sat down to await the arrival of the van. Abingdon, where I lived, was a few miles south of Oxford and en route for Portland, so I was again to be the last person to join the party. One hour passed, which was excusable. A combination of minor delays could lead to that sort of situation. Another half an hour sluggishly passed and then a further hour which seemed to take an eternity. At last, two and a half hours late, an ancient pale grey Dormobile cruised noisily round the curve of Appleford Drive and stopped outside our little house.

Our Equipment Officer, who was at the wheel, looked distraught and showed me the column change gear lever. It bore a remarkable resemblance to the handlebar of a child's bicycle — which, as it happened, it was. He explained how the original lever had come off shortly after the beginning of the journey and that as he was near home he went back there to try to mend it. Failing to find anything else he had sawn off the handlebar of his child's bicycle with the promise that he would put it together again when he returned!

The inside of the vehicle had wooden slat seats and every cranny was filled with bags and cylinders. I looked at my own pile of gear on the pavement and decided there was nothing I could dispense with. After a certain amount of rearrangement and squashing up, to the accompaniment of groans, my equipment was squeezed into the mini-bus.

As newly instated Captain of the Dormobile I took my position on the bridge (one of the front seats), waved goodbye to my wife Wendy and baby Melanie and ordered a course for Portland. Like a decrepit overladen coaster our vessel reluctantly pulled away from its temporary kerbside mooring and headed for the main road into Abingdon. Even at slow speeds the Dormobile rolled disconcertingly on the corners.

We decided to refuel at the Esso garage just outside the town. I jumped out and asked the pump attendant, who viewed us with a mixture of concern and amusement, to fill the tank. As he did so he looked down at our apparently half flat tyres.

'I'd get some air in those if I were you,' he suggested.

'We've already got them at one and a half times the recommended pressure,' retorted our driver from the cab.

'We're fairly heavily laden,' I replied with masterly understatement as he spurted the last squirts of petrol into the tank.

I climbed back into the cab, heaved the sliding door across and the Dormobile again lurched forward.

It was quite dark when we reached Salisbury and stopped for some much needed exercise and refreshments. After the break I took the driving seat, joggled the handlebar lever into gear and we set off for what should have been an easy last leg to our journey. I had told the Manager of the Salvation Army Hostel that we would be late arriving so although we were now hours behind schedule it was no great problem.

I quickly grew accustomed to the behaviour of the Dormobile and drove as fast as safety would permit. All seemed to be going well, until we were climbing a hill out past Tarrant Hinton, when suddenly the noise of the engine increased to an alarming pitch. I pulled to the side of the road and my co-driver released the catch of the engine cover. As he lifted the engine cover the din was deafening. We had lost our exhaust pipe. I switched off the engine and we all clambered out. There were no road lights and there was no moon.

One of our party walked back down the road and returned some minutes later holding the rusty battered remains of our exhaust pipe. One brave member of the party lay under the vehicle and tried to manoeuvre the pipe back into position whilst another helped from inside the cab. The engine was blisteringly hot and burned the hands and arms of the two men trying to get us mobile. Drops of hot black oil were dripping onto the poor fellow underneath. We would have to wait for the engine to cool down. I rummaged into my bag for the pliers and wire I had packed for emergency camera case repairs. All in all it took us about an hour to reassemble the exhaust system and get under way again. It was now one-thirty in the morning.

I was by now very concerned that the 'Sally Ann' would be closed. At the next town we found a telephone box and after much delay directory enquiries eventually found the number. I dialled and waited. There was no reply. I concluded that they were shut down for the night. We would have to find somewhere else to stay. Tired, dirty but not dispirited we pressed on.

The answer to our plight came as we passed a coach station in Weymouth. We pulled into the forecourt and I strode into the lighted garage where several coaches were parked. I put our problem to the friendly old man who was cleaning out one of the coaches, and after a few minutes explanation, he agreed that we could occupy one of the coaches for what was left of the night. We agreed to be off the premises before his boss arrived in the morning. Putting bags in the aisle to act as bridges between seats we were soon sprawled thankfully across them.

I have yet to find out why it is that people who snore always seem to be the first to go to sleep, but my prods and protestations only caused my neighbour to grunt and change key briefly before resuming his porcine slumber. I eventually fell into a fitful sleep from which I awoke just after six o'clock. Fifteen minutes later we were back in the Dormobile having profusely thanked our benefactor. Within a short distance we encountered a milk-man skimming quietly along the road aboard his electrically-powered milk float. We waved him down and purchased a pint of milk apiece. Thus fortified we made our way through the silent awakening town of Weymouth. A white sky was brightening from the east. Suddenly the sea — blue and calm — came into view and our spirits rose like skylarks.

We weaved our way through the town and then out onto the extraordinary geological formation of Chesil Beach. A thread of land, bordered to the west by a steep pebble beach, connects the rocky promontory of Portland with the mainland of Dorset. Beyond the narrow beach on our right was an open shimmering sea ruffled by a gentle breeze. On our left, inside the breakwaters that form Portland Harbour, the sea was grey-blue, flat and calm.

We easily found the jetty at Portland and located the 'Sally Ann'. The staff were friendly, and said we shouldn't have worried and that someone would have let us in no matter how late we turned up; they were used to late arrivals. In its heyday, the Salvation Army Hostel must have provided a useful sanctuary for the sailors who manned the ships that thronged the harbour. That day, however, the 'Sally Ann' had relatively few customers. We were shown to our cubicles; the unslept-in beds had rubber undersheets. After a quick wash and shave we reassembled in the dining room for a substantial breakfast.

When we stepped outside again the sun was shining brightly. Tied up alongside the jetty steps was a strong blue fishing boat. A man wearing an ex-government greatcoat was bent over, tinkering with the engine. He was a thick-set man of average height and of the indeterminate middle-age that many fishermen appear to be. He wore a greasy flat cap beneath which protruded his sideburns which were a mixture of dark and grey hair. From the description given to me I guessed that the man I was facing was Wilkie. At our first encounter he had a slightly shy self-conscious manner, but his sparkling bright eyes indicated a sense of humour; I suspected he was a rogue — but a very likeable one.

Our lack of sleep was not given a second thought as we loaded our equipment into the boat and stowed the aqualung cylinders around the stern. We journeyed out to the Mulberry harbour which proved to be an ideal location, for it was about thirty yards inside the main breakwater and parallel to it. We moored to a ladder, climbed up on to the massive concrete structure and explored the top. There were various openings, some of which were partly covered with wooden hatches. Other hatches were missing and we looked down into dark water inside, for the Mulberry harbour was a hollow structure filled with seawater.

Our Mulberry was just one of many such structures built by the allies prior to the invasion of Europe during the Second World War. The walls of these giant shoe-boxes were made of reinforced concrete and inside was a matrix of strengthening struts. The mode of use was ingenious and simple in concept but difficult in practice. When required a Mulberry could be sealed and the water pumped out. Once afloat it could be towed across to the French coast and positioned where a new harbour was required. When correctly located the Mulberry was again flooded with water and allowed to settle on the sea bed. In this way the Mulberries provided instant berthing facilities for the bigger ships carrying the back-up supplies essential to the men who had gone ashore earlier by landing craft.

Towing the gigantic floating concrete rectangular tubes across the English Channel in times of peace would, I imagine be difficult. During the war it must have been doubly so. The Mulberry at Portland was one of those that never made the perilous journey across the Channel.

The top of the Mulberry provided an ideal place for us to assemble our equipment and organise the diving activities on the *Himalaya* — the remains of which lay between the Mulberry and the breakwater.

I locked my Agfa Isolette camera onto its plate and carefully loaded it into the housing. The rubber glove was fitted into position. I was ready to go. My diving partner Tony (we had dived together at Durdle Door) had caught the underwater photography bug. He had made a housing from fibreglass for his Zeiss Werra camera and had spent the previous months carefully arranging for all of the external controls to operate the camera. A camera housing can work perfectly in the workshop, but the moment of truth comes when it is taken into the sea; that is the all-important moment when theory confronts practice.

The boat that was moored alongside the Mulberry provided a useful platform for getting into the water. We climbed down into the boat and looked into the blue-green water. We waited for the first pair of divers to surface to give us the general layout of the wreck; they told us we were virtually right over it and would have no problems at all finding it.

With one hand inside the glove I climbed gingerly down the diving ladder that was hooked over the gunwale of Wilkie's boat and slipped gently into the sea to check my buoyancy. I tried to swim down but had difficulty in doing so because of the upward pull of the rubber gauntlet of my camera housing which was inflated and acted like a float. I climbed out and put another weight on my belt.

Having found I was now correctly weighted I signalled to Tony. He was waiting patiently in the boat with his new camera housing hanging from a lanyard around his neck. I saw him standing on the gunwale as I sank slowly beneath the surface into the green water. A few seconds later a plume of bubbles appeared beside me as Tony leapt into the water. The bubbles dispersed and beside me appeared the black and white striped (he was wearing a football jersey) rotund figure of my diving partner. He looked at me, gave the OK signal and looked down to catch hold of his camera that had been hanging about his neck a few seconds before. I saw a look of disbelief cloud his eyes. His camera was not there. He peered into the depths beneath him and his look changed from one of concern to panic. His beloved camera had disappeared completely. In addition to the value of the camera itself, he had put months of hard work into adapting it for underwater photography — and he had lost it during the first few seconds of his first advanced dive.

He signalled to me that his camera had gone, despondency written across his normally jovial face. There was fifty five feet of water beneath us. At that moment I happened to look up and could not hold back the hoot of laughter that pulsed along my exhaust tube and into the water behind my back. For bobbing just above Tony's head was his camera. The lanyard was retained by the breathing tubes. Although it was quite heavy in the air, his camera housing complete with camera just floated in the seawater. Tony had not taken this into consideration and instead of his camera housing plummeting into the depths it was safely suspended just above his head!

Tony eyed my signal quizzically when I pointed above his head. He wanted to waste no time diving to see if he could find his camera on the sea bed, but as I insisted, he looked up. When he saw his camera floating above him he beamed with relief. We had both learned a lesson we would not forget.

As we bobbed together on the surface, I did not know that I was shortly to have two even more salutary experiences. The first came quickly.

Having composed ourselves we gave each other the OK signal and headed down towards the dark blurred shapes of green kelp which we could just discern beneath us. As my ears were hurting, I tried pushing the underside of my face-mask against my nose with my free hand, but although I blew hard through my nose my ears would not clear. Next I found that I had to stay vertical and swim hard to remain at the same depth; if I stopped swimming, I sank.

Gradually the pain in my ears eased and I allowed myself to sink until I landed with a bump amidst the kelp on the rail of the *Himalaya*. A cloud of silt floated up into the water.

The glove of my camera housing, which on the surface had been inflated with air, was now forced inside the housing with the pressure of the water. I had put on extra weight to counteract the buoyancy. Thirty feet down the buoyancy had been reversed and the camera and my additional weights were pulling me down. I could still just operate the camera, however, and I cocked the shutter, but I had to move away from the cloud of silt I had stirred to get a clear picture. I managed to shift from my very uncomfortable perch and immediately started to sink rapidly. I finned vigorously and still I sank. My ears started to hurt again as the side of the wreck started to pass upwards past my field of vision. Should I abandon the camera that was pulling me down? Should I jettison my weightbelt? By swimming flat out I was just able to regain the rail of the wreck, but my efforts again disturbed clouds of silt. When I had regained my breath I swam after Tony. I clicked off one shot before sinking back onto the wreck. I was grossly overweight and had to accept the fact that picture-taking on this wreck in my present condition was impossible. I signalled to Tony that we should surface. I had used half of my precious 40 cubic feet of air and had taken one picture, which I knew would be of no value. I decided to leave the camera in the boat and dive back down unencumbered.

As we headed towards the surface, the pressure on the rubber glove was reduced and the air trapped inside the housing expanded to return to me some much-needed buoyancy. We swam over to the diving ladder and I handed the camera into the boat. I stood shivering on the ladder, unfastened my weightbelt and removed some of my weights before sinking slowly back into the gloom to rejoin Tony who was hovering beneath me still clutching his blue fibre-glass housing.

The *Himalaya* was lying on an even keel in about forty-five-feet of water. The top of the wreck was covered with kelp. Below that the spars and plates were coated in silt which swirled off in clouds if a diver finned near them. Our own activities and those of the previous divers had reduced the visibility to about ten feet in places. The *Himalaya* was bathed in a blue-grey fog that gave the entire wreck an uncanny eerie atmosphere. As we swam over the broken deckwork, spars would loom up quickly and then disappear equally rapidly in our wake. A few grey fish hovered in the broken upper structures. They were pollack — melancholy fish winding in and out of the dark grey-brown, twisted metal-work.

We worked our way down the outside of the hull to the soft sandy mud of the sea bed. The *Himalaya* was not a glamorous wreck but we got some idea of her overall shape and size before I noticed that the needle of my pressure contents gauge had moved into the red sector indicating that I was low on air. I signalled to Tony and we started to rise. We were level with the deck when I noticed a rope stretching mysteriously across my field of view. I swam up to it and curiosity took hold of me. I pulled on the rope but could not see what was on the end for it disappeared into one of the open holds. I pulled on the rope again. It gave a few feet and then sank again under its own tension. I knew there was something on the end of the rope, but what was it?

I then did something very foolish.

Without giving the situation a second thought I started to pull myself hand over hand down the rope to see what was on the end. I followed it down into the dark interior of The *Himalaya* until I came to the source of my curiosity resting on the metal ribs above the keel. It was a lobster pot.

I had just reached it and was about to examine it when my air supply became difficult to breathe. I tried to take another breath but nothing happened. I had run out of air. I let go of the rope and headed for the surface as fast as I could possibly fin. Up through the dark shadow inside the hold. Out through the open hatch into the blue diffuse light. I was swathed in bubbles and moving fast when I was brought to an abrupt and immediate stop. I felt as if I had been struck across the back of my neck by a stick. The mouthpiece of my breathing tubes was almost wrenched from my teeth. I was desperate for air and unable to move. I could not see what was holding me down behind my back. I sucked on my breathing tube and a tiny trickle of air mixed with water flowed reluctantly into my lungs as I desperately tried to locate the obstruction with my hands.

At that panic-stricken moment I saw the black and white striped jersey of Tony appear at my side. He pushed my head down and to one side. In a second I was free and continued my frenzied flight to the grey-silver surface overhead. I knew I had to breathe out on the way up if I was to avoid an embolism. As I allowed the expanding air to stream out of my mouth I couldn't believe it would take so long to reach the surface.

At last I burst through the water-air interface into the

bright airy world and gasped a choking breath.

I raised my hand in the approved distress signal of the time — but the surface safety cover was talking to somebody else in the boat and did not notice me. After a few thankful breaths I realised that the emergency situation was over. I did not require any assistance. Moments later Tony surfaced beside me and we made our way the few yards to the diving ladder and climbed aboard Wilkie's boat.

I learned many things about diving techniques on my first dive on the *Himalaya* — one of which was the obvious value of having a diving partner. But I should not have gone down when I was running out of air; I should have released my weight-belt when I found I was in trouble and I should have come up with my hand above my head. For even if I had missed the metal hawser that trapped me over the hold, I might have surfaced under the diving boat and cracked my skull. Finally I appreciated the value of an alert watch-out whose job it is to help a diver who surfaces in distress. My look-out was half asleep.

One member of our group had found a well-screened place on top of the Mulberry harbour. It provided a convenient shelter for the Primus stove, and I was pleased to be offered a cup of hot soup to warm my cold, shaking body. Wilkie was sitting with us idly throwing bits of wood through one of the openings into the water below. He admitted, with a chuckle, that he couldn't swim a stroke but reckoned he would learn quickly if he was ever unfortunate enough to fall in the sea. He thought we were all quite mad — and said so. After my experiences I was inclined to agree with him.

The water that was inside the Mulberry rose and fell with the tide, so there were clearly channels for the sea water to flow in and out. How big these were I never found out. But the inside of the Mulberry was like a huge dark trap. Where the sunlight shone into the cavity we could see the water was very clear. Imprisoned inside this giant fish-tank in the sea numerous jelly-fish pulsed their mushroom shapes in gentle journeys to nowhere.

As Wilkie and I sat chatting and peering into the sea beneath us our attention was suddenly caught by the dark grey head of an eel that slowly emerged from the shadow. The mouth was slightly open and was as large as that of a fully grown Alsatian dog. Just behind the evil-looking jaws the body thickened. It remained perfectly still. A beam of sunlight spot-lit it like the head and torso of a man on a stage.

Its presence had an electrifying effect on Wilkie.

'Get in there — get in there!' he cried. 'Get the speargun and shoot the bugger!' But no, I had had enough experiences for one day, and I declined his challenge. The excitement caused the others to rush across. Wilkie tried to persuade each of them to have a go at the conger eel and told them of a woman diver from London who would have been in the water like a shot. Fortunately for me, they all declined as well. He called us a bunch of cowards and hurled a chunk of wood in the direction of the eel in feigned disgust at our timidity. As the eel turned and the rest of its body crossed through the beam of light, I estimated its length to be about seven feet.

One of the members of our party was making an 8-mm cine film of the expedition. His previous film of our earlier trips to Durdle Door had impressed me and I was keen to try out cine photography for myself. Therefore when we returned to the Mulberry the next day I persuaded him to let me enclose his precious Bolex camera inside my housing. From the previous day's experience it was clear that I would have to stay relatively near the surface. We fitted the wide angle lens and I exposed some of the colour film he had in the camera. When we got the results they were extremely pleasing — far better than any stills I had obtained before. I was instantly converted to shooting movie film.

But I needed a camera with which to experiment. An appeal to the Rank organisation was successful. They gave me one of the new range of Bell & Howell Autoset 8-mm cameras, complete with supplementary lenses. I quickly built a rigid case from Perspex and had to fit only two external controls — the motor wind and the shutter release. I found the coupled exposure meter worked as well beneath the surface as it did above. And for most work the fixed focus wide angle lens gave high quality pictures. To this day

I would recommend any person taking up underwater photography for the first time to start with an 8-mm cine camera with a wide angle lens and coupled exposure meter.

At a later date, I returned to the *S.S. Himalaya* with the Public Relations Manager and a photographer from Rank who wanted to record their camera in use.

One feature of that publicity dive that became imprinted on my memory was my first encounter with a cuttlefish. I was drifting gently down to the wreck (not troubled with buoyancy changes because the camera was in a rigid fixed-buoyancy housing), when the first cuttlefish swam in front of me. It was iridescent and the brilliant colours seemed to sparkle as it gently drifted past, its delicate fin surrounding its body like a skirt. I swam gently after it admiring the fantastic display of colour. When it reached the *Himalaya* it settled on the rail and in an instant adopted the exact brown-green colour of its surroundings. If I had not seen exactly where it landed I would never have known it was there, so perfect was its camouflage.

Later the same day I saw what looked like a mass of green seaweed on a patch of sand. Closer examination showed that each piece of seaweed was actually a cuttlefish with its body faced downwards waving its tentacles in the water imitating seaweed. Its mimicry of its surroundings was as good as that of the stick insects I had studied at school. A prod from my snorkle tube, used at arm's length, sent a startled cuttlefish darting away amidst a cloud of black ink which it injected into the water. All of this I was able to capture on film.

I also learned from that weekend some of the activities of a public relations manager, for a write-up of our expedition appeared a little later as an illustrated article in *Yachting World*. Virtually the same article also appeared in several foreign journals — in some of which the only words I could read were Horace Dobbs and Bell & Howell.

*   *   *

Of the relatively few women I know who have completed a course of training and become proficient divers, each one has had an exceptional and very strong personality, for they are as unique as women who make very high office in business or politics. One such person presented herself at the poolside for my training class during the winter months of 1961. She was the wife of a don at Oxford University and her name was Kay. Kay was tall and slim — but not willowy. She had deep red hair and an air of supreme self confidence that amounted almost to arrogance. She was the sort of person who could shrivel a shopkeeper who dared to give her a rotten apple. At the same time she was generous to a fault and invariably hospitable. Water had a magnetic attraction for her. Her other passion was cooking. These and other facets of her character I was to find out later. But at that first training session I was faced with a mature young woman, whose extrovert personality was immediately apparent, who told me that she wanted to learn to dive and that apart from being a good swimmer she had performed in a water ballet without mask or fins.

At the first pool session it was obvious that Kay was thoroughly at home in the water. As the weeks passed she proved to be a natural diver. She appeared to know instinctively what to do with the minimum of instruction. She made me realise why teachers have favourites in school because the results I saw from my instruction were so fast and obvious. Although I would never have admitted it to her at the time, she mastered the techniques of diving more rapidly than I had done. Within nine months Kay became a very proficient diver.

Kay had two young children, a boy and a girl, and so had I. Our families became friends.

Kay and her family had an extremely successful long holiday in the Greek Islands. By the time she returned in the autumn of 1962 she was bronze-brown and a diving addict. I too had expanded my diving experiences by drift diving with the Torbay divers and I had also had a number of very successful dives out of Salcombe. We were both unsettled by our new diving experiences and felt that the club could no longer offer us the diving opportunities we were searching for. The incessant stream of new members into the club demanded a constant programme of beginners' dives. We wanted more than the odd so-called advanced dive, and so too did a number of the more experienced members of the club.

We therefore decided to form our own underwater research team and The Oxford Underwater Research Group was born early in 1963. The Group was made into a Limited Company to limit the liability of any single member on the advice of our solicitor member, in case, as he pointed out, we accidentally sank a battleship and were sued. Ten men and one woman (Kay) each bought an equal number of shares in the company. The common bond that united us was the desire to combine our professional skills with our spare-time underwater interests.

I already had an idea for a major project and I put it to the newly formed Group. I had heard of a submerged pinnacle of rock, situated five miles south west of the Bolt Tail promontory on the Devonshire Coast. It was marked on the charts as East Rutts and rose to within about thirty feet of the surface in an area where the depth of the sea bed was about 120 feet. Why should such an isolated needle of rock be there? Could it be explained in terms of the geology of the area? I put these questions to a member of the Group, Dave Rawson, who was a graduate geologist.

Dave buried himself in the libraries of Oxford for a few days. When he emerged he delivered a fascinating lecture to the Group on the geology of South Devon, above and below sea level. He explained that the exposed rocks in South Devon were formed during the Devonian period of the history of the earth that occurred about 350 million years ago. This he compared with the age of the earth which is about 3,000 million years. He could not answer the specific questions I had put to him, because so little was known of the underwater geology of the area. In conclusion, he said that a determination of the geological structure of the East Rutts, coupled with a study of other submerged rocks in the area, would make a valuable contribution to the knowledge of England's south-west peninsula.

The prospect of undertaking some worthwhile geological research, which would necessitate diving in one of the best areas we knew, fired the Group with enthusiasm. What was more we had a good prospect of recovering our expenses for

75

I had contacted David Attenborough at the BBC Television Studios, who had referred me to Brian Branston who was responsible for running a series of documentary programmes made mainly by freelance film makers. If we could provide evidence of our ability to shoot good 16 mm film and come up with a strong story-line the BBC would provide us with film stock and a contract.

One member of the Group had made a number of excellent silent 8 mm films above water and I was convinced that if I supplemented his knowledge with my own experience with 8 mm cinematography under water we had the basic filming skills to succeed. The BBC would not accept 8 mm film, however, and we would have to make the jump out of the amateur gauge (8 mm) to the larger 16 mm format. As we needed to acquire a considerable amount of diving equipment, the purchase of new cameras and an underwater housing, which in themselves would have consumed our entire financial resources, was out of the question. We would have to buy second-hand cameras and I would have to make an underwater camera housing.

The first expenditure from Group funds was made for a simple 16 mm Keystone camera which I located at a shop in Croydon. I visited the shop and purchased the camera for the princely sum of fifteen pounds ten shillings. The very wide angle lens (10-mm focal length), which I regarded as essential for underwater work, was bought for thirty pounds from Cambridge. For above water work we purchased a very robust Bell and Howell camera with a lens turret, complete with three good lenses for one hundred and ten pounds from Bond Street, London.

When Brian Branston saw the quality of the above water test films, shot at 24 fps, and I put the full story-line to him, he said he would prepare a contract for a film with the provisional title of 'Operation Pinnacle'. He advised us to shoot in black and white. Once we were assured of getting a contract for a film, preparations for the expedition were put into top gear and every person in the Group was allocated a job.

With the equipment and photographic aspects of the expedition resolved we were left with one major requirement for the expedition: a diving vessel. I already had an idea in that direction — the *Princess* — a small fishing boat skippered by Michael Dornom who had taken out the Torbay divers when I dived with them. Mike was young and understood the needs of divers as he was a diver himself. He also knew the idiosyncrasies of the sea in the region of the East Rutts as well as any person we were likely to find. I contacted Mike and booked his boat for a weekend in late May in order to put our theories, our equipment and our team to the test.

All of those who could make the trip crammed into Kay's VW caravanette and we left just before dawn on Saturday morning. We were all in very high spirits, and in the rising light I drove the mini-bus along the undulating narrow lanes through the wide open fields of Berkshire towards Hungerford. Everything seemed to be going well when suddenly Kay screamed 'Stop!' I braked violently and all of the passengers were shaken into wakefulness. Before I could ask what the problem was, Kay had opened the door of the van and could be seen running back down the road. She returned a few minutes later holding a dead hare by its back legs. It had obviously been struck by another vehicle and was still warm. 'Can't let good game like this go to waste' she said as she unseated one of the members in the back and put the hare in the box under his seat. 'Drive on.'

Ten minutes later we were again lurching to a halt. This time to pick up a dead partridge that had suffered the same fate as the hare.

'Kay, you are incorrigible,' I said. 'What do you think this is — a game safari?'

We saw no more game and by mid-morning we were wending our way along the high-banked Devonshire lanes and dropping into Salcombe. It was an idyllic day. The sea was flat calm, the sky was cloudless and the air was warm. Our diving arrangements worked like clockwork. We were soon out of the harbour and heading towards Prawle Point.

Kay and I dived together. We adjusted our lead weights to suit our novel equipment and set off for a shallow dive close to the cliffs. The dive was uneventful until I spotted a spider crab. I was just about to shoot a film sequence of it when

Kay swooped in front of me and picked it up. I was furious. I signalled for her to surface. As soon as we did so I spat out my mouthpiece and told her never again to take anything until I had first got a shot of it undisturbed and given her the signal to move in. It was the first and only time I remember losing my temper with Kay. She never again acted without consideration of the camera on a filming dive and thereafter she was always able to interpret what I wanted her to do from my often elaborate hand signals.

My anger faded as soon as we re-submerged to continue our dive. The underwater scenery had the crisp brightness of spring. We watched a pair of ballan wrasse, their fat bodies as colourful as rainbows, weave between barnacle-encrusted rocks, and outcrops of vivid green sea lettuce. Other pairs of divers periodically came into view, as they too were enjoying exploring the undersea world and were establishing relationships with their diving partners and other members of the Group. When we left the water the sun was still shining and we stripped off our diving suits, drank hot soup, and allowed the sun to warm us as we chatted about our dives and the future expedition.

I remember distinctly the gentle beauty of the coastline. The elements were at peace with one another. The blue sea gently licked the grey rocks which were covered with lichens of subtle hues of brown, yellow and green. Above them tussocks of dark green thrift were capped with pink flowers. Other wild flowers blossomed on the ledges of the rocks. Young grass on the cliff tops added lush new green to the rhapsody of shapes and colours. The peace and tranquillity of the scene affected us all. We were in harmony with nature and in harmony with one another.

I was to find out later that the true test of a man, or woman, comes not when the going is easy — but when times are hard — when a person has to pit himself against his fellows and against nature when she is angry. And she became very angry before our major expedition was over.

However, without the benefit of hindsight, without a really demanding task to undertake, and in a perfectly peaceful environment, I could not entertain the possibility that we might fail to get along with one another, and that we might not succeed in our major objective, which was to make a film for television.

The first incident that signalled all was not to go well occurred the following day. Our geologist, David Rawson, told us that in the region of Thurlstone there was a primeval forest which had since become petrified. The area was now under water. As the petrified trees were related to our overall objective of a study of the rocks in the area, we decided that some shots of the sunken forest would make an interesting sequence in the film. We set out to see if we could find traces of the lost trees. I dived with one of our most experienced divers, Dave Gill, who was at other times an airman. I loaded the camera into the newly-constructed housing and followed him through the kelp beds as he searched for signs of the ancient forest in the new forest of kelp that now covered the sea bed.

After we had been in the water for about fifteen minutes Dave drew my attention to a tope, one of the shark family, about four feet long. It was lying quietly on the sea bed when Dave swam up behind it and grabbed it just in front of the tail. The startled fish took fright and Dave emerged spectacularly from the weeds, being towed by the fish, which was trying desperately to escape. Failing in its mad dash to regain its liberty the shark started to wriggle violently. Its wide open mouth looked as if it could easily have taken off Dave's hand. At which point Dave let go. The tope took no further notice of Dave but hurtled off out of sight. The incident took place very quickly and I was annoyed that it had been covered by so little film footage.

I signalled to Dave to surface and asked him why the hell he had let go when I was in the middle of filming the sequence of a lifetime. In retaliation to my outburst he pointed out, in colourful language, that it wasn't my hand that the shark was about to sever. Then he pointed to the home-made camera housing which I was holding just beneath the surface. I looked down. It was half full of water.

The rubber 'O' ring seal between the base plate and the body of the housing had become compressed during the dive. When I rose to the surface and the pressure was released the base plate became loose and the water leaked in.

Remedying the fault was a relatively minor problem. Getting the camera into working order again was a major problem.

Fortunately the lens was unharmed. However, despite the fact that I washed it out immediately in fresh water and dried it carefully the camera refused to function. No camera dealer was prepared to even attempt to repair it at short notice — commenting that it would be impossible to obtain spares — and the camera wasn't worth the effort. I knew of nobody who would be prepared to hire, or loan us a 16 mm camera in an underwater housing. Our expedition was due to begin in three weeks and the future of the Group rested entirely upon a film with plenty of underwater sequences. The only solution to the problem was to repair the camera myself.

I dismantled the camera, replaced two small components that were badly corroded, and reassembled it. With trepidation I wound the spring and pushed the shutter release button. The mechanism whirred for a few seconds and stopped. I dismantled the camera, checked every component and tried again. The same thing happened. I could not understand why. Four times I dismantled the camera without success. Although I was getting quicker at the job each time I did so it took several hours, and another day passed. Finally, on the fifth attempt, I interchanged two washers that appeared similar, but were of different thickness. They must have been accidentally switched round the first time I dismantled the camera, for after that it worked perfectly. I ran a spare spool of film through the camera without a hitch.

Whilst I had been working on the camera the rest of the Group had been making and gathering together the equipment we needed for the expedition. We chartered the *Princess*, skippered by Michael Dornom, for two weeks and reserved caravans for our accommodation at Beadon Farm.

The back of Kay's VW was piled to the roof with equipment — including a large aquarium. Everyone was at a key pitch of enthusiasm and excitement. The expedition upon which we had all expended so much effort was going to happen.

It was the last week in June — Wimbledon week. Kay and I arrived in Salcombe before the rest of the party. As conditions were good we decided to waste no time and were soon on board the *Princess*. We were looking for locations close to Salcombe where we could take essential fill-in sequences for the film. We were therefore looking for sites where the underwater scenery was typical of the area and the water was clear.

Mike suggested that we should try round the rock formation on the west side of Salcombe Bay known locally as the Masons and his suggestion proved to be a good one. As the dive was to be for reconnaissance I did not take the camera.

It was a delightful dive, the underwater visibility was in excess of thirty feet and we found some interesting rock formations that I noted mentally for a number of general sequences we needed. Also there was plenty of underwater life.

As we climbed the diving ladder to reboard the *Princess,* Kay's knife slipped from its sheath and spiralled down towards the sea bed twenty-five feet below. I swam down after it but my ears were painful, and although I could see it on the bottom it was several minutes before I could safely descend the last few feet to retrieve it. As I hovered impatiently, with the last of my air running out, I was tempted to make a quick dash for the knife despite the pressure on my ears. But the pain told me to hold back and only an event in the Arabian gulf years later has since told me how close I was to bursting an eardrum. Had I made an impetuous plunge for the knife and perforated an eardrum it could well have changed the outcome of the entire expedition and that in turn could have changed the course of my life. However, I did recover the knife and quickly surfaced as the last of the air in my cylinder ran out.

When all the party finally arrived in Salcombe they were in high spirits.

The following day there was a lot of sorting-out and setting-up of equipment to be done and we devoted the morning to these tasks. By mid-day we were ready to dive but as the wind was rising we decided to confine ourselves to diving locally. Different pairs of divers explored various sites, collecting specimens for the aquarium we were establishing and looking for suitable areas and subjects for the film. Kay and I were the last to dive and we chose a place in the middle of the estuary. We made our way to the bottom to a depth of about fifty-five feet. This time I had the camera and I filmed the prolific life that we found there despite the fact that the visibility was falling rapidly and in places decreased to two or three feet. I filmed a large, spiny starfish and the delicate filter feeders that deserve a more attractive name than tubeworms. Every nook and cranny was covered with marine life including sponges and seasquirts. Fish abounded.

The following day the wind was still strong and the underwater visibility was very poor. Diving was confined to a single party, led by our biologist Geoff Crockford, who was collecting live specimens for his aquarium.

The following day the weather deteriorated further and the frustrations at not being able to dive and achieve our objectives were starting to tell on the previously harmonious group. Tempers were beginning to fray.

On the fifth day of the expedition the wind and rain were still piling in from the south-west. Despite rough seas we made an attempt to get the *Princess* out to sea but huge waves were breaking over the sand bar at the entrance to the estuary. A party on the shore filmed the brave boat as she punched her way through the waves and bucked like a bronco, but it was obvious to everyone that even if we were able to cross the bar, diving four miles out to sea would be impossible. Reluctantly we turned about. When we were sideways on to the waves the *Princess* rolled like a drunken sailor, and all aboard had to cling to whatever fixture they could to prevent being thrown across the deck. After we had turned round the following sea pushed us quickly back into the relatively quiet waters of the harbour.

That night tempers were reaching breaking point. When everyone was going to bed I left the caravan that I was sharing with three others and walked down to Salcombe. I had to be alone. I had to get away from everyone and think things out. I heard the church clock strike midnight. The

82

streets were wet and black and glistened yellow under the road lights. The town was completely deserted. I walked down to the car park and boat yard where we had our aquarium. The rain spattered the surface and through the side of the aquarium I watched a small thornback ray swimming to the surface exposing its white underside that had the appearance of a ghoulish deathly face. When it had gulped some air it sank back to the bottom. I walked to the edge of the jetty and watched the dark water swirling and gurgling against the stonework. I was aware of the wind and the rain on my face but could not feel them.

I had worked on every member of the group before we departed and my efforts had been most successful — like a chain reaction — with each person generating more and more enthusiasm which had reached a peak when we all departed for our expedition. The analogy with atomic power seemed to fit our situation exactly. I had a group of people who collectively could generate a tremendous force that if harnessed correctly could create something great and durable. But if the power got out of hand the results, like a nuclear generator, could be disastrous.

After five days of emotional stress and frustration how differently they all behaved from how I had anticipated. Dave, our geologist, whom I had thought might be difficult to handle under stress, took the situation with equanimity. Our above-water cameraman had shown himself to be completely unable to shoot film under the stressful conditions. He happily took up other duties and willingly gave the camera to another expedition member who had never taken any cine film before in his life. But the person with whom I was in almost open conflict was our engineer, who had perhaps poured more emotional and physical effort into our project than anyone else apart from myself. I think in the most expansive of his dreams of the future he had foreseen our becoming a really professional full-time organisation. The first step along that road was to produce a successful film and he had put more than his fair share of effort into making it happen. His heartfelt plans were being shattered by the weather and my incompetence as expedition leader.

The following day (the sixth of the expedition) the weather was still cruel and we were again confined to local diving sites. In the morning Kay and I dived at the site known locally as 'The Creek' which was particularly rich in marine life. In the afternoon the weather eased slightly and we moved a little further afield to Starehold Bay where I was able to film the battered remains of one of the last of the great grain clippers, the *Herzogin Cäcilie*. It was sad to think that the scattered, twisted and buckled metal plates we saw on the sea bed were all that remained of a beautiful sailing ship whose masts once strained to the pull of over an acre of sail. But as we were finding out, the sea could be very cruel.

At last, one week after we had arrived the weather showed some signs of improvement and we set off to find the East Rutts. We had some lines of sight bearings, which the fishermen called 'marks', for finding the exact location of the tiny underwater outcrop of rocks. These simple guides to locating diving sites are remarkably accurate provided the points of reference on the shore can be seen. As one of our marks involved lining up a white tower near the coast with a peak on Dartmoor it was with some anxiety that we watched the deteriorating above-water visibility. For if we lost that mark we would never find a lonely needle of rock four miles out to sea.

After a run of two and a half hours out of Salcombe we knew we were in the right vicinity. Our essential mark appeared and disappeared in the mists and low cloud on the moor and we watched the echo sounder anxiously. Then, all of a sudden the scale went from 120 feet to 60 feet and down again to 120 feet in seconds. We had passed over one part of it. We swung round immediately and after several more traverses the echo sounder recorded 40 feet. We threw over a buoy immediately. We'd found it. We'd made it at last, after seven long days of waiting.

Kay and I changed immediately and brought a boudoir smell to the fishing boat as we liberally dusted our diving suits with talcum powder. Wearing a pair of our heavy high-capacity cylinders I sat on the gunwale and dropped backwards like a brick when the *Princess* rolled conveniently. We had timed our arrival to coincide with slack water and I could see the anchor rope stretching in front of the boat which was pulled back in the gentle stream running over the pinnacle. Beneath me, about thirty-five feet down, I could just discern the kelp-covered top of the needle. I made my way to the anchor rope and was joined by Kay. We exhaled and allowed gravity to pull us gently towards the streaming tablecloth of kelp on the flat top of the rock.

The summit of the rock was teeming with fish, most of them heading into the slight current. We continued to swim forward and descend down a steep slope. The kelp plants thinned, and at a depth of fifty feet had disappeared altogether. Away from the top of the pinnacle the water was absolutely still and the visibility increased dramatically. We could see at least sixty feet and what a vista unfolded before us. I had never before seen such intensity of life below the kelp line. Every nook, every cranny of the rock was covered with a profusion of life. Was this part of the fair land of Lyonesse that was said to have sunk and disappeared for ever? The variety of the sea life astounded me. Large colourful edible sea urchins abounded and the fish seemed completely unfrightened by us. One wrasse eyed us alertly and guided us below into an underwater wonderland. There were fronds of pink gorgonian coral growing out of the rock like miniature bushes in a landscape dotted with yellow and black sponges. At 110 feet the rocks shelved away onto a sandy sea bed. Despite the depth the light intensity appeared to be very good and the underwater visibility we estimated to be about sixty feet. It certainly was the most beautiful underwater scenery I had ever seen. I took the plastic net shopping bag that was strapped to my leg and collected samples of the multifarious forms of life for our marine biologist, who was proposing to document the species we found. Such was the variety we could have filled it many times over. Our reconnaissance dive was a success.

We climbed back aboard the *Princess* and waited for our other three most experienced divers, who had followed us into the water, to complete their survey. Allan Hancock, who had dived in many parts of the world with the Royal Air Force, was the first to return. He said he had never seen such a profusion of life — even in the China Seas. Next came Dave Gill, who had also dived in waters reputedly much more exotic than the English Channel. He too said he had never seen such a wealth of plant and animal life. In his specimen bag he carried a number of small chips of rock he had removed from the needle with a hammer. Even before he had climbed the ladder, our geologist took them from him and started to examine them. The rock chips were full of holes like a Gruyère cheese. Dave said that he could not recall any rock like it in the entire area. The needle was a unique geological structure of relatively soft rock and that was probably the reason why the number of sea creatures it supported was so bountiful.

While we had been underwater the sea conditions had noticeably deteriorated. The waves were getting higher. Mike Dornom was getting agitated. We were so excited with our finds that we were quite unaware of the radio playing in the background until the programme was interrupted and the announcer declared to the suddenly silenced group on board the *Princess* that a south-westerly gale force 8 was imminent in sea areas Finisterre, Sole, Plymouth and Portland.

When our marine biologist surfaced and climbed up the diving ladder he stopped and held onto the gunwale. He let the mouthpiece fall from his mouth and uttered one word 'Fantastic!'

As we helped him climb aboard he said 'This place should be made into a nature reserve.'

I could not have agreed with him more. As soon as Geoff was safely aboard Mike Dornom, who normally moves slowly, showed just how fast he could move when the situation demanded it. He hauled the diving ladder inboard and lashed it down. He quickly got us to stow our aqualung cylinders where they would not roll and cause damage. By the time we had completed that task he had started both engines and raised the anchor. With both engines going we ran for Salcombe as fast as we could, the strengthening following wind helping us.

Day seven of our expedition was our lucky day. We had located the needle and shown it to be something quite unexpected — geologically. What was more it was teeming with life. It was just the fillip we needed to dispel the depression and get the group into a more harmonious frame of mind. But as yet we still had our major task before us — to film the needle under water.

After eating our evening meal we crowded into one of the caravans to review the situation. Because of the lost days we needed to substantially increase our under water filming capability. Could this be done by creating another under water cameraman? We had already done so above water. Why not underwater? Underwater photography was more demanding, requiring diving skill and complete compatibility between the cameraman and his partner. But it was worth a try. Two other members of the group who had come together and worked extremely well as a team were Dave Gill and Allan Hancock. Kay and I had already established an excellent cameraman-model relationship. Could Allan and David do likewise? Dave said he would be happy to use the camera and Allan agreed to take on the film star role.

With renewed enthusiasm and hope for success we departed into the blustery night to fortify our spirits still further in the hostelries of Salcombe, knowing that before we could put our new plans into practice we would need the Gods on our side. And they were. For the gale blew itself out during the night. The following day conditions were perfect.

We had left a red marker buoy on the top of the needle and had no difficulty relocating it. We arrived in time to take full advantage of the slack water period between the tides. Kay and I dived first and our pre-arranged sequence of shots went perfectly. We dived only to eighty-five feet and returned to the surface twenty minutes later. Our engineer, now much happier, immediately took charge of reloading the camera for Dave and Allan. Shortly after they had gone overboard a powerful and official looking boat drew up alongside. It was the ever vigilant customs men who wanted to know what we were doing so far out to sea. I explained that we were making a film of a geological survey. When they saw a bag of rock specimens being brought up by a diver they said science was legal, waved us a cheerful goodbye and departed at a very impressive speed.

On thinking about the incident later it was apparent to me that the top of the needle would be an ideal location to leave a cache of smuggled goods. On the assumption that customs men are not fools — and I am sure they are not — I have no doubt the same idea had also crossed their minds.

Kay and I dived again on the needle. Despite the fact that I shivered with cold for over an hour after we had returned to the surface I was extremely happy to have got my target of five minutes' underwater film 'in the can'.

Most people find wrecked ships fascinating. During the following days, when we were unable to visit our needle of rock, we filmed some of the many wrecks in the area. The highlight of our wreck dives was on the *Maine* on the very last day of the expedition. Everyone had worked very hard and most of the divers had lost weight. So on the final day we decided we would have a 'Jolly' — a purely fun dive. A unanimous decision was that we should visit the *Maine*. For me, however, photography had always been fun, so although everyone else was prepared to dive and just look around, I took the 16 mm cine camera with me — and I have never regretted that decision because I got some of the best wreck footage I had ever taken.

Conditions were as near perfect as they could be in the English Channel. The visibility was in excess of sixty feet. Kay, Steve and I followed the buoy line down to the stern where the coral-encrusted gun was still pointing diagonally towards the sky. We were all weighted correctly and perfectly at ease in the water. I filmed Steve examining the breach and muzzle of the gun watched by Kay, who hung in the water as if suspended by an invisible line to the surface. There was no current at all. We swam towards the bow and we could see the vessel stretched out before us. Her huge bronze propeller under her stern had gone, salvaged by the Torbay divers. The spare iron propeller which had no scrap value was still secured on the top of the foredeck and was there for all to see. Shoals of pout whiting swarmed over the deck like swathes of chiffon blowing in a gentle wind. They moved aside as Kay descended through an open hatch. I watched from above and could see her moving over the tangled wreckage inside. She drifted lazily upwards out of number three hold. In the hull of the vessel was a gaping hole made by a torpedo fired from a German U boat in 1918. The 3,600 ton cargo vessel — a victim of war, not the fury of the sea — lay resting peacefully in its grave on the sea bed.

The horrors of her sinking have been forgotten but that sudden death at least saved her from the ignominy of being dismembered in a breaker's yard. After forty-five years she had become an object of both romance and adventure, which if I succeeded with my film would be seen by millions instead of the handful of divers who were now touring her remains like explorers wandering around the overgrown remains of a derelict and previously inaccessible castle.

The word 'rushes' is the name given to the unedited print from a film which is 'rushed' to the studio as soon as possible. Although the name rushes was given to the print from the 4,600 feet of film we shot on our expedition, it was hardly appropriate for it was not until six months later that John Eveleigh, our above-water cameraman, and I were able to view the film at the BBC studios at Ealing. As John and I sat for two and a half hours in the small viewing theatre and watched our film jumping silently from one apparently unrelated sequence to another, I was much more aware of the bad parts of the film (e.g. out of focus, badly framed or incorrectly exposed) than the good. Without the added feature of sound it was a silent, dismembered spectre of our expedition.

We discussed the film with the programme producer, Harry Hastings — who said he was unable to give us a definite answer. We feared the worst. Two weeks later our fears were confirmed. The BBC would not use the film. From our talks with Harry Hastings and Brian Branston we knew why — it lacked a final exciting climax that 99% of those who watch television want and expect every time they switch the wretched thing on.

John and I spent hours probing our minds to see if we could uncover an idea for the one ingredient that we could incorporate in the film to make it a success. Suddenly we found it. David, our geologist, had said he would like a big sample of rock from the pinnacle. We would dynamite a piece off for him. We worked out a new story line and I sent it to Brian Branston telling him that we would be prepared to shoot more film.

Brian expressed enthusiasm for the new story and sent us the rushes of the film in order that we could prepare a 'rough cut', that is, edit out all the bad film and put the remainder together to fit our new story.

John and I spent many evenings in his dining room drinking malt whisky and converting the film, which was nearly a mile long, into a usable form. In March we showed it to the group and told them of our plans. The problem on the use of explosives had been resolved by one member of the group who had given up his office job to become a full time diver-fisherman. His partner, Edwin Tessyman, was experienced in the use of underwater explosives and would do the job for us.

On the last Saturday in May Kay and I again sallied forth before dawn and headed towards Devon. I was driving her VW mini-bus. It was still dark as we crossed the Salisbury Plain. There was no traffic on the road and after leaving Amesbury we sped through the night down the hill towards a major fork in the road. We took the left hand side, signposted Exeter, when Kay requested we should stop. On the right hand side of the road the pillars and arches of Stonehenge were silhouetted black against the navy blue sky. With engine switched off the world outside was completely silent. There was no sign of human life apart from ourselves.

'It's nearly dawn and Midsummer is not far off,' said Kay. 'Let's see the sun rise through Stonehenge.'

It was as good a place as any to stop for a break. Why not?

I parked the VW and we climbed the low perimeter fence and made our way to the centre of the circle of stones just as a hint of grey light eased its way into the eastern skyline. The massive stones stood in a circle about us, silent sentinels to our secret visit and the rites of our forefathers over 2,000 years before us. We were alone in a capsule of history. What enormous spiritual force must have driven the men who, without the aid of the wheel or iron, were prepared to haul the gigantic blocks of stone from Wales, a hundred miles away, to erect them in this special place?

How insignificant the two of us were.

On the most distant horizon a bright orange crescent appeared and silently grew into a yellow disc. The shadows from the pillars lay across the ground as long and straight as fallen pines. The colour of the grassy slopes around glowed yellow-green with life-giving light. A skylark climbed an invisible stairway into the sky and crowded the air with its joyous, melodious song.

We could have been witnessing the creation of the earth. Instead, we were watching the creation of a new day. As the warm orange sun rose in the sky it gradually burned into brilliant white. As it did so the magic of the dawn dissolved into the bright blue sky.

The hum of a car along the road reminded us that we, too, had a journey to make and film to complete.

On that and other trips to Devon during the summer of 1964 we shot another 2,000 feet of film and it was November before I saw the results of our efforts. There was far less wastage than in the first set of rushes — we had learned many lessons the previous year. Harry Hastings was delighted with the new material and said it would fit ideally into a new series he was working on. By January 1965 he had cut our 7,000 feet of film down to 1,500 feet and John and I went again to the studios at Ealing to view the edited version and discuss the commentary and the final editing.

Harry Hastings was not very keen on the title 'Operation Pinnacle' and of the many alternatives we discussed, 'Neptune's Needle' suggested by John, had the necessary alliteration and hint of the subject matter covered in the film. So the title of 'Neptune's Needle' was fixed.

Harry also felt that the wreck sequences which had become a major sequence in the film needed highlighting in some way. I contacted Derek Cockbill and he sent me an old sepia coloured postcard of the *Maine*. Harry copied it and made a sequence in which he panned the camera across the print. The sequence was built into the film and most people who watch the film think they are seeing the *Maine* move through the water.

In April 1965 there was to be an International Film Festival in Brighton. It was an event during which the best underwater photographers in the world challenged one another to display their artistic skill with pictures taken in the marine environment. Competition was extremely keen and I asked Brian Branston if we could submit 'Neptune's Needle'. He agreed, subject to its being finished on time. It was. Just. The film arrived for viewing by the judges on the last day of entry. I had not seen it in its final form.

With other members of the team I went to Brighton and sat in the auditorium anxiously awaiting the film presentations and the announcement of the awards. We did not even know if 'Neptune's Needle' would come high enough on the list to be shown, let alone win an award. We watched film after film and we were getting near the end of the programme when the announcement was made. 'The next film to be shown is 'Neptune's Needle' submitted by Horace Dobbs on behalf of The Oxford Underwater Research Group.'

I sat through the twenty-five-minute film reliving every second of every sequence. Then came the ecstatic moment when it was announced that 'Neptune's Needle' had been given the highest award for a professional film shot in British waters — a gold medal. Then came a surprise further announcement. 'Neptune's Needle' had also won a bronze medal in the International Competition where it had to compete with professional films shot in colour in seas as far apart as Hawaii and the Red Sea.

For that moment alone it seemed all worthwhile.

It took two years to make the film, and 'Neptune's Needle' left its mark on all members of The Oxford Underwater Research Group. When it was all over I felt I had learned more about people than I would ever have done on a dozen courses on personnel management. Most of us involved in the making of 'Neptune's Needle' were in the region of thirty years old and it was a watershed in our lives. The person upon whom it had the biggest impact was probably Kay. By the time the project was over Kay was more restless than ever. She took up a Voluntary Service Overseas post which took her to the Far East. She travelled to Asia on the Trans-Siberian Railway and spent some time with women who dived naked for pearls. On another occasion she moved to the Hawaiian Islands and on a brief return visit to England she told me she was the best diver on Oahu island. Kay was a superb raconteur but I never knew her to exaggerate a story, so I would not be at all surprised if she really was the best diver in Hawaii — male or female. In one of her letters to me she wrote, 'I only hope that age — instead of taking everything away from me as I always feared — will bring me some peace and calm'.

She never found out because she didn't grow old. On a trip into the vast Pacific Ocean the small ship on which she was sailing was lost without trace.

3

In the Cradle of Diving
THE MEDITERRANEAN

The sport of diving was born in the Mediterranean for it
was in the South of France that the American Guy
Gilpatrick first donned a pair of waterproofed flying goggles
and started the sport of 'goggle fishing'. It was Guy
Gilpatrick too who introduced Hans Hass to the underwater
world. And it was in the South of France that the man who
was to popularise the sport beyond all others — Jacques
Cousteau — first tried out the new demand valve
engineered by the Belgian, Emil Gagnan. To divers in
England in the late 1950s the Mediterranean was a
Shangri-La — the warm sea of the legendary 100-foot
visibility, a sea teaming with large groupers such as Merou
the Bonehead, who entertained Guy Gilpatrick for many
hours.

In 1959 as a young married man with a family to support,
the expense of a trip to the Mediterranean would have
placed an impossible burden on the family finances. A
group expedition, in which the travelling expenses would be
shared, however, was within my budget. So one cold winter
night I put it to the diving club that a holiday to the
Mediterranean should be organised for the following year.

The idea was received with enthusiasm and the preparations were put in hand. After studying the various
possibilities carefully it was decided that a new location —
the Costa Brava (the rugged coast) — would be the cheapest
place to go. But it was not without its problems. In the days
before the tourist boom, simply getting diving equipment
into and out of Spain posed considerable difficulties.
Despite correspondence with every conceivable body we
thought might be able to help us, I failed to obtain the

apparently necessary permits to take our equipment into Spain and dive. Plans on the other fronts, however, went as smoothly as such plans ever go, and by the appointed date for departure we had hired two brand new mini buses and

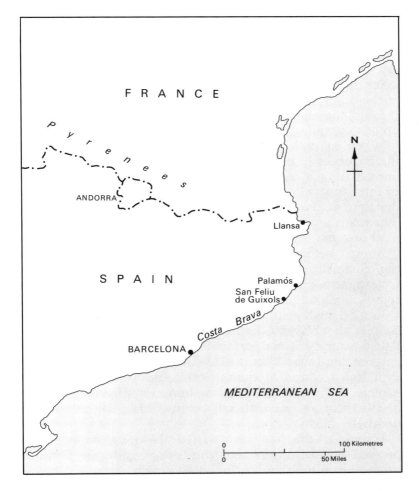

were resolved that we would have a good holiday — if nothing else.

Loaded with camping gear and practically every piece of diving equipment belonging to the club, we sallied forth from Oxford in the early hours of the morning, bound for Lydd airport.

Right from the onset of the trip a friendly rivalry existed between the occupants of the two vehicles. As we drove through southern France the rivalry degenerated into almost open hostility which came to a climax when the question of an overnight stop was raised. As one of the party in our mini-bus was on a heavy drug regimen and Wendy my wife was six months pregnant I felt it important for their sakes that we should have an overnight rest. The occupants of the other vehicle however, wanted to press-on and drive through the night. So we decided to part company and meet up at a camp site near Palamós.

When we passed through the frontier post at the foot of the Pyrenees in bright sunshine the next morning we were immediately aware that we had entered a much poorer country; a donkey burdened with a heavy load was one of the first native forms of goods transport we encountered. The roads to Palamós varied from smooth, freshly laid main road to some very rough minor roads.

Shortly before we departed from England I had contacted the Spanish diving club Centro de Recuperaciónes e Investigaciónes Submarinas (CRIS) in Barcelona and had some correspondence, couched in charming pidgin English, with a Spanish gentleman, Roberto Diáz. He advised me to contact the Naval Commander, as soon as we arrived in Palamós, and get his permission to dive. So as soon as we entered the town I set out to find him. Most places were shut but I found a waiter who could speak French and explained my requirements to him. He directed me to a house bearing an official-looking insignia above the doorbell.

I pressed the bell and waited. Nothing happened. I pressed the bell again and from deep inside the building came a rumbling indicating that somebody was moving. After a further long wait the heavy oak door was opened by a very short fat man dressed in an off-white nightshirt and a night cap. He could speak no English or French, and as I could muster no Spanish, communicating with him was extremely difficult — except he made it clear I shouldn't have woken him from his siesta. However, when he found that I was not to be dismissed easily he made me understand by sign language that I was to report to his house again next morning at 9.00 am. I was to find out later that I had made a major diplomatic blunder by calling on him during the sacrosanct hours of the mid-day siesta.

Being only partially aware of the magnitude of my *faux pas* the next problem to be tackled and resolved was that of locating the camp site and the other members of our party. Finding the site, Camping La Fosca, recommended by Roberto Diáz, was not too difficult. But it did not demand a grain of common sense to see that the site was packed to capacity. A quick search revealed no signs of our companions and on the advice of the manager we headed disconsolately back towards the town to an alternative site. This was not only in a far less desirable position, but was equally crowded. The harassed manager, who could only speak a few words of French, was far less friendly than the previous one and directed us brusquely towards San Feliu de Guixols. By then it was mid-afternoon and the occupants of my mini-bus were hot, hungry and not surprisingly, getting irritable.

We headed out of Palamós along the winding coastal road towards San Feliu de Guixols. We had not gone far when we saw heading towards us an identical white mini-bus. It contained two members of the other half of our expedition and they told us they had located a splendid camping site just a couple of miles outside San Feliu de Guixols. Camping Val d'Or was an excellent site. It had just opened and boasted a bar, a shop and immaculately clean toilet facilities. I had to admit they had come up trumps. The site ran down to a very long vividly white beach composed not of sand but of tiny pebbles. As soon as we had pitched the tents I unpacked my snorkelling equipment to make my first contact with the sea which I had been looking at so longingly, on and off, during the past six hours.

A gentle swell sent the sea creaming up the sand-pebble beach. Beyond the row of tiny white breakers the sea bed shelved steeply and I was soon peering into the vivid blue water. I was no more than a few yards from the beach when

I saw a strange black shape zig-zagging towards me. It looked just like the head of a large fish, with no body at all. Its dorsal fin was mounted where its shoulders would have been had it been human. It had another fin underneath, as if to counterbalance the top fin. And joining these two fins was an apology for a tail. Although this strange creature appeared to be all head it had only a tiny mouth. I recognised it as one of nature's bizarre but successful modifications of the basic fish shape. It was a sun fish, though why it was so called I did not know for it did not look at all sun shaped and it was black in colour. In a few seconds it had disappeared. I looked into the blue expanse to see if I could detect any more of these strange forms but I could not. Although I have dived in the Mediterranean many times since I have never again seen a sun fish.

Seeing something unusual during the first few minutes at a new diving site has been a recurring pattern in my diving experiences. Although I did not realise it at the time I was learning another lesson in photography — always take a camera with you — even on a reconnaissance dive. For such is the perversity of life in the sea that if you leave your camera behind, as I had done, you may miss a unique opportunity.

As I swam away from the beach, I peered intently into the clear blue water. The problems of the long journey fell from my body like particles of sand and I enjoyed the simple pleasure of being able to see further underwater than I had ever been able to see before. The clarity of the water gave the impression of purity: I could see every grain of sand on the sea bed twenty feet below. I took a deep breath and swam down. A few small almost transparent fish scattered as I joined them on the sand and swam over the bottom. I looked across the plain and swam along for ten yards with my chest almost touching the sand before gently floating to the surface. I took a few quick breaths and again finned down to the sea bed which stretched like a desert in all directions until it disappeared into the blue haze at the limit of the underwater visibility, which I guessed was well in excess of 100 feet. Looking along the sea bed the water immediately above the sand had a slight milkiness that dissolved into the pellucid blue of the almost empty sea.

I had entered the sea from the long white beach which was terminated several hundred yards to my right by an outcrop of rocks. I made my way towards the rocks, porpoise fashion, swimming underwater, surfacing and blowing the water out of my snorkel tube before diving again. I passed by several isolated boulders on the sea bed before reaching my objective.

Out of the sandy sea bed the rocks grew, pale-grey and rough. Seen from below they climbed up through the water towards a moving, uneven ceiling of blue. When they reached the surface their rough texture divided the air into a necklace of white bubbles that rose and fell regularly with the slight swell. The sun which was falling behind the rocks burst into the water like a swaying array of search lights, seeking the sand beneath and dappling the sea bed with a moving pattern of bright and less-bright yellow light. Just beneath the wreath of bubbles a shoal of silver bogue glided close to the rocks, rising and falling with the motion of the sea, feeding on morsels of food, unseen to me, that were dislodged from the rocks by the surge. Beneath them the rocks were speckled with the black spiky pincushions of sea urchins each the size of a small apple. The hard needle spines of the sea urchins provided them with a good defence as they browsed on the rocks, constantly devouring any tiny organisms that settled on the surface, keeping the rock surface almost bare of any other forms of life.

The picture, of which I was a living, moving part, was a cameo of the basic ingredients of life: air, water and light. It was beautiful and elemental. I could feel the urge that a few years before had drawn the pioneers of underwater swimming into the virgin coastal waters of the Mediterranean.

When the sun set behind the rocks casting a dark shadow over the scene I realised I was starting to feel cold. I swam back to my entry point and climbed the still sun-warmed beach tired but happy.

The next morning I drove back into Palamós and called at the house of the Naval Commander. This time he was ready for me and presented a totally different image for he was dressed in his official uniform. I followed him as he strutted arrogantly towards his office. When we reached his office he sat himself pompously at his desk beneath a huge framed picture of General Franco. Having established himself as a man of considerable importance he looked at me impassively across his polished mahogany desk. I explained in both English and French that I had a party of divers and wanted permission to dive in the area. But I felt as if I might as well have spoken to the picture of Franco, for not a flicker of understanding passed across his face. I decided that verbal communication between us was impossible without the aid of an interpreter. So I departed to one of the many bars nearby and found a waitress who could speak French. She was reluctantly persuaded to accompany me into the presence of the Naval Commander.

I went through my situation slowly and after a protracted and somewhat exasperating debate he asked me for evidence of the diving ability of my party. I produced my own British Sub Aqua Club log book. Upon seeing that, he asked for the log books of all my party, which I had omitted to bring with me. I could sense that further debate would be of no use. So I agreed to return with the documents the next morning.

I returned along the hot dusty road to the camp site and found the rest of my party sunning themselves on the beach. That evening I gathered their diving log books together and the next morning saw me motoring back to Palamós whilst they prepared themselves for another idle morning. I parked the mini-bus and collected my barmaid interpreter before once again presenting myself to the Commander.

At the appropriate moment I produced from my pocket the fourteen log books and spread them impressively across the desk. The Commander picked one up, flicked through the pages and tossed it back on the table. The barmaid translated his remark. 'You are too many to dive.' Despite my protest he would not change his mind and I left his office and thanked the barmaid for her help. The only person I thought could help me now was my contact in Barcelona with whom I had corresponded. I found his letter amongst my papers and set out to telephone him. I located a telephone in a bar and a waiter who could speak English said he would get the number in Barcelona for me. He told me he would have to book the number and that I should return in one and a half hour's time. I could not understand how such a telephone system worked, but agreed to do as I was told. In a dejected mood I strolled around the tourist shops in the increasing heat. When I returned it took only about ten minutes for the call to get through and I spoke to Roberto Diáz for the first time.

It is not until you come to discuss something with somebody in a foreign language over the telephone that you realise how important gestures and looks are when communicating with a person. After several frustrating attempts I eventually understood that I should contact the local agent of the CRIS club, Señor Francisco Gubert, whose address I was given. I tracked him down in a sack-making factory. He agreed to meet me the following afternoon, after his factory had closed, and that we could jointly visit the Naval Commander. By the time we had completed our arrangements it was well past lunchtime on day three of our previous ten days on the Costa Brava.

On day four, well after the siesta period, we joined forces and I again tackled the Commander. By this time the situation had degenerated into a scene from a farce well beyond *HMS Pinafore*. The Commander agreed that we were all well qualified to dive and that really the size of our party was of no significence. He claimed that we would have to get permission from the naval authorities in Barcelona before we could dive. My new-found ally translated this latest piece of nonsense for my benefit and then launched into a passionate argument in the time-honoured Latin manner. He pleaded with his voice, with his hands and his eyes. I could not have wished for a better man to put our case. But all was to no avail. The Commander sat in his chair beneath his picture of Franco, and refused to accede to my request. The answer was an emphatic 'NO'.

To drive one thousand miles and then be unreasonably refused by a pompous official angered me beyond measure. Could we risk diving without the Commander's permission? If we did we stood the chance of losing virtually all of the club's diving equipment for armed militia patrolled the beaches. If we were to go into the water wearing aqualungs we were certain to attract attention. Could we risk it? I decided to put it to the rest of the party when I returned to the camp site.

I drove back along the now familiar long winding dusty and almost uninhabited road between Palamós and San Feliu de Guixols. I turned down the unmade road that led to the camp site and clouds of dust stirred up by my passage settled on the corn-on-the-cob growing in the field alongside. Most of the party were in high spirits. They had been into San Feliu. One of them said he had found a shop selling diving equipment. On describing our plight, the proprietor had replied that if we all joined the local diving club, a branch of CRIS, we would all be allowed to dive. Thereupon he produced the membership forms.

The next morning I was in the shop with the requisite fees and photographs and we were all signed up on the spot. It was day five — exactly half way through our ten-day stay and at last we could dive. That moment brought home to me an important lesson. It is that reward is often completely unrelated to effort. I had spent half of my holiday battling with bureaucracy. Yet the situation had been resolved in a few minutes by the laziest member of the party who was out enjoying himself in nearby San Feliu whilst I was angrily battling with the Commander in Palamós.

We had already reconnoitred the coast for suitable diving sites and immediately we had our diving cars we set off for a rocky promontory that looked to us to be a good location. Before we left England I had painted a metal disc with the primary colours and a few mixtures of them to observe and photograph the effects of changing depth on colour. I had also set myself another objective — to find and photograph an octopus.

My diving partner on that occasion was to be Ann Symons, the secretary of the club and one of its most experienced divers. I gave Ann the coloured disc and we cautiously made our way down the rocks to the sea. The rocks were extremely uneven and sharp. And just getting into the sea encumbered with aqualung and weightbelt, without damaging myself, and more importantly my camera, was not without difficulties. At last I launched myself forward into the water. Ann was beside me and we swam clear of the coast before switching from our snorkels to our aqualungs. We finned to a submerged pinnacle of rocks and swam slowly downwards. I watched the disc as we sank and at a depth of only ten feet the red sector had darkened considerably, whilst the yellow blue and green sectors appeared relatively unchanged. Ann waited patiently whilst I took a reading of the light intensity and adjusted the various camera controls. The sea was very clear and as she had weighted herself exactly to be neutrally buoyant she remained suspended in the water with the ease of a lazy goldfish. I took my picture and we turned head down and finned gently to a depth of sixty feet. At this depth the red sector of the disc had apparently changed to a dark purple and the white central section looked pale blue. The other colours had become darker and less vivid but were still recognisable.

At a depth of seventy feet we were nearing the sea bed and I tapped Ann on the shoulder and signalled in the direction of another pinnacle towards which I wanted to head. She swam off and I followed close behind. After travelling twenty yards she turned to check that I was following. She gave me the 'are you O.K.?' signal by holding her thumb and index finger together in the shape of a circle. I replied 'yes I am O.K.' with the same hand signal which we had practised many times before during our training sessions in the pool and in the sea.

She turned and swam off. As she did so one of her fins clipped my face, knocking the breathing tubes out of my mouth and my facemask up onto my forehead. She was obviously quite unaware of what she had done, for she swam away from me towards our pre-determined destination.

At that precise moment I was very thankful for all the training I had undergone. I was seventy feet down, I could not see clearly because my mask was dislodged and I had no air, for my mouthpiece was floating above my head pouring unbreathed air up to the surface. I released one of my handholds on the camera housing and reached up for my breathing tubes. I put my mouthpiece in position and thankfully breathed air vital to my continued existence. I pulled my mask back over my nose and eyes. Holding the top of the mask with my hand I held my head back and exhaled gently through my nose. As the air displaced the water my vision became clear and I could see Ann still making steady progress towards the pinnacle — mistakenly confident that I was following her because she had just given me the O.K. sign.

An incident that could have had fatal consequences was over in less than a minute. I gathered my composure and swam after her.

As we swam over the sand I saw a silver shell glinting in the bright light. It was the shape of a tiny ear and had a row of small holes in it. As I picked it up I noticed another object protruding from the sand. It was grey and covered with algae. I put my camera housing onto the sea bed and grasped the strange object with both hands. It moved but the base was well buried. I joggled it back and forth and after a short time I was able to wrench it free. It was a bi-valve shell, shaped like a mussel but well over twelve inches long.

It seemed as if my dive had only just started but when I looked at my air cylinder contents gauge I could see that the needle was approaching the thirty atmospheres mark. It was time to return to the surface. I signalled to Ann and clutching my camera and the shells we drifted slowly upwards.

When the large shell was opened later at the camp site we were surrounded by other campers, who were unashamedly inquisitive. The outside of the shell was covered in growth which had appeared dull in the depths. On the surface however, it became bright red in colour. I slid my diving knife between the two halves and severed the abductor muscle which held the two components tightly together. When I had prised the two shells apart I found that only a relatively small part of the inside was filled. I scooped out what was obviously an organ designed to filter food from the sea and found a crab, whose body was the size of a very large pea. The shell with the crab inside it probably enjoyed a symbiotic relationship — the crab eating any mites or parasites that might fancy imposing themselves on the mussel in return for protection within the shells that could clamp shut like a drawbridge. My public dissection of the *pinna nobilis*, or pen shell, revealed that the inside surface at the broad end of the shell, had the smooth brown texture of polished tortoiseshell. At the pointed base the brown melted into a small area of opalescent mother of pearl. I have since been told that large pen shells are much prized as *hors d'oeuvre* dishes. Indeed one member of our party was invited to join a local Spaniard who dived commercially for such shells.

Once we had broken the authority barrier our diving was relatively unhindered for we were able to resolve with little difficulty another problem which can prove tiresome (the supply of high pressure air for our cylinders) when we located a convenient compressor in San Feliu.

We also located a couple who had set up a diving school in the town. They were Pat and Joan Harrison. Wendy and I visited the Harrisons one evening and they recounted to us the tremendous number of financial and bureaucratic difficulties they had experienced when trying to establish their diving school. Remembering my own recent encounters with the Naval Commander in Palamós I understood exactly how frustrated they must have felt. The evening passed convivially and we looked at underwater photographs and discussed picture-taking technique in the Mediterranean.

The next day I joined Pat and Joan for a dive at one of their favourite sites. I gave Pat my cine camera and took the still camera for my own use.

Pat Harrison obviously enjoyed using the cine camera and as we drifted slowly down I saw him swimming around me filming happily. The cine camera was fitted with the fixed focus wide angle lens. The coupled exposure meter took care of all changes in the light intensity. So all he had to do was wind the camera and film. I, on the other hand, had to reset all of the camera controls for every still picture I took, with my Voigtlander Vito B camera inside its home-made Perspex case. It would sometimes take up to a minute before I could get the camera properly set up for a single photograph. And as the total duration of a dive with the equipment I was using was only about twenty minutes, my picture taking capacity was not high. Finally, the flash gun which I had incorporated in the camera housing was unreliable.

Before we set off for the dive Pat had told me of a feature that he would point out to me. It was a chimney through the rocks. At a depth of about sixty feet he signalled to me and I joined him under an overhanging rock. I looked up. The view was like looking into a telescope filled with fish. The sides of the chimney were not even but a disc of light with the surface of the sea beyond was clearly visible as a silver blue dics at the end of the tunnel. Inside, the black silhouettes of dozens of fish lazily drifting up and down and from side to side were framed by the irregular sponge-encrusted rocks.

It was another cameo of placid underwater life that I have since treasured as a memory.

When we reached the rocky sea bed about eighty feet down I could not take pictures because my flash had ceased to function, and the light intensity was too low for natural light pictures. Pat was still happily filming however.

As we glided over the uneven boulders something strange caught my eye. The conformation of one group of boulders looked somewhat unnatural at close quarters. I drifted away slightly and suddenly the previously unidentified images I was looking at crystallised in my brain. I was looking at a cannon, covered in marine growth, jumbled amidst the boulders. Once I had identified it I could not understand how I had not recognised it immediately. I swam excitedly over to Pat and signalled to him. I pointed out my find to him. As soon as he recognised it he pointed his first and second fingers at me, as if he was a schoolboy using his fingers as a gun. Sign language in the deep. He filmed me indicating the cannon before we made our way slowly back to the surface.

When we were discussing our dive later Pat said he had never observed the cannon before — despite numerous dives in the area. I have heard of similar reports from other divers which identifies one aspect of diving which I would rate as one of its attractions as a pastime. The total area scanned by a single diver may be quite small, and so much can be missed that every diver stands a chance of seeing or finding something unique, even at a popular diving site.

I telephoned Roberto Diáz in Barcelona and told him the news concerning our resolution of the problem of diving permits and that we had confined our activities to the San Feliu vicinity. The language barrier again proved a difficulty but I agreed to meet him in Palamós on Sunday. I did not fully comprehend the arrangements but my understanding of the purpose of the meeting was to organise a dive. Thus, when I set off in one of the mini-buses to Palamós with just a few of our party the aqualungs were put in the back almost as an afterthought. When we arrived in Palamós we were greeted by the Barcelona Branch of CRIS who had driven to Palamós for the specific purpose of diving with us.

As soon as I met Roberto Diáz, the difficulties in communication that we had experienced over the telephone disappeared. We were quickly able to resolve our problems and agreed to dive there and then.

To this day I have a pin sharp image of that descent into the open sea fused into my memory. The sea was a brilliant transparent turquoise blue. I sank slowly feet first. As I did so I rotated gently and it seemed as if the sea was as clear and blue as the sky. Around me the divers were making their way to the bottom at different speeds. I tried to descend more quickly but my ears hurt and I knew that a rapid descent would be foolish.

I could see every detail on every diver. It was as if there was no water between us. I had never experienced such clarity. From their demand valves air billowed in spurts and the bubbles coruscated as they chased one another upwards. Near the surface the bubbles were like oscillating silver puddles that expanded and divided into a joyous rush for the freedom of the atmosphere.

Seeing that I was having some difficulty in my descent one of the Spanish divers swam over to me. I pointed to my ears in an attempt to explain my slow descent. The Spaniard removed his face mask, pinched his nose and blew. He then replaced his mask and cleared the water from it by exhaling through his nose. All of his movements were extremely precise and I understood immediately the point he was trying to make — probably thinking I was a novice. In order to appease him I went through the same ritual. But I knew from experience that I could not descend as rapidly as most divers.

By this time the majority of the divers were below me and had formed pairs. I looked around and a shapely figure in a black suit approached. I recognised the silhouette at a glance. It was the only female in the Spanish group. Did she also think I was a novice? She did. And took me by the hand. At that moment I decided that being a novice had its advantages and I was going to enjoy being one. I looked into the facemask of my new-found diving companion, whose eyes were still made-up and looked more alluring than ever due to the magnification of the water. I again pointed to my ears and tried to signify that I would have to descend slowly. She appeared to understand.

Because of the misunderstanding concerning the diving arrangements I had not taken an underwater camera with me and for a change I was able to concentrate entirely on what I saw around me. I could see the sea bed from the surface although not clearly as the haze gave it a slightly out of focus appearance, but I could recognise the rocky nature of the terrain. As we approached the bottom we passed through a cloud of small black damsel fish that parted company to let us through and then reformed over our heads. My partner, who had been watching me during our entire descent, was still obviously concerned about my safety.

She swam over to me, took my hand in hers and pointed in the direction in which she wanted us to go. As she did so, I looked at her and she looked at me — the blinkered vision of facemasks making such visual communication a very positive gesture. I nodded my head to signify that I was happy with the situation. We were heading for a valley between the rocks and swam slowly forward — still hand in hand. I scanned the bottom: a rubble of boulders on sand. I noticed a spike of white gorgonian coral attached to a rock like the bleached skeleton of a tree in an arid landscape. I was peering into the crannies of the rocks looking for an octopus. Beyond the gulley and hidden from view were another group of divers. Their presence was revealed by the plumes of bubbles that rose like smoke signals from behind the rocks. We finned lazily towards the ridge. As we floated over the top the entire group came into view. Clouds of silt were suspended in the water where they had disturbed the bottom. On the bottom I saw what looked like a stone sphere. I released myself from my partner's grasp and managed to pull the object off the rocks. As I did so a cloud of silt swirled up into the water and I noticed the characteristic dark brown stain of iron on the rocks. The sphere I was holding was not made of stone at all. It just had the appearance of stone because of calcareous concretions in which it was covered. It was a cannon ball.

I knelt on the rocks with the prize in my hand and considered my chance of getting it to the surface. I decided that it would be possible, but the effort involved in doing so and getting back down to the sea bed would almost certainly use up the remainder of my air. So I abandoned the idea. I let the cannon ball fall from my grasp. It hit the rocks with a dull but perceptible thud. I was later told that the French had beseiged Palamós during the Napoleonic wars. When the town capitulated the French destroyed the fortifications and dumped a number of the cannons and their ammunition in the sea.

Had the cannon ball I found been fired in anger? Or was it one that had been junked? The answer to that question I shall never know, but there was evidence that the French had suffered some losses. I found a piece of wood, riddled with worm holes, that obviously looked like a piece of wreckage. I picked it up and we swam on towards the group into an area that was more obviously a dumping ground. Cannon balls lay scattered over the sea bed and amongst them, randomly arrayed as if they had been thrown on the sea bed like dice onto a table, were an assortment of cannons. They too were encrusted with the concretions of the marine organisms that had built their homes on the new firm solid substrates kindly provided by man.

I noticed, that two of my party were leaving the sea bed,

sixty feet down, and heading towards the surface. The air supplies of the British divers were running low. When I commenced the dive I had been trying to keep my air consumption to a minimum by deliberately taking shallow breaths. In the excitement of finding the cannons I had forgotten to do so and I suddenly realised that I was using up my air fast. I was beginning to feel chilled. I looked at my white skinny arms and noticed they were covered in goose pimples. I shivered slightly and was momentarily annoyed that lack of air should bring to a premature close the adventure that seemed to have only just started. But I still had enough air to stay down for a further five precious minutes and that time I spent exploring the sea bed. If a French ship had been sunk here there was always the chance that I might find something exciting. Gold does not decay in the sea.

When the needle on my air cylinder contents gauge was well into the red I signalled to the black-suited lady who had so gallantly escorted me. Very lazily I let myself drift upwards still clutching my worm-eaten piece of timber. I was aware that the world was becoming brighter and more intensely blue as we neared the surface. I could hear the slow throb of the engine of the fishing boat and could see it clearly from below. The propeller was not turning. I surfaced beside it and quickly released my aqualung harness after handing my trophy to someone on board.

Having chaperoned me back to the boat my diving partner disappeared silently below the surface to rejoin her countrymen who were still rummaging below. Finding them was easy. She just had to look for their plumes of bubbles and follow them down.

The sea had got up whilst we were below and the boat rocked with irregular movements in the swell. A thin layer of cloud veiled the sun, but the air was warm and I lay on the deck to get what heat I could back into my cold limbs. I had not been lying on my towel for more than a few minutes when I heard a 'Hey' from over the side of the boat. I went to investigate and found one of the Spanish divers alongside with his life jacket inflated. He was not in trouble but had a cannon ball clutched to his chest. I leaned over the side and lifted it on board — delighted to have the opportunity to examine one at my leisure on the surface. The diver released the air from his jacket and swiftly descended again in a flurry of bubbles. A few minutes later he reappeared with another cannon ball and then another.

It was almost an hour after we had left the water that the last of the Spanish divers surfaced and climbed into our boat. Roberto Diáz ordered the boats back to harbour and we sat together talking. He apologised for the fact the sun was no longer shining, and for the misunderstanding over the arrangements. I told him that as far as I was concerned everything was perfect. When he offered me one of the cannon balls as a souvenir my pleasure was complete.

As we arrived at the jetty we were met by a sinister-looking member of the Spanish military police, wearing a green uniform and a black hat with the flap turned-up at the back. He clutched what looked to me like a sten gun. It was suspended from a black strap over his shoulder, and he held it with one hand at hip level. He examined every article we removed from the boats and placed on the jetty. Finally came the cannon balls. They were placed in a neat pyramid on the stone jetty. At which point, the *guardia*, whom we had all pretended to ignore to that point, became intrusive. He was a coarse-featured man, who did not look too bright. The type I felt who would pull the trigger of the gun he was fondling first, and then ask the questions after. 'Aha!' he said 'What are these?' in gruff Spanish. Roberto Diáz stepped forward and explained that they were cannon balls and there were lots of them lying on the sea bed.

Thereafter the rate of conversation accelerated until it developed into a full scale shouting match which ended with the soldier placing one of his jack-booted feet on the pile of cannon balls and pointing his gun, still at hip height, at Roberto Diáz with his finger round the trigger. Thereupon Roberto threw his hands into the air in a gesture of despair. He walked over to me, his face still alight with passion.

'That man is a peasant — a moron' he said. 'He says we must get the Naval Commander's permission to take the cannon balls!'

We cleared our diving equipment rapidly from the jetty

and loaded it into the cars. Needless to say, getting the Naval Commander's permission was out of the question. When we drove away the soldier was still standing with one foot on the cannon balls and clutching his gun. I have never been back to Palamós and I wonder if he is still there. After all he could not have carried the cannon balls away with him. And if he left them behind, someone may have pinched them whilst he was away at the Commander's house asking his permission to move them!

★　★　★

My first excursion into the cradle of diving took place during the fortnight in August 1960 when various industrial works in Oxford took their summer holidays. In December of the same year my son Ashley was born. During his very early schooling days he was asked if he had been under the water with his father. He said that he had. When questioned as to how one so young could have such an experience he replied 'I was inside my mummy's tummy'. When he described underwater scenes and was asked how he came by such knowledge he replied 'I peeped out through her belly button.'

My daughter Melanie, who was just over two years old stayed behind in England with her grandmother whilst her unborn brother was peering into the depths through the navel of her mother snorkelling in the Mediterranean.

In subsequent years we made several memorable family holiday excursions to the Mediterranean.

In 1969 we found and raised a large Roman vessel called an amphora which was used for storing wine. It was made in about 150 BC, and we have often speculated on how it came to be off an island near Llansa where we found it in a crevice in the rocks partly buried in sand. Was it discarded when the contents had been consumed in a drunken revelry? Or was it thrown overboard as an offering to the gods (a common practice amongst Roman sailors in the pre-Christian era)?

On another holiday to a completely different location — the island of Elba — we came across treasure of a different kind. It happened off a tiny island called Gemini, on the day the very first American Gemini rocket was successfully launched into space. I was aqualung diving with Melanie, who was 13 years old, and we saw something glinting in the sand. We picked it up. There was no doubt about it — it was a solid gold ring with mystic symbols embossed on it. Melanie has worn that ring to this day. Nobody has been able to decipher the symbols and because gold is not affected by the sea we have no idea how old the ring is. Is it more than co-incidence that Melanie's birth sign is Gemini?

One of my disappointments on my first visit to the Mediterranean was that I didn't see an octopus; I have seen dozens since. On a sentimental pilgrimage back to Llansa in 1984 I was out diving with Melanie's husband Don when we cane across two octopuses mating. It was a fascinating sight, and the two were so engrossed in their sixteen-armed embrace that they stayed out in the open despite a little manipulation for the purposes of photography. Melanie, who was pregnant at the time and interested to witness how octopuses procured their progeny, snorkelled overhead to view the scene.

I am now the excessively proud grandfather of a beautiful granddaughter Rebecca. I wonder if, like her uncle Ashley, Rebecca will one day tell fanciful tales at school about a pre-parturition excursion under the Mediterranean with her grandfather — after all I have called this chapter 'The Cradle of Diving'.

4

Caribbean Corals

THE ATLANTIC OCEAN

About four fifths of our planet is covered with water. The variety of scenery just beneath the surface is as varied as that on the land although the *type* of scenery depends upon many factors — one of the most important being the water temperature. Corals can only flourish if the water temperature remains above 18 °C. There is therefore a girdle round the equator where the richest coral growths can exist. In the Atlantic Ocean it reaches as far north as Florida. And after years of dreaming and longing to dive in truly tropical seas an opportunity came my way in 1970 when I was invited to give a paper at a scientific conference in San Francisco. It was combined with several other business meetings in the USA. By stretching my expenses, my savings, my leave and my employer's good will I was able to tack on to the business trip a brief visit to the Florida Keys for my wife and myself.

As we flew towards Miami on the daily BOAC flight from London, we could see the Keys projecting like a sickle from the Florida mainland towards the Gulf of Mexico. The islands, or Keys, were set like amber studs in a multi-hued turquoise sea.

It was the colour of the sea that occupied my interest, because when I gazed through the window of our Boeing 707 and could see the submerged areas of sand and coral reef clearly differentiated as shades of blue, I knew the 'viz' in the warm waters around the Keys was good.

A line of clouds clustered over the Keys was overshadowed at one point by a thundercloud like a giant mushroom on a tray of white candy floss. We skirted the thundercloud. The yellow-blue expanse of Biscayne Bay sped underneath us, soon to be replaced by the rubber-plant green and water-strewn swamps of the Everglades.

I did not think the crowded airport at Miami was air-conditioned until we stepped outside into the Turkish bath climate that is summer in Florida.

'It's 85° and 95 per cent humidity here in down-town Miami,' proclaimed the weatherman on the local radio station.

We were greeted by an American family who had driven their 'camper' down from New York. Campers were already

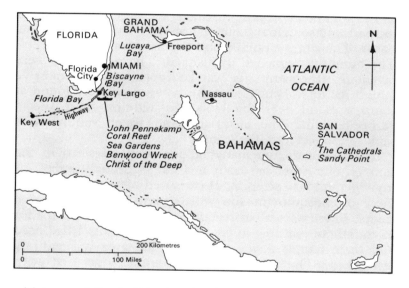

widely used for holidaying in the USA. They are compact caravan-like homes which fit on to pick-up trucks. They have the advantage that they virtually become an integral part of the truck, and can therefore be occupied when the vehicle is on the move. The camper, however, can be quickly detached from the truck and will stand free on legs.

Miami used to connect with Key West (the southernmost city in the USA) via a railway. But part of the railway was destroyed in a hurricane and a road now joins the Keys together like a string through a row of beads. Alongside the road, the water pipeline, clad in aluminium to reflect the heat, extends like an infinite knitting needle. The highway, US1, is the umbilical cord to Key Largo and places like the ports of Ferandina and Jacksonville.

Fifty-five miles out of Miami, we pulled off the US1 into the entrance of the John Pennekamp Coral Reef State Park. At the lodge we were greeted by a friendly, heavily-built ranger with a lugubrious but efficient manner. Bib-shaped sweat patches darkened his khaki shirt beneath the arms. He mentioned that it was 85° and 95 per cent humidity as he nonchalantly swatted a mosquito taking its supper from his soft brown arm. It was 8.30 in the evening East Coast time, and 1.30 in the morning in Britain. We were given a map of the park and soon found our allocated site beside the Marina Basin. The sun set rapidly and the temperature fell to 80°. The humidity remained unchanged. The mosquitoes were ravenous. Our camp site was equipped with the massive table with fixed benches, of the type which were found at camp sites all over the USA. In addition there was a barbecue grill. The electricity and water supply were rapidly connected to the camper.

As there were too many in our party to sleep in the camper, our American hosts had kindly brought a tent for my wife and I to sleep in. It consisted of a cottage-shaped piece of mosquito muslin which hung from an external frame. There were no instructions and it took some time for us to fathom out how to erect it; all other tents I had used had their frames inside. The camping area was entirely tarmacked. The guylines were eventually secured with metal pegs which we hammered directly into the hard ground. The tent was big enough to enclose the picnic table and two beds. What went on, or came off, inside the tent was clearly visible from the outside, but such exposure was of no consequence to us, we were thankful to drop on to the beds.

We lay there listening to the humming and then the dreaded silence as a trapped mosquito settled down for a late supper. Our hosts, accompanied by four of their children, bade us 'goodnight' and were engulfed in their camper. The yellow rectangles of light which were the windows, turned black as the lights went out. Silence. Minutes later, the still night air erupted to unstifled howls of anguish as the 'bugs' which had been lurking in the camper moved in for a feast on any exposed young arms and faces. Yellow rectangles of light again punctured the silver walls of the camper. The hum of the mosquitoes was overrun by sporadic bursts of fire from an aerosol insect repellant can. The lights went out again as our friends tried to settle their tired children, in the humid insecticide-filled camper. I was pleased that we were outside.

Opposite the entrance to the John Pennekamp Coral Reef State Park was a sign, very modest by American standards, which told us that we were at the Carl Gage Diving Center.

At ten o'clock the next morning there was no sign of the mosquitoes. The temperature close to the buildings was rising to 100 °F and the machine dispensing ice-cold drinks gobbled nickels like a Las Vegas fruit machine.

The inside of the building, a strikingly cool 80 °F, was a cornucopia guaranteed to delight the eye of a diver. Cylinders, harnesses, life-jackets, watches, cameras, depth gauges, fins, masks, knives, demand valves, weightbelts and even underwater scooters were displayed in extravagant profusion. Amidst the melee of patrons of assorted ages, shapes and sizes, a team of bronzed athletic youngsters served the customers and made arrangements for the day's diving expedition.

I was ushered through to the workshop to meet the owner of this fine diving centre. The inscrutable Carl Gage was short and built like an ox. His shaved head was the same bronze colour as the rest of his muscular frame. I felt like Anna being introduced to the King of Siam. The blurb on the hand-out leaflets told me, amongst other things, that Carl Gage was an air-line pilot, a sky-diving photographer, a military parachutist and jump-master and decorated veteran of the Korean conflict. He held the rank of Major in the Marine Corps Reserve.

He invited me to join the expedition, to the reef leaving that morning, and asked me what equipment I needed. Nancy, a shapely diving instructress, produced the diving gear immediately. After a further exchange of terse sentences, I left his somewhat daunting presence and wandered back into the bazaar-like shop. Eventually, all those joining the expedition were lined-up outside in the white sunlight for 'life-vest drill'. The man leading the expedition who introduced himself as Captain Mike Voigt, was the American dream youth personified: over six feet tall with short hair bleached almost white by the sun, and a muscular body tanned evenly to a deep golden brown. In a totally monotonous voice, he went through the ritual of explaining how the lifejackets should be worn and inflated in case of emergency.

Then with the essential preliminaries at last completed, we set off in a convoy of cars for one of the boats which was moored about two miles from the centre. I joined the instructors in the leading truck, which was easily identified by the yellow mini-submarine perched on the roof like a bulbous cigar. With the heavy gear stowed evenly around the stern of the boat, and the packed sandwiches and multitudinous cans of aerated mineral water deposited in the ice box, we set sail in the direction of the reef five miles offshore. The green-blue water sped under the boat like snow past a toboggan. We were soon at the first site, and anchored over a shallow outcrop of coral called Sea Garden.

The party was divided into three groups of about ten. I joined Nancy's group. We put on snorkelling equipment: facemasks, snorkels and fins. Instant tuition was given to those who had not worn the equipment before. The experienced snorkellers stood poised briefly on the gunwale, and then leapt into the sea with bravura. The more timid and less experienced had to be coaxed to launch themselves from a height of three feet into the water. Some just couldn't pluck up enough courage, and retired at the last minute to mingle discreetly with the small bunch of non-diving passengers.

Our party of snorkellers, clustered round Nancy like a family of ducklings, moved on an arc-shaped course away from the boat. For security the novices kept close to mother-duck Nancy. One large, middle-aged male straggled behind the party. Despite vigorous efforts he could not make very fast progress. His leg movements, those of a cyclist, were very inefficient at propelling him through the water. If he had used the correct leg stroke, that of a slow crawl, his fins would have propelled him efficiently through the water with the expenditure of much less of his failing energy. Nancy was soon by his side. He wanted to go on, but couldn't get the hang of the correct leg strokes, so Nancy towed him to the group. Hand in hand with her charge, she led the unlikely armada over the glassy sea.

Our party, who had been swimming over a sandy sea bed, suddenly reached the outcrop of coral which was the destination. Our eyes scanned the fairyland of soft and hard coral which was revealed beneath them with startling clarity. No other landscape, natural or unnatural, has the diversity of form or texture of a coral reef. The coral reef has been likened to a petrified forest. But appearances are deceptive. For this is not a dead forest. Each coral is a colony of microscopic animals removing salts from the sea and depositing them in a never-ending do-it-yourself housing programme. Each variety builds in an individually characteristic manner.

The results of most of man's efforts at architecture are puny when compared with the wealth of shapes which have been evolved by these tiny simple creatures. Some of their homes resemble leafless trees, with the trunks firmly anchored to the reef and their slender branches spreading outwards and upwards with arboreal elegance. The order of corals, the gorgonacea, which build the sea whips and sea fans, give their structures flexibility. Like palm trees bowing before a hurricane, they bend in the water currents and survive the sometimes violent surges of sea.

In contrast, the true or stony corals, have adopted a recalcitrant attitude to their environment. Their structures take the form of fortresses, designed to withstand the poundings of the sea. Some are elaborate and bizarre whereas others take simple forms. They are all beautiful.

The corals feed on the minute organisms suspended in the sea. Some varieties of these zoological construction workers reside permanently on the exterior of their homes, endowing the coral with a characteristic colour and surface appearance. Many of these microcreatures however, are shy of the light. They retire into the labyrinths of their fortresses during the day and all that is visible to the diver is the grey architecture of their labours. Such is the brain coral. As dusk falls, the intricate contours of its surface become emblazoned with colour as the hungry inmates emerge to take their just harvest from the sea.

There is relatively little life to be found in shifting sand. But wherever there is an outcrop from the sandy sea bed — be it rocks or a wreck — then there is sanctuary, and all forms of sea life come crowding in. The coral reef we saw below us was no exception. It abounded with fishes.

Nancy let go the hand of her ward and snorkelled fifteen feet down to a sea-whip coral with an angel fish flirting in its branches.She hovered momentarily, almost touching the fin of the fish with her finger; the fish idly moved to the far side of the coral. Nancy surfaced and announced to her party that we had just seen a grey angel fish. She obviously loved the sea and enjoyed her role as guide to Neptune's treasure house. She sounded again and again. She blew into her snorkel tube each time she surfaced and the trapped water fountained into the air. With the soft seductive tones of the American South, she told her retinue the names of the fishes and corals they were floating over.

The party, entranced by the beauty of the subaqua scene, were unaware of the passage of time or distance. In fact, they had idled their way in a giant semi-circle and were closing in on the boat, which sat motionless on a sea without swell. Submerged ladders attached to a platform over the stern of the boat made leaving the sea no more difficult than clambering out of a swimming pool.

The burble of excited voices merged with the piped music emerging from the cabin. Gesticulating husbands, their masks pulled up on their foreheads and still wearing their fins, plodded like clowns about the deck as their incredulous wives were told of their experiences. The women snorkellers had a greater sense of dignity than the men. They removed their fins and masks, and shook their heads so that their wet hair fell into style, before eagerly describing the reef to their wide-eyed, less adventurous companions.

The other snorkelling parties were quickly on board and the anchor was hauled in. The boat shuddered as the powerful engine throbbed into life. The piped music died and we skimmed out to the main reef for the next stage of the expedition — the aqualung dive. Whilst the boat was speeding towards the reef the aqualung divers assembled their equipment. Regulators were attached to cylinders. The more image-conscious divers strapped formidable-looking knives to their legs. Depth gauges and compasses were clamped to their wrists. The rotating bezels of their waterproof watches were twizzled and the water temperature gauges attached to their watch straps were scrutinised. They registered 105 °F in the sun!

The anchor went overboard. The engines cut. Silence. The white boat rolled very slightly on the almost imperceptible swell. The reef was clearly visible beneath the zircon-blue sea. The water looked cool and inviting.

We again formed groups — smaller this time — as fewer people were aqualung diving. Nancy lined up her team and checked each person's equipment. One by one they sat on the gunwale and rolled backwards, cylinder first, into the sea, myself amongst them.

With Nancy as our leader we headed off into the submarine wonderland, drifting into the coral fantasia of the reef. The density of life on the reef was phenomenal. The brilliant blue and yellow colours of the queen angel fish were dazzling. Every speck of the base of the reef was covered with sponges and other exotic forms of life.

For me, as an underwater photographer the John Pennekamp Coral Reef was paradise. Because of the total ban on spearfishing the fish had nothing to fear from divers. Indeed, by stirring up the bottom with their fins as they passed, the divers attracted fish as birds are attracted to a freshly ploughed field. Our dive was at Church Rocks which is roughly at the centre of the Park. A bronze statue of Christ with arms outstretched, anchored to the reef about fifteen feet down, provided an excellent 'prop' for underwater photographs. A friendly Bermuda grouper, which followed the divers around, added further to the site as an underwater tourist attraction. There are numerous sites differing within the John Pennekamp Coral Reef State Park, and I visited many of them with Carl Gage.

We inspected the wreck of the *Benwood* sunk in 1943. The twisted rusting frame of this doomed ship now lies sprawled across the submerged reef like a dead man. No longer do sailors swab her decks and polish her brass. Instead, a new crew of grunts, porkfish, snappers, jewfish and snoek have taken over. Gorgonian fan corals, spreading more slowly than the pink spikes of rosebay willowherb which covered London's war-time scars, are transforming the hideous metal hulk into a bower for the sea's inhabitants to weave their timeless tapestry.

A totally different wreck lies several miles outside the Pennekamp Park. She is the wreck of the *San José*, a Spanish galleon sunk in 1733. She lies on incredibly white coarse coral sand in about thirty-feet of water, her dark wooden timbers projecting starkly from the sea bed like the rib cage of a half-submerged skeleton. Encrusted cannons rest on the sand. Were these reminders of the climate's less permissive moods for the winds can and do reach hurricane force in this region? Or was this wreck the corpse of a victim of the English pirates who plundered the Spanish galleons that passed this way carrying their often ill-gotten cargoes back to Europe? I don't know. Despite assiduous hunting amongst the debris, I did not uncover a single doubloon.

A huge iron anchor lay just off of the wreck of the *San José*. Swimming down to it, I was surprised to see an intensely packed shoal of grunts and pork-fish hiding in the penumbra of the stock. Even when approached closely by divers, the fish refused to leave the safety of the comparative gloom under this man-made object, which to me at least, appeared to afford the minimum of sanctuary.

Carl Gage and I sat motionless on the sea bed on opposite sides of the anchor waiting for the silt, stirred by the passing divers, to settle. We were both wanting to take photographs, and knew that we would be rewarded by clearer pictures if we waited.

During my brief stay at Key Largo I got to know just a few of the secrets of a coral reef. The photographs I had taken enabled me to relive my dives and identify some of the species I had seen which were far too numerous for me to take in during the relatively short time I had spent under water. Indeed, during the few days I had spent on my first visit to a coral reef I had more beautiful pictures of sea life than I had painstakingly gathered during the previous ten years in British waters and the Mediterranean. For years I had struggled to overcome the difficulties of timid fish, lack of light and cold. After so much frustration, underwater photography in Florida seemed unbelievably easy and simple.

My first visit to a coral sea also caused me to modify my entrenched views on diving practice. The idea of taking untrained divers into the sea was abhorrent to the British and also to many Americans who had been trained in colder waters. For safety's sake it was considered essential for trainee divers to have a thorough understanding of the equipment and the effects of cold and pressure etc. before they put their heads under the sea. This required an intensive and often protracted period of training. Yet in Florida I saw people, who obviously had very little, or even no previous experience, diving in the sea. Yet I felt that the people who went on sub-aqua safari with Carl Gage were safe because of the excellent organisation, because they were in warm, clear, currentless waters, because they had all been put through a rigorous life jacket drill, and because they were always under the surveillance of an experienced diver. Indeed, it was just like diving in a giant swimming pool in water that was clearer and warmer that most of the indoor pools I had been in. Even getting back into the boat was easier than climbing out of a swimming pool. Many of those who swam round the Christ of the Abyss statue were underwater tourists who had never dived before and were never likely to again. Out-and-out novices did not dive below ten feet and were very closely supervised. They did not endanger themselves, or anyone else. And what an experience they had! Can you imagine doing your very first dive on a coral reef instead of in a swimming pool?

That is not to say that I disagreed with the strict training schedules laid down by the British Sub-Aqua Club and other recognised diving organisations. I still adhere strongly to the view that only when you are completely familiar with the limitations of your equipment and the hazards involved can you safely enjoy exploring the undersea world. But for the first time I saw that it was not essential to slavishly follow the rules and regulations devised for cold, tidal waters in order to enjoy quite safely an escorted underwater tour in a warm coral sea.

Although I thought the corals in the Pennekamp Park were rich, good fortune has since taken me to other parts of the world where the water is clearer and the underwater life is considerably more prolific and exotic. I have also seen how the American style of diving has been adapted to cater for the holidaymaker who wants to do more than take a cursory at a coral reef.

★ ★ ★

An opportunity came to experience for myself how such diving holidays are run when I went to the Bahamas on the trail of an elusive dolphin who had been dubbed Sandy. I had been commissioned by the Bahamas Tourist Board to film the dolphin, Sandy. Sandy lived off the island of San Salvador which boasted only one hotel, The Riding Rock Inn, which catered almost exclusively for divers. It was arranged that I should stop en route at Lucaya Bay, Freeport on Grand Bahama to visit UNEXSO — the Underwater Explorers Society. So with my seventeen-year old son Ashley as my assistant, I flew to the Bahamas. Firstly we were shown the facilities that were available at the UNEXSO Centre.

When we passed through the large plate-glass doors we discovered that virtually everything a diver could need was available. For the complete novice instruction could be had in the swimming pool. In addition to the usual lecture facilities, a darkroom was available for the diver-photographer plus laboratory space for the underwater scientist. There was even a museum of diving equipment — which included a camera housing that collapsed at depth. Full air cylinders and regulators were always on hand. Boats taking people on diving trips left the jetty with the regularity and punctuality of buses leaving a London depot. The fact that you missed the boat if you turned up late had a remedial effect on those who practised the sin of unpunctuality.

The diving sites visited were graded, and only those with the appropriate training and experience were allowed on the deeper 'advanced dives'.

Ashley and I went out with several different groups to various reefs which gave us an opportunity to sample the underwater scenery the waters off Freeport had to offer the diving holidaymakers.

It was an exotic location with exotic diving in exceptionally clear water, with an abundance of stony corals and friendly fish, including groupers, which we came to appreciate more and more especially when we moved on to San Salvador. However, off Freeport we were also introduced to the excitement of exploring surge channels. These are tunnels that run under the coral on sloping reefs. We were shown how to find the entrances to such channels under large coral heads. Sometimes the channels were quite narrow with just enough room to pass through. In places sunlight streamed through cracks in the roof, sending beams of light dancing through the water into the tunnel. Looking up we could see the outlines of the corals and the fishes that sought sanctuary in the shade. We would swim through the tunnels until we found an opening large enough for us to pass out through — back into the dazzling sunlight on the reef.

In addition to the surge channels through the coral reefs there are also tunnels that run completely under Grand Bahama. From the air the underwater shafts at the entrance of these tunnels can be seen as deep blue discs — the so-called 'blue holes'. As the tidal height varies around Grand Bahama it provides a pressure head which can drive sea water from one side of the island to the other via these long natural tubes. Thus at certain states of the tide there is a whirlpool over a blue hole and anything suspended nearby is likely to disappear down into the depths with the water which is being sucked down like bathwater down a plug hole. At other states of the tide the process is reversed and water comes spilling up to the surface. Diving the blue holes calls for meticulous planning. Unfortunately we did not have time to engage on such an enterprise at sea, but we were able to do the next best thing. That was to dive into a cave in the middle of the island, which was also called a blue hole and was connected to a tunnel passing under the island.

We reached the opening of the cave after a trek through dense scrub undergrowth in the company of Dennis Williams, a blue hole expert. In addition to our diving equipment we carried a lightweight ladder which enabled us to descend through the small cave entrance to a platform of rock about twelve feet below. From there we dived into a huge cavern filled with fresh water. The fresh water being less dense than sea water rose and fell with the tides like a piston being pumped up and down by the sea water in the tunnel underneath.

It was a fascinating dive. The entrance to the cave was always visible. Light from above shone like a lighthouse beam into the crystal-clear water signposting the exit route to safety.

In the centre of the cave was an enormous stalagmite, which must have taken centuries to form. Parts of the roof were covered with stalactites. Our air bubbles collected on the roof and looked like pools of mercury in the beams of our underwater torches. Close inspection of the crannies in the rock surface revealed small transparent crustaceans and fishes which had adapted to the unique environment of a fresh water blue hole.

We would like to have stayed longer in Grand Bahama but we had an even more exciting adventure ahead of us — or thought we did — an appointment with a wild dolphin off San Salvador.

From Freeport Ashley and I flew to Nassau and only just caught the plane to San Salvador. Our camera equipment was extremely heavy and cumbersome and when I saw it being squeezed into the tail of the tiny aircraft I wondered what kind of safety margin the island hopping airline worked to. When Ashley and I ran across the tarmac to climb aboard the engines were revving and we took the only two remaining seats. I sat between two black ladies, one of whom should really have been allocated one-and-a-half seats, such were the dimensions of her rear quarters. She had a smiling, shiny milk-chocolate-brown face. On the other side of me sat an old woman who was as thin as a lath. Her wrinkled skin was as black as coal and on her lap sat a very young child who seemed to be utterly bemused by the situation. He looked silently at me through big eyes. Because of the dimensions of the lady on the opposite side of me I felt like an uneasy slice of tomato in a somewhat lopsided sandwich. Squashed in from both sides, close physical contact with my travelling companions was inevitable. Even before we had left the ground I was aware that the reason why there was a vacant seat beside the old woman was because she radiated a kind of musty smell.

As soon as I was securely dovetailed into what portion was left of my seat, the part of the fuselage which folded down to form a gangway was pushed back up into position. The wooden pole and nylon rope which formed the handrail in the climb-aboard position had long since lost the catch which should have secured it when the door was raised. So as the door was shoved up from the outside the handrail dropped into the inside of the aircraft just missing me. As I was in the rear seat of the aircraft I could see that the recently closed hatch was outlined with light. Indeed, on inspection I found the gap round some parts of it was sufficiently wide for me to still see parts of the runway quite clearly. From this observation I deduced that the aircraft was not pressurised. The aircraft shuddered and accelerated forward. Through the cracks round the door I could see a buckled wheel galloping across the runway. After testing the suspension on a few potholes the pilot lifted his craft into the sky and through the gap round the door I saw clouds instead of concrete. I could also see through the partially open door to the cockpit that the black pilot was reading a paperback book at the same time as he got our aircraft into the sky.

The old lady next to me was very nervous and frequently poked me with a long finger before enquiring where we were in a dialect which I could barely discern. From her expression I don't think she understood a word I said. To console herself she started puffing at an old clay pipe despite the sign which said NO SMOKING. The stench from the smouldering weeds did nothing to mask her own unique bouquet which was invading my clothing where it pressed against her. In sympathy for the child on her lap whose ears were obviously hurting due to the change in pressure during take-off I offered him a sweet. Whereupon the old lady took the sweet, shoved it in her own mouth and continued puffing at her pipe.

Ashley, who sat opposite me, watched the scene with obvious but discreet amusement. His entertainment was increased still further when my companion reached into her hand baggage and produced a bottle, wrapped in plain brown paper, which she uncorked. Raising the bottle on high she took several generous swigs before wiping her lips with the back of her hand. The subtle smell of rum added a new note to her very personalised perfume which penetrated the cloud of smoke in which I was engulfed.

Our destination was the easternmost island of the Bahamian archipelago and we stopped briefly a couple of times en route. On one occasion we flew low over an island and it was not until the pilot saw a man standing on the runway waving a screwdriver and a pair of pliers in the air that he decided to put the aircraft down. The rumour that passed amongst the passengers was that the aircraft was in need of a little electrical maintenance. When we thumped onto the runway the NO SMOKING sign fell off.

However, the incident which brought the biggest sparkle to Ashley's eyes occurred just before we left the aircraft. My companion, who had extinguished her pipe, but had resorted frequently to the bottle in the brown paper bag, dug once again into her baggage. This time she produced some pieces of cold Kentucky Fried Chicken plus a large sugar-coated bun that was liberally loaded with jam. This she gave to the infant on her lap. When he bit into it the trapped red jam spirted through the hole. Some of the jam managed to find its way into his mouth but the rest of it spread over his face, his hands, his clothing . . . and me.

The warm air of San Salvador is totally unpolluted. However, I don't think it had ever smelt sweeter than it did to me when I stepped out of the aircraft to be greeted on the tarmac by the manager of the Riding Rock Inn who had come to meet us and ferry us the short distance to the small hotel that was to be our base for the next ten days. He said a flight was considered to be 'on time' when it arrived on the right day.

As all of the accommodation in the bungalows attached to the hotel was occupied Ashley and I were assigned to a large caravan, or trailer in American parlance. We were quickly ensconced, and shortly after our arrival a slim young man wearing shorts and sporting a Mexican-style moustache arrived on his scooter. It was Chris McLoughlin — the senior dive master — who was to introduce us to Sandy the dolphin. Chris explained that Sandy had not been seen lately but he was hopeful that the dolphin would join us when we went to Sandy Point. He also pointed out that as all three diving boats were committed to following their routine dive schedule, he had decided to put Ashley and myself on his boat which would ferry a group of doctors, who were attending a one week course on diving medicine, to the various diving sites around the island.

When we arrived at the jetty the following morning we discovered just how efficiently the dive and lecture schedules for our group of doctors were organised. At the appointed time the group appeared from their lecture room. Each person was responsible for seeing that his or her personal diving equipment plus two aqualung cylinders, or tanks as they were referred to, were put on board for the two morning dives. Within ten minutes of leaving the lecture, the entire group was settled on the boat and we were heading out of the marina towards the open sea. The sun was shining from a sky of unbroken blue onto an unruffled sea to match.

Diving sites are frequently given names by those who visit them and the dive organisers at Riding Rock Inn were no exception. Our first dive was to a place which they had named 'The Cathedrals' because of the spectacular underwater rock formations. I had encountered a similar name before in several parts of the world including Mauritius and Scotland. Indeed, I had often visited a place called 'Cathedral Rock' off St. Abbs in the cold waters of the North Sea. The differences between the two sites were as great as those of the proverbial chalk and cheese. Both were spectacular in completely different ways. In Scotland 'The Cathedral' was covered in soft marine growths including dead men's fingers and anemones that looked like large powder puffs on stalks stuck to the volcanic rock. 'The Cathedral' was a large natural archway through which I was carried by the current. When I emerged I could see neither the surface nor the sea bed despite the fact that underwater visibility — 'the viz' in divers parlance — was good by local standards.

In San Salvador 'the viz' approached 200 feet and at all times I could see the surface and the sea bed. Indeed, the visibility was so good that the dive master could keep his eye on all of his class — which would have been totally impossible in the murky waters off the Scottish coast where it was even easy to lose one's diving partner if one was not vigilant. Here 'The Cathedrals' consisted of a series of spectacular archways on the edge of the 'drop-off' which is the region where the sea suddenly plummets to enormous depths. It really was a superb diving site and it provided us with an opportunity to try out our new cine camera and housing before the hoped-for meeting with the dolphin. As is almost always the case with new equipment we ran into snags. We were happy to have discovered the faults on a trial dive.

As soon as the last divers returned to the boat the anchor was hauled in and we set sail for another site in shallower water. It was the wreck of a ship that had gone aground on the reef in 1902 and now lay strewn across the sea bed. Much of the ironwork had been colonised by sea growth but the twisted shapes and large unnatural features such as the boilers were clearly indicative of structures fashioned by man. The wreck of the vessel provided an artificial reef superimposed upon the coral reef itself. Shoals of multi-coloured fish glided around the wreckage in a continuous ballet which was only temporarily interrupted if danger threatened and the fish darted into the numerous nooks and crannies between the ironwork. After an hour on the wreck, the divers returned to the dive boat and made the short journey back to base for lunch.

After our meal we returned to the jetty where the tanks had been recharged with air in preparation for the afternoon dive which was to be at a location called Grouper Gulley. With some of our camera problems resolved Ashley and I dropped into the clear blue sea to meet the fish after which the site had been named. The grouper is a territorial fish, different varieties of which are found in the various seas of the world under a great variety of local names such as merou or jew fish in the Mediterranean and rock cod in the Red Sea.

Grouper Gulley was on the edge of the drop-off and as we made our way through the valley in the reef toward the outer wall we saw several Nassau groupers. They were not large as Nassau groupers go — being about two feet long. They weaved quietly in and out of small caves in the coral watching us carefully — indeed for most of the time they kept their heads pointed in our direction — partially through curiosity and partially through apprehension, as if they did not quite trust us. There were many other fish on the reef but the groupers obviously held a senior position in the hierarchy — indeed they might well have been considered as the kings of the reef dwellers.

It was thus with high hopes that we set out the following morning with two powerful engines on the stern of our diving boat pushing it ahead at a fine speed. Riding Rock Inn was situated approximately in the middle of the island of San Salvador on the west coast. Sandy Point, where we hoped to encounter Sandy the dolphin, was the southernmost headland.

When we arrived we found that the water was exceptionally clear — with a visibility in the region of 200 feet. Thus from the surface we could clearly see the bottom immediately beneath us about fifty feet down. We were just on the edge of a reef which dropped down almost vertically to about 140 feet. As we glided down through the pellucid water the underwater vista stretched away from us with unbelievable clarity before it eventually disappeared into the pale blue curtain which represented the limit of our undersea view. Some of the divers had raided the breakfast table just before we set off and they carried their bounty in polythene bags. The fish obviously knew of such activities, for as soon as the divers reached the reef they were greeted by a great variety of fish all anxious to supplement their own breakfasts.

I was hoping that the dolphin would suddenly appear to join in the fun with the divers. So in addition to enjoying the presence of the multitudinous fishes I took frequent looks into the far distance to see if he was homing in on us. It was on one such scan that I saw a large shape approaching us from way down on the reef. It approached steadily and was making a course in a straight line directly for us. When the grouper arrived we were in the company of an Australian doctor who was distributing the last pieces of soggy bread from his food bag. The grouper snapped them up and we started to film. The fish was the largest specimen of a Nassau grouper I had seen, and I estimated its weight as between sixty and seventy pounds. It was about four feet long and it circled us with dignified slowness which was not matched by the divers who became very excited at the arrival of the king-size grouper.

Whilst the grouper circled the diver I circled both of them, filming as I went. Ashley also joined the group, which without realising it was sinking towards the sea bed. In such exciting situations divers breathe fast. Their air consumption also increases rapidly with depth because each breath contains a greater quantity of air. I glanced at my depth gauge and was surprised to see it recording a depth of 140 feet. At such a depth the duration of a dive with a single tank is short. As I did not want to become involved with long decompression stops I signalled to the party that we should climb to shallower water. I hoped that the grouper would follow us. And he did. In fact he stayed with us for the rest of the dive. It was not until we started to head back onto the reef table prior to our return to the boat that the grouper suddenly veered off and I watched him return in the direction from which he had come. As he disappeared into the deep blue haze I envisaged him returning to his own special cave deep on the reef. The large grouper obviously had a big territory.

Although we were disappointed not to have seen the

spotted dolphin at Sandy Point we had had the consolation of meeting the grouper, and as we had come equipped to shoot a film we considered using the grouper in place of the dolphin as the main character.

The more Ashley and I debated the subject the more convinced we became that we should shoot a film about the grouper instead of the dolphin. As I had come prepared to carry out a number of studies on Sandy in order that I could compare the behaviour of one wild dolphin with another, I wondered if I could switch to a comparison of a dolphin's behaviour with that of a fish. It would all depend upon the willingness of the grouper to join us again on our dives at Sandy Point. We agreed that should the dolphin appear we would immediately switch to our original programme. This thought gave us new heart that our visit, although enjoyable, would not be wasted from a filming standpoint and so we started working on ways of introducing the grouper to a viewing audience.

We both considered that his arrival at Sandy Point had a stately dignity to it. He was obviously master of the reef and had nothing to fear in his own extensive territory. Indeed, we had already begun to think of the grouper as having a slightly disdainful air with a superior manner. With his discreet yet tasteful Cooper's Oxford Marmalade colouration we could afford him no lower status than that of an hereditary peerage. So the grouper became Lord Marmaduke. As soon as we gave him a name he took on a personality. And just for the fun of it we drew parallels between undersea life on the reef and life on the land. We saw the reef at Sandy Point as a huge underwater park where a deep cave provided a stately home for Lord Marmaduke. Life on the reef was just as organised as it would be in a well-run ducal estate. There were schools of grunts and porkfish which roamed across the undersea world like sheep in the fields. Then there were the gardeners — the parrot fish who kept the coral neatly trimmed by constantly nibbling at it — and beneath them, numerous support staff such as the cleaner fish — tiny wrasse which kept the larger fish free of parasites. The surgeon fish provided a major work force with their heads down cropping the coral as if they were farm workers at harvest time. Then there were the tenants on the estate. Some of them, such as the angel fishes, glided in and out of their coral homes with grace and dignity, whilst some of the butterfly fish were so overtly flashy in their dress and coquettish in their manner they became Lord Marmaduke's fancy ladies who might also lead astray an unsuspecting male passer-by. The reef which Lord Marmaduke had inherited was one of the most beautiful in the Caribbean with unsurpassed views of coral seascapes. Lord Marmaduke presided over his estate with the unquestioned authority of a member of the aristocracy.

This, then, was how we saw the star of our proposed film. Later events showed however, that his behaviour was not always what one might expect from a fish of such high rank.

On the first return visit we took with us some bread which we carried down into the sea in transparent plastic bags. Lord Marmaduke arrived on cue and joined the other fishes who were engaged in a mad scramble for the food. But whereas the other fish darted in and gobbled up the particles of bread that drifted into the water, Lord Marmaduke, with his superior sized mouth trolled around consuming his free breakfast like a lazy vacuum cleaner. When all of the food had disappeared, which happened in a few minutes, he started to look around for more. He even managed to look offended when his benefactors ceased to produce their handouts.

At this point Ashley decided to take a photograph of Lord Marmaduke and pointed his exposure meter towards the grouper. The meter was enclosed in a clear plastic housing which was attached to Ashley's waist by a stout nylon lanyard. Mistaking the plastic-encased meter for a bag of food the grouper darted forward and attempted to grab the meter much to Ashley's horror and astonishment. Ashley spun round in the water trying to pull the meter away from the grouper who aggressively pursued it with his huge mouth ajar. As Ashley's hand, plus meter complete with arm could easily have been engulfed into the maw of the grouper I was not surprised at my son's obvious fright. However, the incident was quickly over when Ashley pushed the grouper away with his camera.

To avoid a repetition of this incident we took a much bigger supply of bread on our next visit. I suggested that I should film Ashley giving Lord Marmaduke pieces of bread one by one.

This idea, however, did not take into account one of Lord Marmaduke's least admirable qualities — greed. As soon as the grouper saw the bag of food he rushed at it and snatched it away from a wide-eyed Ashley, who was only too happy to let go of the bag. The grouper darted away with the bag firmly gripped between his jaws, then slowed down, let go of the bag momentarily, and opened his huge mouth wide. This act was sufficient to cause an inrush of water and the plastic bag of bread disappeared into his mouth like a feather into a suction tube.

I watched horrified. The thought of what the plastic bag would do in the gut of the grouper was not pleasant. However, before I could dwell on that thought for too long the grouper regurgitated the bag into the water with such violence that most of the bread it had previously contained was expelled.

When we discussed the uncouth behaviour of our piscatorial film star I explained to Ashley that the bread we had been offering Lord Marmaduke was making the water very cloudy and this would spoil the quality of the film. It was at this stage that we decided to see if he was interested in other foods which did not disintegrate so readily when in contact with water. An obvious answer was the hot dog, or frankfurter sausage, of which the hotel had a good supply in its deep freeze. Thus on our next visit we went down with a supply of sausages which Ashley tucked into the pocket of his lifejacket. Now this turned out not to be the ideal place to store food because Lord Marmaduke immediately got a liking for sausages. When Ashley somewhat timidly produced the first sausage the grouper gulped it down with incredible speed. Having seen where the first one came from and having decided that he was a sausage gourmand, Lord Marmaduke rushed at the source of supply. Whereupon Ashley quickly emptied his pouch of the remaining sausages and beat a very hasty retreat. All of this took place in a very short space of time and in such confusion that it did not constitute more than one short unsatisfactory sequence for a film.

We needed a longer sequence, but how could we slow down the action of Lord Marmaduke's prodigious eating speed. We decided to use a string of sausages, or literally sausages on a string. As the sausages were deep frozen we decided to collect them the night before in order that they would thaw out and be in a soft condition for threading. We took them to our caravan and left them in a plastic bag together with a bag of bread. When we found them the next morning we discovered that we had another resident in the caravan with us. A mouse. The plastic bag containing the sausages had been nibbled through and part of one of the sausages had been eaten. The bread was untouched. The previous occupant of the trailer had been the world famous photographer Al Giddings. We decided therefore that Al had left one his friends behind, and for want of a better name we called our unseen fellow resident Al. We decided that he was a very discriminating mouse as he could tell bread from banger through the thickness of a plastic bag.

When we arrived at Sandy Point the next day we threaded up what was left of the sausages on a stout nylon string, one end of which was secured to Ashley's wrist to ensure that the grouper did not end up with the string inside him, or if he did, Ashley would be in there as well. At last this ruse worked, and I was able to film Lord Marmaduke snatching the string of sausages and then engaging in a tug-of-war with Ashley. We were both happy after the experiment because I managed to shoot the sequence on film whilst Lord Marmaduke was able to pull the bangers off the string and consume them.

I had taken to San Salvador a number of objects which I thought would interest a dolphin. How, I wondered, would the grouper react to them instead?

There was one way to find out. Try them.

Lord Marmaduke showed a complete disinterest in everything unless it was edible. Everything that was except for an object which had evoked one of the most startling responses I ever encountered from a dolphin — a mirror. Donald, the dolphin, studied it first and then attacked it with his beak, smashing it to smithereens.

Immediately the grouper saw the mirror he rushed at it as if it were a bag of food and hit it, smashing it into a dozen pieces. Even then the silly fish did not realise that it was not edible. I watched dumbfounded as Lord Marmaduke then proceeded to snap up the glinting fragments of glass as if they were fry. Having gobbled down every jagged piece of glass before it had a chance to drift more than a few feet down the stupid animal circled us as if looking for even more food. I immediately regretted the entire experiment convinced that I had inadvertently committed the likeable but stupid Lord Marmaduke to death. However, I had not taken into account the fact that nature can build in defence mechanisms when appropriate. And a few seconds later the grouper regurgitated the contents of its mouth and the fragments of the mirror were scattered over the reef like confetti. Before any further misfortunes could occur we gathered up every piece of glass and took it back to the boat.

When we reappeared at Sandy Point a few days later Lord Marmaduke rose up to greet us from the depths apparently none the worse for his experiences — and hungry as ever.

We never saw Sandy the dolphin and returned home with film of Lord Marmaduke, a Nassau grouper, instead.

5

Diving for Treasure in Bermuda
THE ATLANTIC OCEAN

My arrival in Bermuda had all the trappings of the opening of a James Bond film. I looked out of the window of the aircraft onto a vivid Technicolour blue sea with a semi-circular sandy bay alongside the landing strip. A helicopter flitted across the bay like a dragonfly followed by its shadow. My plane touched down with a gentle bump. The engines screamed as the pilot reversed the thrust to bring the giant silver bird to a stop.

On the tarmac an official, wearing earmuffs and waving two table tennis bats, guided the aircraft onto its correct spot in front of the airport terminal. A small crowd of black and white faces on the roof of the building scanned the arrivals. An airport official carrying a clipboard under his arm and wearing a cap, white shirt, white socks and white shorts that came down almost to his knees, gave an immediate impression of a bygone colonial age. It was a noisy, unreal scene.

I was quickly through Customs, and stepped through the doors from the air-conditioned terminal into the balmy air outside. The exit was thronged with people waiting excitedly to greet the new arrivals. I had no idea who would meet me.

Out of the crowd emerged a very portly man (Mr. Big) with dark, wavy hair and a serious expression. He stepped up to me and held out a podgy hand.

'You must be Horace Dobbs,' he said.

'That's right,' I said, flattered that he should recognise me.

'I'm Bob Davey, Chairman of the Bermuda Branch of the British Sub-Aqua Club. Welcome to Bermuda.'

His expression changed to one of friendliness as he took one of my heavy suitcases and introduced me to another member of the club.

Since my arrival outside the airport I had been aware of a very attractive girl with short, dark, curly hair who had been

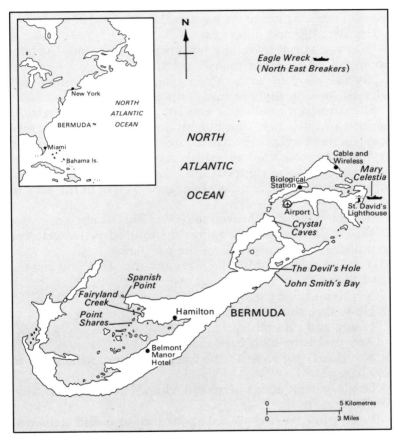

watching me demurely from the edge of the crowd. She wore a pair of very large sunglasses which added a hint of mystery to her. Despite the glasses I could feel the sparkle of her eyes.

Our group separated from the rest of the crowd who were being busily bustled into taxis. The attractive girl attached herself to the small knot of people who surrounded me and we headed off towards a row of parked cars. My bags were tossed onto the back seat of an open white sports car and the attractive woman climbed into the driving seat. My next move seemed obvious to me. I looked towards Mr. Big, who clearly had the situation under his control, for a gesture that would authorise me to sit next to the driver.

But Mr. Big had other plans.

'No, you're not travelling by sports car,' he said. 'At least not yet. I've got other plans for you.'

'By the way,' he said, introducing me to the young lady who sat looking shyly at me. 'This is Lettie.'

She smiled revealing a row of enamel-white teeth. I nodded towards her. She quickly looked away. Her brown arm reached towards the dashboard. She turned the ignition key and backed the car swiftly and expertly out of the parking space. She stopped, spun the wheel and accelerated rapidly towards the exit. My baggage was still in the back of her car.

'You're staying with her,' said Mr. Big. 'Come on.'

'Where on earth are we going?' I enquired as the welcome committee headed away from the car park.

'You'll see,' said Mr. Big. 'Follow me. Did you have a good flight?'

'Yes thanks, very good.'

'How were things when you left?'

'Foggy and miserable.'

'Any problems with Customs?'

'No. But I still have a little question of excess luggage to sort out.'

'Don't worry about that old chap,' beamed Mr. Big. 'We'll soon fix that.'

By this time we had walked about 100 yards and arrived at a wooden jetty. Moored alongside the jetty was a sleek power-boat. I stepped on board.

'Cast off forward,' ordered Mr. Big to the one member of our party still on the jetty as the engine roared into life.

'Let's go — oh it's hell in the colonies,' he chuckled. The boat turned in an arc and headed out into the bay.

As soon as we were clear of the jetty the engine was

opened up and the boat came up effortlessly onto the plane. In the calm water of the bay she hardly seemed to touch the water and I got that strange walking-on-air feeling that one has on a boat that is skimming over the water.

'We like to do things in style out here,' said Mr. Big. 'Want a beer?'

'Yes please.'

'So do I,' he beamed — an expression I was to hear many times later. 'Peter, get out some beers.'

I was handed a can of lager and ripped off the metal tag. I was ready for it.

'Christ!' exploded Mr. Big. 'It's not cold. I don't know what this bloody place is coming to. Sorry about that old boy — I should have fixed it.'

The warm air sweeping smoothly over my face felt delightful and I leaned into the curve as the boat arced like a slalom skier out of the bay and into the open sea.

'We thought we'd show you some of Bermuda,' grinned Mr. Big.

On the north side of the island the sea was choppy and the boat started to thump into the waves. The man at the wheel eased back the throttle slightly to a stage where the bumps were not of sufficient ferocity to impede the consumption of the beer which was disappearing at a prodigious rate. I held on to a bulkhead with my left hand and stood with my legs slightly apart and relaxed to absorb the successive thumps.

Mr. Big pointed out numerous features on the coastline. 'That's the TV mast,' he explained. We took a course about a mile off-shore.

'We have our own TV station you know. It's okay except when the mast gets blown down in a hurricane.'

Between sight-seeing I was asked questions about the state of British diving. The conversation became quite animated and Mr. Big was standing with his back to the cabin door taking a swig from yet another can of beer when the boat hit a large wave. Mr. Big momentarily lost his balance and bumped rear end first, against the cabin door, to the sound of splintering wood.

He turned round and looked at the hole in the door. He had knocked out two of the louvre slats.

'That's one of the problems of having such a big arse,' he exclaimed as he ruefully examined the damage. 'Another beer?'

I was warming to this carefree bunch of expatriates in their immaculate Bermuda shorts.

We skimmed in a huge semi-circle round Spanish Point. Once in the lee of the headland the sea flattened and the throttle opened. We barely seemed to touch the surface as we headed like a mayfly over the water into Fairyland Creek. In the creek we reduced throttle, the boat immediately dropped onto its hull and we cruised along the island at a gentle pace to a private jetty where we moored alongside a slightly dilapidated-looking boat.

'A fine craft isn't she?' said Mr. Big.

'Great,' I said.

'Not this,' he said, referring to the boat in which we were standing. 'That,' he said pointing at the battered boat moored at the jetty. 'Fine craft. She'll do all of eight knots with the wind behind her. I'll take you out in her. That will be a real ride.' He swelled with pride.

I stepped onto Bermuda soil for the second time in two hours. I peered down into the blue-green water and could see a shoal of sergeant major fish scurrying to and fro below the surface.

A young woman with a delightful young toddler came down to meet us.

'Come into the house,' said Pat Haynes.

We walked through a garden, past trees loaded with grapefruit, into the house. A large fan coral decorated the fireplace — a diving souvenir no doubt.

Mr. Big produced a sheaf of papers from his pocket. The heading on the top sheet was ITINERARY – DR. HORACE DOBBS. Each page carried an hour by hour plan for my entire stay on the island.

I thumbed through the itinerary.

'It's a very comprehensive fixture list I've got here,' I said.

Not sure whether he would be sensitive about his bulk and the slightly sinister implications of a name like Mr. Big,

I mentally renamed him Mr. Fixit and then put the idea to him.

'I think I'll have to christen you Mr. Fixit.'

He clearly liked the implications of the nickname. So Mr. Big became Mr. Fixit from that point on during my stay in Bermuda.

The next morning I walked into his office in Hamilton. The air conditioner kept the temperature down to a very comfortable working level and Mr. Fixit greeted me with a smile. He walked with the rolling gait of Father Christmas and his muscular thighs filled the legs of his Bermuda shorts to an extent that they fitted him almost as closely as a pair of stockings. He wore full length white socks and merged perfectly into the machinery of running an office. Immaculately dressed black girls punched comptometers and tickled typewriters. It was nearly lunchtime and he was making last minute arrangements as he was to take the afternoon off.

Outside the office we were met by a young man with an enormous mop of blonde hair and a bright ginger beard. His name was Martin. Martin was a noisy, extrovert mechanic who had also taken the afternoon off, though less legitimately than Mr. Fixit.

Towards the end of our meal in the Lobster Pot our friend with the red beard suddenly assumed an alarmed expression and immediately tried to hide his face. Anyone less easy to conceal I could not imagine. He kept his back to the door and pointing over his shoulder he wailed in a stage whisper, 'That's my boss and I'm supposed to be off sick.' The boss sat down by the door and glanced our way but did not appear to recognise Martin's back view.

The problem was how to get Martin out without being spotted by his boss.

One thing that could be said about Martin was that he did not allow anyone to be unaware of his presence in normal circumstances. Life to him was one long drama. He called the waitress — a very tall slender negress in an immaculate grey outfit and wearing black steel-rimmed glasses. She came across and looked down on the dishevelled Martin.

After two minutes' ardent conversation, the excitement of

which caused Martin to raise his voice higher and higher, she agreed to let him leave via the kitchen.

At the appropriate moment Martin leapt to his feet and hustled out towards the kitchen to the accompaniment of a trail of distress signals like a startled blackbird. His boss, however, was engrossed in his lunch and did not notice. We passed him as we made our way out of the official exit. Martin, bobbing up and down like a yo-yo, was waiting for us a little way from the Lobster Pot.

We filed into a car and headed for the jetty and Mr. Fixit's 'fine craft'. We boarded the boat and chugged out towards Spanish Point to a buoy marking the outermost deep channel.

Suddenly came the deafening, deep-throated bellow of a ship's siren. Behind us appeared an enormous vessel. It looked like a section of New York's Fifth Avenue adrift in the sea. The siren again bellowed its message of 'move aside' and our tiny boat resonated with the sound. It was the cruise ship *Sea Venture* on her way back to New York. She was coming up the narrow passage at Point Shares. I looked over the side and could see the bottom clearly with its treacherous shoals of coral. It was difficult to imagine how such a vessel did not run aground. We watched in awe as she passed through Two Rocks Passage between the islands. The gargantuan vessel appeared to have only inches to spare on either side of her huge bulk. Some of the encapsulated community on board peered down at us: the "see-ers" looking at the "do-ers".

I looked up and up to the shining black Spanish *guardia* hat that sat on top of her funnel towering above us – far higher than any building on Bermuda. There is something very impressive above such a vast floating bulk when seen at close quarters. But even such leviathans are vulnerable as the story of the *Titanic* reveals only too well.

The *Sea Venture* sailed past us in stately grace around Spanish Point. Our boat lurched up and down in the wake as we followed her out to one of the deep channel buoys, which was the area selected for our dive. I was longing to get into the water. The wind was rising and by the time we reached the site, waves four to five feet high were curling alongside the boat. The water had a yellowish hue which indicated suspended sand particles. The underwater visibility was not going to be verygood. I put on part of my wetsuit and wearing snorkel, mask andfins, jumped overboard clutching my camera. My first dip into Bermudian waters.

The water was almost twenty-five feet deep. The bottom was sandy and was just visible in places. Scattered across the sand were coral outcrops that came to within five feet of the surface. I snorkelled down and explored them holding my breath — again enjoying just looking at the intricacy of the basic structures that make up a coral reef. Fish were not abundant and those I saw quickly took to their heels. A few angel fish wheeled in and out of the reef. These frail-looking fish are very decorative when viewed from the side, but when they turn head-on or tail-on, they are extremely slender and become insignificant. One queen angel came to within five feet of the camera and would come no closer during the brief time I could hold my breath. I lay on the surface and watched her movements. She patrolled a certain small area of the reef, spending most of her time in a gully between very large coral boulders. I snorkelled quietly down to her lair time and time again, holding my breath until my lungs were bursting, waiting for her to adopt a good pose close to the camera. But she behaved in typical female fashion. She would come coyly towards the camera fluttering from side to side in a seductive, flirtatious, photogenic fashion whilst I waited with my finger on the button. Closer. Closer. Almost there. Then just as I was about to take the picture she turned tail and swam away. All that was left in my viewfinder would be a vertical grey stripe instead of the gloriously colourful diamond shape she had presented a second before.

I got the distinct feeling that she was nervous and wondered if she had acquired the sense of self-preservation and awareness of man that prevails in all fish in an area where spearfishing is practised. The only type of spearfishing equipment that was allowed in Bermuda was the Hawaiian sling. This consists of a spear that passes through a short metal tube with an elastic catapult at one end. The metal tube is usually held in the left hand and the base of the spear in the right. When a fish is spotted the end of the spear is pulled back against the tension of rubber and released at the appropriate moment.

Spearfishing with an aqualung was not allowed. One of the members of our party periodically appeared in my field of vision brandishing a spear. But, as I suspected, the fish were only too familiar with the hazards of allowing themselves to be approached too closely by such intruders and stayed well out of range. The lobster is less able to flee from man the predator and even at the back of his hole in the reef where he would be safe from attack by a large fish, a long metal spear can find him out. And indeed one lobster did come to an untimely end at the hands of one of my companions.

I still had not got any pictures of sharks. My one consolation at seeing the impaled lobster making its last contortions on the end of the spear was that it would attract something really worth photographing. I peered into the murky water looking for the undisputed savage of the sea. But to my disappointment and the intense relief of Mr. Fixit, no sharks appeared.

The inshore reefs around Spanish Point were under colossal pressure. In these sub-tropical waters spear fishers could stay in the water for hours at a time and during the course of their dives could cover large areas of the reef depleting the territorial fishes such as the grouper who make their homes and stay within specific areas. Pollution too was adding to the hazards of the inshore life and the huge boats that barged through the water stirred up vast quantities of silt with their propellers. The fine particles settled on the corals and choked them.

Finally, there was a tremendous pressure on the fish population from the commercial fishermen who strove to satisfy the ever increasing demands for fish — both from the many tourists who came to the islands and the Bermudians themselves. A popular method used by the Bermudian fishermen was "pot fishing". Huge open baskets with tunnels leading into them were laid on the reefs. The fish swim into the traps and cannot find their way out. Unfortunately, a large number of the traps get lost or hooked on the corals and are then abandoned by the fishermen. They then become jails for the trapped fish. During my stay I was to see a number of these discarded traps on the reef. I came across the first whilst snorkelling over an outcrop of coral. The trap contained one pathetically thin cow fish that nervously retreated to the back of its ineluctable home when I snorkelled down to take a photograph.

Some divers open up cages that are obviously derelict. This one was, and Mr. Fixit snorkelled down, took a knife from its holder on his leg and slit the nylon net to let the emaciated fish swim once again to the freedom of the reef and the open sea. I hoped it would survive.

Many ships have come to grief around Bermuda. Some losses were understandable — ships coming into unfamiliar waters in rough weather. One loss however appears to have been brought about by the sheer carelessness and incompetence of an experienced pilot. On 20th September 1864 the Bermuda *Royal Gazette* carried the full story of the unfortunate loss of the *Mary Celestia*. Having dived on the site of the wreck of the ill-fated *Forfarshire* in the Farne Islands, I was anxious to see the wreck of another paddle-steamer that foundered in the same period.

The remains of the *Mary Celestia* are to be found near St. David's Lighthouse. I did not swim to the sea bed but allowed myself to drift slowly down into the pellucid pale-blue space around me. The physical pleasure of weightlessness and the gentle warmth of the water engulfed me. I looked down. Beneath me I could see, clearly defined, the remnants of the two paddle wheels. All of the woodwork had rotted away leaving the iron framework — like a metal scaffold put there for the convenience of the corals that had colonised it. Between the lattice-work of the two skeleton paddle wheels was a solid structure which I deduced was the ruin of the engine. Standing on the sea bed forty feet below me stood a tiny black-suited figure in a small cloud of sand swirled up by his fins. He was peering into the wreckage. Bubbles from his demand valve streamed up past me to burst through the water-air interface and escape into the atmosphere twenty feet above my head.

147

I drifted slowly downwards, swallowing to clear my ears, and as I did so my vision narrowed to a single paddle wheel and its inhabitants. Fish weaved in and out of the man-made metal tree with its branches of iron and its leaves of coral. Above the sun was shining down giving the entire scene a tropical softness.

How different this was to the remains of the *Forfarshire* in her North Sea graveyard where the water is cold and green. The paddle wheels of the *Forfarshire* have been smashed by the waves and dispersed by the current that rips through Piper Gut while the *Mary Celestia* lies quietly rotting in a tranquil graveyard.

Other divers poked amongst the wreckage. Some were taking photographs. I twisted my way between the iron framework of the paddle wheel quietly pursuing a file fish that was reluctant to let me close enough for a picture. A diver came across to me and conveniently posed as he also swam through the ironwork. Twenty minutes passed in an instant and when the needle on my pressure gauge was in the red, I headed gently towards the surface reluctant to leave the fascinating pale-blue grave of the *Mary Celestia*.

I climbed on board the boat and felt the sunshine on my back as I heaved off my aqualung. When it was on the deck I noticed that the cylinder was the type with a reserve supply of air. I had not pulled the reserve lever, and when I did so the needle on my air pressure gauge sprang out of the red into the white scale. I had enough air left for another short dive. I couldn't miss the opportunity. Moments later I was back in the water overjoyed to be descending again into the blue depths. This time my ears cleared quickly and I swam over to the boiler.

Mr. Fixit, clearly identifiable by his generous waistline, was probing the wreckage, intent on finding another souvenir with which to adorn his house. When he saw me he quickly adopted a pose. Standing on the sea bed he leant back against a steel member projecting from the sea bed as if he were leaning on a lamp-post in the High Street. I could see his eyes laughing as I gave him the OK sign with my fingers. A large blue parrot fish that had previously been happily picking up morsels uncovered by Mr. Fixit's attacks on the boiler with his knife, hovered nearby waiting patiently for some more easily come-by food.

There were so many subjects to photograph and so much going on I would have sung with joy if I could. But all too soon my pressure gauge again showed my air supply was running out. All of the other divers had left the water and I enjoyed a few brief minutes of solitude, alone with that indefinable force of the sea.

In his effort to see that my days in Bermuda were as interesting and fully occupied as they could be, Mr. Fixit arranged for me to go big game fishing. So one morning, at the crack of dawn, together with various members of the diving club I climbed on board the *Ubique*. Beer cans were packed into the refrigerator until it was full. The remaining cans were stowed in the sink. I was told that it was to be strictly an above-water fishing trip. However, I had heard that sharks often appear on such occasions. So in the hope that I might get some shark pictures I had secretly packed my mask, fins and snorkel together with an underwater camera at the bottom of my holdall containing my food and drink for the day.

There were white horses all round us as the boat, powered by two 350 hp engines, bulldozed its way out to sea through the mounting waves. The mixture of black thunder clouds and brilliant clear sky overhead changed the colour and mood of the foaming sea in our wake from soft Cambridge blue to forbidding cobalt blue and back again as we sped out to the fringing reef. As orders for fluid refreshment came down from the flying bridge, beer cans started to leave the refrigerator in quick succession.

The echo sounder was switched on as we went over the top of the reef and soon the water became deeper until the echo sounder showed a depth of 160 feet and it was time to fish.

The anchor was heaved overboard and the engines stopped. The force of the wind against the boat pulled the anchor rope taut and the *Ubique* started to pitch and roll. The waves rose and fell like small mountains all around us and I sat in a chair on the stern trying desperately to retain my breakfast. The delicate condition of my stomach was not improved when Gavin, the Captain, produced a bag full of half-decayed fish, which he flung over the side in handfuls as ground bait. I watched them drifting down through the water along with the breakfast I could retain no longer. Gavin excitedly put a rod in my hand when I sank thankfully back into the chair.

I let the heavy lead weight carry my hook with its impaled bait into the depths and out of sight. After about thirty seconds I felt the line change tension slightly. I reeled in my line out of curiosity. As it came to the surface the line flicked from side to side. I had hooked a grunt weighing about a pound.

'A fish! A fish!' Gavin cried.

The effect on the others on board was explosive.

'We're in amongst them.'

'Horace you're going to get the big one,' Gavin cried as he threw handfuls more bait over the side. He expertly removed my fish from the hook and attached another small dead fish as bait.

In a few minutes another fish came in. Then another. Martin seemed out of luck, however, despite several flamboyant and noisy strikes. And then he had one. He struck viciously. His line went as taut as a bow string as he reeled in furiously.

'Give me the bloody belt somebody!' he screamed.

I thought he would burst a blood vessel with excitement. Gavin rushed over to him as he struggled with his rod. He strapped to him a heavy leather belt with a socket where a jock strap would be situated. Martin placed the butt of his rod in the socket and heaved with all his might with both hands on the shaft of his rod.

'Get out of the bloody chair, man,' he roared through his beard at me.

I was not familiar with the routine on such occasions — which is to vacate the throne on the stern as soon as a big fish is hooked to give the angler the best chance of bringing in the catch.

I quickly got the message and launched myself sideways just as Martin threw himself, backside first, into the seat which I had been occupying. All the other anglers cleared their lines so that the king on the throne could fight his duel with his piscatorial adversary.

I noticed that the stress was far greater when the boat rose on a wave and relaxed slightly when we slid into the next trough. I noticed too that he was not reeling in any line and that his line maintained a constant angle into the sea over the stern. The fish certainly wasn't moving. I decided that he was either bringing up the biggest non-moving fish off the coast of Bermuda or attempting to lift a brain coral which was securely attached to the reef. His face was red and his tousled blonde hair stuck out at all angles. I was just thinking how impossibly strong both the rod and the nylon line were when Martin plummeted backwards into the chair as his line at last gave up the struggle and parted.

His outburst at that point was unprintable.

'Now you know why we don't bring women on these trips,' said a grinning Mr. Fixit as Martin replenished his tackle.

A beautiful rock cod — a fine red fish with bright blue spots — was landed next.

My bait disappeared several times and replenishing it was something I seldom succeeded in completing without a visit to the side of the boat which was still bobbing up and down like a cork on the Atlantic rollers.

Then it was Peter Haynes' turn to take the throne. As he reeled in his line I looked over the side. A snake-like fish with a large yellow head was writhing in the water. When it broke surface a moment later the yellow head resolved itself into a porkfish jammed in the jaws of a green moray eel. The interlocked fish were hauled over the side and flopped squirming on the deck. I was contemplating the misfortune of the porkfish which had been hooked at one end and eaten at the other when Martin took a truncheon and bludgeoned the moray to death in a fearful frenzy. He hurled it back into the sea. As he did so he expressed his loathing of the moray because of the damage it could do if it managed to take a bite at someone on board.

After that the fishing went dead.

'Sharks around,' announced Martin. 'The fish are taking cover.'

'We'd better move on,' said Gavin. 'Let's have the anchor up. Someone must go into the forepeak and arrange the rope as it comes in.'

I thought I should volunteer, but knew just two minutes in the forepeak would finish me off. Seeing my plight Mr. Fixit, cheerful as ever and completely unaffected by the movements of the boat, went down into the forepeak. I had never felt so much like a useless passenger on board a boat before.

Once we got under way I began to recover and it was suggested we would troll for fish. The two outriggers which projected from the deck alongside the cabin like two huge fishing rods were swung out until they were at right angles to the line of the boat. The lines from the fishing rods were passed through two pegs at the ends of the outriggers. The function of the outriggers is to keep the two outside lines well clear of any other lines that may be trolled from the stern. If a fish bites, the pegs release the line and the fish is played with the rod. The lines were baited and streamed over the stern as we moved forward. More of our diminishing stocks of rotten fish were thrown overboard.

In a few minutes the checks on the rods whirred as fish took the bait. The engine slowed and two pompanos were reeled in. As soon as they were landed we set off again but after a further thirty minutes no more bites were had despite the copious quantities of dog food that were tossed into the wake.

'It's those damn sharks again,' moaned Martin.

I thought of my fins, mask and camera in the bottom of my bag, and again mentioned my desire to get shark pictures to Mr. Fixit.

'You can't possibly go in out there,' he explained, his cheerful expression changing to one of real concern. 'Besides which we agreed this was to be a fishing trip.'

I was sorry I had mentioned it.

'If you really are desperate to get shark pictures I think I may just be able to fix something.'

Dusk was falling. All the bait had been used. The engines were slowed and we hauled in all the lines in preparation for the long return trip.

ve left: Lorenzo Ricciardi loads one of his guns with bullets he kept hidden in
llowed-out book.
ve right: The author at the wheel of the Arab dhow, Mir-el-Lah.
w: A wreck in the English Channel appears mysteriously out of the green
.

Underwater photography
relatively murky British
waters made a major step
forward with the
introduction of cameras
with wide-angle lenses and
domed portholes.

diver finds the neck of an amphora, which has lain on the floor of the Mediterranean for over 2,000 years.

The submerged stalactites and stalagmites I discovered in a blue hole in the middle of Grand Bahama Island indicate that at one time the now flooded cave was above sea level.

e: The Nassau grouper we named Lord Marmaduke had a prodigious
tite for sausages and we threaded them on a stout nylon string to save Ashley
g his fingers.

w left: The author took this picture of himself gazing at a beautiful soft coral
e Red Sea by using a camera with a wide-angle lens held in his extended left

w right, top: A clownfish nestles with impunity in the stinging tentacles of an
one in the Red Sea.

w right, bottom: The wrecks in Truk Lagoon were loaded with war cargo –
this gasmask.

At Ras Muhammed in the Red Sea a Napoleon Wrasse keeps one eye focused on the author's still camera whilst the other eye watches another diver filming with

ry wreck in Truk Lagoon is a time capsule. A bicycle still remains where it

The sealions, gentle clowns with amazing speed and agility, performed for us everywhere in the Galapagos archipelago.

As we headed for base I lay thankfully on one of the bunks amidships where the motion of the boat was least and dozed. As I passed into a state of semi-consciousness I mused on the day's proceedings and the extent to which man will go to catch a few fish. Six fully grown men armed with ten rods, dozens of weights, miles of nylon line, hundreds of hooks and pounds of fish caught by somebody else, had attacked the fish from a multi-thousand-dollar craft powered by Twin Criss Craft 350 horse-power engines. What chance did the fish stand against such an onslaught? Actually quite a good one if our unspectacular catch was anything to go by!

Having vowed that I would never ever go big game fishing again I went to sleep. I was awakened with a start by a scream from the engines when they were suddenly put onto full power. I was awake and alert in a flash as the motion of the boat changed from forward to stop to reverse. I rushed out of the saloon amidships onto the stern. I looked around and could see the light of the shore and various navigational marks as we rocked violently from side to side. I grabbed the rail to steady myself.

'Sorry about that Squire,' called down the helmsman. 'Thought we were going to hit a shoal so I shoved her into reverse at full throttle.'

Mr. Fixit clambered down from the flying bridge. He was swathed in oilskins that were dripping with water. A smile spread across his face.

'Time for another beer,' he said.

*　　*　　*

Mr. Fixit was as good as his word when it came to finding a shark for me. He obtained permission for me to lead a group of divers into the waters of Devil's Hole.

We arrived with the first trickle of tourists at 9.30 am on a dull, windy morning. The entrance to the hole was via a shop and narrow passage way. My party of divers, in crocodile formation, wound their way along the path to the edge of a natural water-filled hole some twenty yards across. The hole was close to Harrington Sound and appeared to be connected to it via an underwater tunnel. Passage of the occupants out of the hole was controlled by a metal grid, like a portcullis, that dropped into the culvert. The edge of the hole was lined with trees that cast their shadows over the water and gave it a malevolent appearance. I leaned against the guard rail and peered into the depths. I could just see the bottom about twenty feet down. A nurse shark, about five feet long, swam languidly round the edge of the pool at a depth of about ten feet. From above it looked black. After a few more lazy strokes it settled on the bottom like a log of wood.

I was going to realise my ambition to get some shark pictures at last. This shark was not free ranging in the sea as I would have liked — but it was a start. At least this one could not escape — or so I thought at the time. I changed quickly into my wetsuit, strapped my knife to my leg and heaved an aqualung cylinder onto my back. I ducked under the hand rail and slipped as quietly as I could into the dark green water. I exhaled gently and sank slowly down into the dark water of Devil's Hole.

Near the surface was a mixture of fresh and salt water, which was not completely mixed. As a result I could not see anything clearly defined due to the differences in refractive index of the saline and fresh water. It was like looking through a heat haze on land.

The shark was obviously nervous at my presence and swam past me at speed. It was useless trying to take pictures in such conditions. As I sank down however, I passed into clear salt water. That was better. The shark made another circuit, staying well out of camera range, and disappeared from view completely. The huge turtles in the pool were far less apprehensive and appeared to ignore me completely as they flippered energetically to and fro. I touched the bottom and tried to avoid stirring up the silt. There was no sign of the shark. Across the Devil's Hole I noticed part of the green-grey wall diffused into a black undefined area. As I swam over to it, it took the shape of a cave. So that was where the shark had disappeared to. I hovered at the entrance waiting for my eyes to adjust to the gloom before I moved slowly forward.

I was not sure what tactic the shark would adopt when it

found itself trapped and face to face with my camera and I wasn't helped by poor visibility from a cloud of suspended silt inside the cave. My eyes slowly became accustomed to the gloom as I inched my way forward. My quarry was in residence. I reduced my rate of breathing to a minimum. As the images inside the cave became clearer I realised I was not facing a shark but a gigantic grouper.

Keeping its massive head faced in my direction it moved imperceptibly backwards as I moved forward. When it could retract no further it sidled to the back wall of the cave, still keeping a bright eye focused in my direction. It was a magnificent fish and must have weighed well over 100 lb. Suddenly from my left came a tremendous flurry. A huge dark shape hurtled past me swirling the silt into impenetrable blackness. Another occupant of the cave that I had not seen lurking in the shadows, had decided to beat a hurried exit. The silt it stirred up reduced the visibility and light intensity to nil. I was suspended in black ink and did not know if the shark was still in the cave with me or not. There were obviously recesses in the cave that I had not seen when I approached the giant grouper which I assumed was still just a few feet away in the total darkness. It was one of those moments when one's adrenalin level is very high and the impulse to flee is almost overwhelming. Inside I was coiled like a tightly wound spring. But I had to control my fear. I couldn't see a thing. I had no idea what action the shark — if it was still present — or the giant grouper, would take if I blundered into them in the dark.

I stayed absolutely still and waited. Time became elastic and stretched; what must have been a few seconds seemed minutes. As I waited, holding my breath, the silt started to settle and a pale grey glow appeared on my right. It was the exit to the cave. I beat a deliberate but unhurried retreat towards the light that brightened with every inch of progress I made towards it.

The green water of Devil's Hole looked bright by comparison with the cave. By the time I emerged, several divers were in the water sporting themselves amongst the turtles. With my one free hand I grabbed the front of the shell of a passing 200-lb turtle to hitch a lift to the middle of the pool. But after a brief tow it took exception to me as a passenger and twisted round so that I lost my grip.

I made my way to another hole in the wall from which earlier I had seen projecting the head of a large moray eel. Remembering the stories of these eels, with their rows of teeth that point backwards so that once they have taken hold they cannot let go, discretion dictated that I should not investigate its presence with my hand. I peered into the hole, but if it was at home it was clearly not keen to receive visitors.

My shark was nowhere to be seen.

From the middle of the pool I looked up and could clearly see the tourists leaning over the rails and watching my underwater antics. Then they started to blur. Little circles appeared and disappeared all over the ceiling above me. It was raining. After the dive I stood by the rail alone in the warm rain and looked down again into the now quiet and sombre pool. I hadn't got my shark pictures after all.

⋆ ⋆ ⋆

One of the other tourist attractions on Bermuda was Crystal Caves. The water-filled caves were open to the public for sightseeing, but diving in them was strictly prohibited — so that when I was asked to take some underwater pictures in the caves for the tourist board Mr. Fixit was delighted, as he had always wanted to dive them. Arrangements were made for a select group of experienced divers to assemble at 4.45 pm outside the entrance to the caves which were located on a narrow neck of land between Harrington Sand and Castle Harbour. The tourists had all departed when we arrived. So we changed into our diving suits by our cars in the fading evening light.

We were all excited and somewhat apprehensive. The water temperature was reputed to be 45 °F — colder than the North Sea. Thus everybody was kitted in a full wetsuit — myself included. As most of the party had only dived in gentle waters off Bermuda they (unjustifiably) considered me tougher than them due to my frequent immersions off the British Coast. Not wishing to tarnish the myth by leaving the water too hastily due to the cold, I decided to insulate myself to the maximum and wore every scrap of neoprene rubber I could muster, including hood, boots and gloves.

It is strange that in time of stress and apprehension the English resort to jokes. The famous cockney sense of humour was at its greatest during the war when the bombs were falling on London. Humour appears to relieve tension. Thus some of the divers hid their fears of the forthcoming dive in the cold and dark with a series of bawdy comments on the effects of cold on a man's primary member.

Casually mentioning a dive I had made under the ice in Blenheim Lake, I slipped into the water as gently as possible. Despite every care a cloud of silt obscured my vision. I proceeded forward with the utmost caution. To my surprise the water was not cold. In fact it was as warm as a luke-warm bath. I looked at the thermometer on my watch and it registered 74 °F. I laughed at the slightly comical nature of the situation. It was as if I had gone out with a fur coat on, expecting snow, and found I was in the tropics.

Hardly moving my fins I crept gently forward and switched on my electronic flash gun and photographed a stalactite surrounded by sand. I finned slowly forward and the sand again swirled up. Picture-taking was going to be difficult. I started to move down into a cavern to my left and was startled to find a mass of stalactites under the overhang. They were completely invisible from the surface. I was totally engrossed and just admiring their beauty when a hand touched my fin and beckoned me to the surface. I recognised the excited face in the mask immediately as Martin's. To my surprise there were now six divers in the water behind me and all were swimming rapidly back to the pontoon. Martin, who always gets excited, was swimming close to the bottom and every stroke of fins sent clouds of silt and sand floating up into the water. I filled with anger. What did he think he was doing after I had made it clear to everybody before we entered the water that people must swim gently? Once we surfaced I exploded with rage.

'What the bloody hell do you think you are up to?' I bawled. 'You have filled the water with silt. How the hell can I get pictures in those conditions?'

At this point a person I did not recognise explained very calmly that there was a deep underwater passage out of the cavern. He was afraid I might go into the passage and asked me to stay in the main cave. I found out later that the man who addressed me was the owner of the caves. I reluctantly promised to stay in the main cave and sank again into the chamber. I tried to take some pictures close to the surface and beckoned Peter, my partner, to pose by a stalagmite, but there were two layers in the water and as he moved towards the stalagmite, the layers mixed. The clear image was immediately diffused into a shimmer like a heat haze distorting the view of a distant landscape on a hot day. Photography under such conditions was impossible. At the base of the stalagmite a pair of pliers, probably dropped by workmen engaged on setting up the lights, were embedded in the sand. I touched them but they would not move and were fused into the rocky floor. Not wishing to disturb the environment further I left them to swim deeper to the cave. I looked back and saw a cloud of sand rising from the base of the stalagmite as Peter tried to release the tool from the bed of the cave. I muttered angrily to myself and headed down into the deep cavern.

At a depth of approximately twenty feet the water was beautifully clear and the cave opened out into a huge cavern which was not penetrated by the above water lights in the main cavern. I swung the beam of my powerful lamp towards the roof. It swept through the water like a spotlight in a darkened theatre, the circular disc of yellow light illuminating one glistening stalactite after another. What beauty. It was like the ornate architecture of a submarine cathedral. My anger dissolved like steam in air. In my mind I could hear the sound of a choir rising into the icicled ceiling. Below me were some huge stalagmites. To me they were the pipes of a stone organ that added its own deep, resonating, majestic sound to my imaginary chorale. It was a moment of magic. I was at peace with myself floating alone in my submerged temple.

Another beam of light flashed across the scene. It was from Peter Haynes' torch. We continued our exploration together. In one place a heavy stalactite ran from the roof to the floor of the cave. The middle of the stone pillar was split as if somebody had cut it through and removed a four-inch section. I got Peter to peer at my camera through this extraordinary natural fracture.

On the sloping floor of the cave a long fissure bore witness to the forces that had been brought to bear on the cavern. Forces great enough to shear rocks in two. At some time in its long history the cave must have been subjected to an earthquake or earth movements that had caused the floor and the ceiling to move apart. The pillar that Peter had peered through had just snapped in the process. But many others could not stand the strain. Large broken cylindrical columns of stone lay strewn across the ground like pillars of a ruined Greek temple.

I followed the cavern down to its maximum depth of about forty feet where it funnelled into a narrow chamber towards which I felt very strongly drawn. But I had agreed not to leave the main cave, and I returned into the brightly lit area under the catwalk. There were about six divers in the water which had stayed remarkably clear, despite the churning eddies from their fins because the sand on the floor in the middle of the cave was coarse and settled quickly. Thus my early anxiety over the visibility was unfounded.

On the cave bed beneath the pontoon were many objects dropped and tossed in by the numerous visitors. These included a number of old English pennies which had become cemented to the stone. The white rock surrounding them was stained a turquoise green indicating that the copper was gradually dissolving to form the coloured salts that tinted the rocks. One of the final pictures I took before I left the water was of an old Polaroid camera fused to the rock with a brown stain from the iron of its decaying components spreading like blood from its broken body.

★　★　★

One of the events on my visit to Bermuda which made a deep impression was a visit to a large hotel to attend a film lecture. The speaker was twenty minutes overdue. The room was filled with about 150 American tourists. Then into the room strode a portly, middle-aged man with the slightly bow-legged, self-assured swagger of an Elizabethan captain presenting himself at court. Instead of the ruffed breeches and stockings, which flattered the shape of a man's legs, he wore an immaculate pair of grey Bermuda shorts, yellow socks and polished brown shoes. The rest of his attire, which was as colourful as that worn by Raleigh or Drake, consisting of a red jacket, white shirt and dark, small-knotted club tie was the epitome of sartorial elegance amongst the old-established white Bermudian population. He had a hawk-like nose and his receding red-gold hair was swept back from a broad ruddy forehead. He eyed his audience through a pair of horn-rimmed spectacles.

How could he gain the attention of this large self-interested garrulous audience?

I was soon to find out.

Every light in the room suddenly went out, and as they did people stopped talking. Ten, twenty, thirty seconds passed and not one word was spoken. The black darkness was punctured occasionally by a glowing red spot of light as members of the assembled expectant crowd in the Belmont Hotel, Hamilton, Bermuda, drew on their cigarettes. Forty seconds passed. Still there was silence. The audience were becoming apprehensive.

From the middle of the silent dark room came the laconic introduction.

'All men have dreamed a dream.'

He paused as he allowed his words to register.

'Ladies and gentlemen, I have lived my dream.'

A projector started to whirr and a scene of the sea and sailing ships vividly splashed onto a screen and filled the room with a pale-blue light.

Harry Cox — diver, treasure-hunter, philosopher, businessman, gourmet and character extraordinaire had his audience in the palm of his hand. And he never let them go after that. He launched into an account of the underwater life around Bermuda with the passion and zeal of a Welsh preacher. He told the story of how the old sailing ships came to grief on the treacherous outer reefs and how the reefs had recently claimed the yacht of one of his dearest friends. Finally he launched into the dramatic story of how he had found a treasure of gold and jewels worth a fortune.

It was a story I knew already, but I had not learned it from sitting in an air-conditioned luxury hotel watching slides on a screen. I had gained the knowledge on board Harry's boat, *Shearwater*, whilst out with him on an unforgettable diving trip to the very reef where the treasure was found.

The trip had been arranged by one of Mr. Fixit's many deputies. I presented myself at the appointed hour of 8.30 am at the PW Dock in Hamilton not knowing quite what to expect. Adjacent to the dock was a supermarket. I have an abhorrence of the crowded, soulless de-personalised supermarkets that have become part of our way of life and I find these temples to the fake gods of speed and convenience particularly loathsome when they become shabby and tawdry. But the supermarket by the dock was airy, spacious, clean and with a superb selection of foods — a Fortnum and Mason of supermarkets. I liked it.

Inside I met Harry Cox and he clasped my hand in a firm handshake.

'Help yourself to anything you fancy,' he said waving his right hand in an expansive gesture.

Harry had a friendly chat with the smartly dressed lady who came and stood by the till as we approached. Loaded with cans we stepped outside and walked along the quay in the bright November sunshine. I found out later that Harry Cox owned the cornucopia we had just visited and had once commenced a lecture to the diving club with the phrase 'I am but a humble grocer'.

We made our way to the *Shearwater* which was moored alongside the jetty. There was an air of activity about the place. Water was being piped aboard and after depositing our food supplies in the saloon we left the boat to attend to the air cylinders which were being filled at a compressor on the jetty. As the bottles were charged we laid them in a neat row along the ground. A strapping young man then came and whisked them aboard the boat.

'You know Horace, I love this boat,' said Harry leaning on the guard rail of the *Shearwater*. He uttered the words with deep sincerity.

'Let me show you round.' He gave me a conducted tour of the vessel which had a fibre-glass hull.

'She's forty-four feet long and fifteen feet in the beam and was built to my own design in the United States.'

The orange peel surface texture of the fibre-glass gave the *Shearwater* a utilitarian appearance that was not relieved by the overall shape or design. There were no frills. It was a boat designed for the job of diving.

She was powered by a single 350 hp engine whose exhaust pipe was hidden inside a fibre-glass funnel which was perhaps one of the boat's few concessions to appearance.

'She does about one mile to the gallon,' commented Harry when I enquired about her fuel consumption.

We ended our tour on the roof of the saloon where there was an additional steering wheel coupled to the one in the cabin. It was a good vantage point from which to navigate in a coral crowded sea.

At the wheel was a slender eleven year-old boy with straight golden hair and a clear complexion tanned a pale brown. It was the face of an intelligent boy that beamed a mischievous reserve and reminded me of my own son Ashley. We shook hands as I was formally introduced to Harry's son William. I took an instant liking to the shy, slightly embarrassed boy. Harry looked round the ship and scanned the jetty as we walked round the upper deck.

'Take her out Willie,' he called to the boy standing alone at the wheel as we clambered down to the main deck.

Harry disappeared into the engine room whilst his son started the engine. One of the Negroes on the jetty cast off the moorings. The boat swung gently away into the harbour and we put to sea under the control of a boy, who had a 350 hp engine and the fate of a very expensive boat under his control at the pull of a lever.

'I am going to take you to one of the most beautiful sites on the whole of the coast of Bermuda,' said Harry. 'I'll take you to the spot I have named "a window in the sea".'

Our destination, which Harry did not disclose to me at

that moment, was to be John Smith's Bay.

When we arrived I saw a flat coral outcrop that just broke surface, set in a deep-blue sea. Most times the water rose and fell gently over the rocks, like a cloth falling over a table. But occasionally the rocks would slash the sea into ribbons of glistening white foam. The *Shearwater* edged her way in towards the outcrop. Two anchors were heaved overboard. It was time to dive.

People were leaping into the sea. I joined Harry and a young lady, Nancy, who agreed to model for me underwater. In a moment I was over the side and peering down into the coral seascape below. Nancy and Harry were each temporarily swathed in a shroud of silver bubbles as they dropped into the water beside me. A few seconds later the bubbles had floated to the surface and the leaders of the diving troupe were clearly visible. Harry wore just the jacket of his diving suit. Nancy wore a jacket and trousers but at my special request she had not put on a hood. I noted with pleasure how her golden hair, swept by the bubbles of air escaping from her mouthpiece, floated like a candle flame around her pretty face.

Looking down I felt briefly as if I was flying in a helicopter amidst the skyscraper blocks of London or even New York. The grey coral rose in slender pinnacles and in massive conglomerates around me. Paths of sand meandered around the natural architecture of the coral city. But there the similarity ended. Instead of people scurrying determinedly along the streets, as only pressure-burdened city people do, these submarine avenues were peopled by a few piscatorial pedestrians. They finned lazily to and fro like Italians strolling languidly round a country piazza in the hot midday sun. It was a submarine community at peace with itself, its surroundings and the endless sea beyond.

The gaggle of divers drifted down as Harry took the lead, sometimes following the line of the sandy paths, occasionally flying over the small grey hillocks.

Trailing behind a group of divers is not the way to get good pictures as their fins stir up the sand. Also shots of divers swimming away from the camera are far less attractive than divers swimming towards the camera. I therefore hovered above the party and tried to anticipate their route. When I had decided which way they were likely to go I would swim vigorously ahead and then drop down in front of them so that I could catch them coming towards me — a tactic which called for bursts of energetic swimming. After one such manoeuvre I saw a large natural arch ahead of the party. I recognised it immediately from Harry's earlier description. It was Harry's 'window in the sea'. From inside the view beyond was one of fish, sea and coral.

After pausing briefly to absorb the beauty of the scene I swam quickly through the opening to get a shot of the divers as they emerged. Harry was in the lead and swimming close to the roof of the cave. Near the entrance he turned to see that his party were still in convoy. As he did so he struck his head on a piece of coral projecting downwards. A pale cloud of green blood diffused into the water around his floating hair. I immediately swam over to him and gave him the 'are you OK' sign by touching my thumb and forefinger together in the shape of an 'O'. He replied with a similar sign, which indicated 'I am OK', and swam on gently fingering the cut. I looked at Nancy who had also seen the accident and noticed that her lips looked pale blue. We were about forty feet down and I was again seeing the colour-modifying effects of water which preferentially absorbs red light.

About twenty minutes after entering the water I was aware of a dark cloud overhead. Looking up I could see the keel of the *Shearwater* with its single stationary propeller. The guided tour was over. We had a quick conference whilst treading water on the surface beside the boat. Harry climbed aboard and Nancy and I sank slowly back into the sea on a private exploration and photographic expedition to use up the remainder of our air. In the same way that I like to explore the backstreets and alleyways of a city, so I wanted to get closer to the heart of the reef. The first twenty minutes had given me an overall impression of the area. But like any guided tour, having once got my bearings, I now wanted to delve into the cracks and crannies and peer into the holes. I wanted to meet the real inmates of the reef. I wanted to look at the bricks as well as the buildings.

In close-up the reef was not at all like a city for there were no straight lines and the building bricks were a wondrous mixture of shapes and sizes. Even the Antonio Gaudi's Church of the Holy Trinity in Barcelona, with its irregular shapes and diversity of structure, would be rated as plain when compared with the architecture of John Smith's Bay.

We swam slowly back towards the window in the sea. In addition to the brain corals and fan corals, with which I was by now familiar, I saw shapes I had never come across before. One of the most unusual was akin to three pyramidal pixie hats stuck on top of one another. Another pillar had the appearance of a half burned candle with its chunky run of wax down one side. I signalled to Nancy that I wanted her to pose between the candle and an adjacent vertical coral face, but she could not understand my mime. I thought back to years before and how Kay and I worked together; Kay would have known what I wanted.

The situation with Nancy illustrated one of the many rules of photography that I had learned over the years. It takes time to establish a relationship with a diving partner. When Kay and I were filming together we knew instinctively where the other would be, and knew immediately what a gesture or a signal implied.

However, Nancy, my unpaid model, was intelligent, and a competent diver. We made good progress. The housing containing my electronic flash unit was connected via a long coiled cable to the camera. I detached the head and handed it to Nancy and signalled to her to illuminate a coral cave by holding the flash unit in front of her. She understood. The flash fired and she handed the flash unit back to me. As we turned a corner of the reef to explore another gully I tried to wind on the film but as I depressed the wind-on lever it stuck. I had used all my film. I glanced at my pressure gauge; the needle was half way across the red section. I showed it to Nancy. We circled a large pinnacle and drifted slowly upwards. It is very satisfying to use all of one's air and all of one's film on a single dive and then to surface beside the boat.

I thanked Nancy for her patient co-operation and made my way to the portion of the deck I had allocated myself. As

165

I dropped my dripping fins on the deck and peeled off my jacket I had an internal feeling of great happiness. I stowed my camera carefully on a towel and after drying off went into the cabin. Nancy was singing in the shower and Harry handed me some hot chili con carne. What more could I have asked for?

Harry said he was very disappointed at the poor visibility, which by North Sea standards was exceptionally good. Harry insisted that a visibility of fifty to sixty feet was not exceptional in John Smith's Bay. The reason for the slight turbidity in the water was the state of the sea which was gradually deteriorating as the wind veered round to the south. I told him that as far as I was concerned it had been an outstandingly good dive and diverted the subject to his forehead on which a deep-red scab had formed.

The swell was now breaking continuously over the emerging coral table and it was clearly prudent to move out. We were soon under way again and continued eastwards. We completed a full circuit of the island to get back to Hamilton. As soon as we docked, I helped unload the cylinders and haul them to the compressor whilst the other members of our assorted party bid Harry goodbye.

'You must come up to the house for a drink,' said Harry. 'Charlie will give you a lift.'

I was reluctant to agree for fear of outstaying my welcome but Harry insisted and I was certainly not tired of listening to Harry, who had a wealth of knowledge, not only of the sea but of Bermuda itself. Having fortified himself and myself with an extraordinarily large rum on the rocks, Harry showed me some of his collection of rare artefacts salvaged from the seabeds. Many of them entwined the romance of majestic sailing ships with voyages to distant and exotic lands. His collection included bottles, pottery, spoons and a large ivory tusk. I built an imaginary picture of myself aboard a seventeeth-century sailing ship as I handled the objects that must have been common-place to sailors of the period. It was not difficult for me to dream of the past for the house itself was built in 1720 and was filled with beautiful old furniture.

The first human inhabitants of Bermuda were white

sailors. Harry explained how the old houses in Bermuda, of which his was a magnificent example, were built like upturned ships' hulls. To emphasise his point he indicated the thwarts in the ceiling at one end of his long lounge. Houses in Bermuda were, and still are, built from blocks of limestone coral cut out of the ground. The hole produced by this process provides a convenient tank for water storage. The limestone bricks are held together with a mixture of lime and shark oil which gradually reacts with the air to form an extremely hard and binding cement. After our fascinating discourse on the colonisation of Bermuda we came back again to the subject of wrecks.

'I would like to take you out to the wreck of the *Eagle*,' said Harry. 'Let's see what we can find out about her.'

He led me to his bedroom which housed a magnificent four poster bed. He removed an old tome from the bookcase and put it on the deep green velvet bedcover. One of the many dogs in the house, upset by the lack of attention we were paying him, leapt upon thebed. Grabbing a corner of one of the pillows in his jaws, he shook it violently and then tossed it into the air over his back. Harry appeared not to notice this extrovert behaviour and informed me that the *Eagle* was wrecked on the outer reef on 12 January, 1659. Appropriately, she was an English ship under the command of a Captain Whitby. The *Eagle* was loaded with trade goods and passengers and was en route from Plymouth, in England to Jamestown before she came to her untimely end.

After further browsing through the fascinating old books, the generous drink Harry had poured for me had worked through my system and I felt the need to relieve myself.

'Where's the loo, Harry?' I enquired.

'I'll show you where the loo, as you call it, is,' he said and strode out of the room. I was somewhat surprised as he led me through the house into the garden which happened to be where he stored his barrel of superb rum and from which we had both had a liberal libation.

'No, Harry,' I protested. 'I don't want another drink, I want a pee.'

'Horace,' he said, managing to get into the expression of that single word the resigned irritation of a schoolmaster addressing a dull pupil on the same topic for the third or fourth time. 'This is Bermuda.' He unbuttoned his fly. 'The only water we have here we collect off the roof of the house. If we run out we have to buy more. Every time you flush the lavatory, gallons of it are used. So why waste it?'

So saying he urinated onto a flower bed.

The day allocated for my trip to the *Eagle* was near the end of my stay in Bermuda. Harry gathered on board the *Shearwater* a collection of his treasure-hunting friends. For Harry had decided not to go straight to the site of the *Eagle* but to do a little treasure prospecting en route.

The pre-sailing formalities on the jetty were quickly and efficiently coped with by a small band of men who knew the routine and had carried it out many times before. I couldn't help thinking they looked an unlikely bunch of treasure hunters. A group of successful Americanised Bermuda businessmen, past middle-age and soft from easy living — not the hard, scarred villainous crew I might have expected. A few more visitors including Nancy joined the group and we headed for the outer reef over a calm sea.

I wandered into the cabin where Harry was clasping a black-bound volume with gold lettering on the front cover. It was the log of the *Shearwater*. Harry handed it to me. It was written in a bold, simple, unfaltering hand and it contained not just a record of the activities of the *Shearwater,* but Harry's thoughts as well. It was fascinating to read, and in a few moments I was totally engrossed.

I was startled from reading when Harry called out that we were approaching the outer reef and it was time for two members of the party to 'drag' — the technique Harry used when hunting for wrecks that may contain treasure. As two of our party kitted up on the poop deck I returned to the log and shortly came to the following section dated 26 July, 1968 and entitled '*Sebastian* Wreck'.

'Gillies' mask stared — his eyes didn't move at all. I fanned powerfully and sand eddied up and scattered with the gusts which my hands created, and then there fell out of the niche of centuries-worn convoluted rock a gold bracelet in three bands — the sand left it, half encrusted and lying heavily where we both saw it in this instant of discovery.

'I snatched it up and Gillies said later he could hear me shouting at the wall of water "GOLD — GOLD — GOLD." I handed the bracelet coil of heavy yellow to Bill.'

By the time I had finished reading about the finding of the treasure two frail-looking old men were clothed in full wetsuits. They leapt into the water and swam to two long ropes trailed over the stern of the *Shearwater*. With the engine out of gear the boat floated lazily on the sea. Each man grabbed a rope with his hands and put one of his feet in a loop at the end of the rope.

Harry was on the flying bridge and scanned the coral outcrop over which we hovered. He looked astern at the two men floating like black logs on the water. One of them raised his arm and made a circular movement indicating to Harry to start the propeller turning. Harry put the engine into gear and moved the throttle very slowly forward. The ropes, which had lain like snakes on the surface of the sea, straightened. The divers took the strain. The white crest of wave broke in front of each man's mask as they accelerated slowly forward. The first 'drag' had begun.

We towed the two men from the inside of the reef to the outside of the reef which had a sharp drop off indicated by an abrupt change of colour of the sea from light blue to deep blue. As soon as the divers reached the blue water Harry turned the boat and headed back towards the shore dragging the two divers over a strip of coral adjacent to the strip they had covered on their first traverse. When they reached the inner edge of the reef, again marked by a change in colour of the sea, this time to the yellow-blue colour of shallow water over sand, Harry again turned the *Shearwater* through 180 degrees. He began another traverse, parallel to and adjacent to, the last.

After about half an hour of dragging backwards and forwards across the reef, one of the men raised his hand and let go of the rope. Had he found a new wreck? His partner also let go of the rope and the two of them snorkelled over the area peering intently at the reef beneath.

The *Shearwater* was quickly brought to a standstill and manoeuvred back to the divers.

'Horace,' said Harry. 'I hope we've found a wreck for you.'

I gazed over the side but could see nothing different from the other areas we had traversed.

'False alarm,' yelled one of the black-suited dragmen as he swam over to his rope. His partner also took a rope.

'Sorry, Horace,' said Harry.

He immediately put the engine into gear and the drag started again.

As the *Shearwater* moved back and forth over the reef I passed the time with Harry on the upper deck. He explained how the navigators on the old sailing ships had no compasses but could measure latitude with the aid of an astrolabe. They used Bermuda as an essential reference point when travelling from Spain to the New World and more importantly, when sailing, loaded with treasure, back from the New World to Spain. The lookout would spot the low hillock of the main island of Bermuda when the vessel was perhaps twelve miles offshore.

'Land ahoy!' would come the cry from the crow's nest. The course would be changed and the ship would sail towards the island to refill with fresh water. Then six miles offshore, when the island was still only a strip on the horizon, the sea would suddenly change colour from cobalt-blue to grey-blue. Before she could change course the ship would be over the coral of the outer reef. It would be too late to give orders to lessen sail and change course. A sailing ship cannot be stopped in an instant. As the ship moved relentlessly forward the brain corals and staghorn corals would tear through the hull like a rip saw. And into the sea would spill her ballast and cargo, before the ship itself finally came to a halt probably with some of its deck still well above water. In good conditions the crew might take to the boats and row ashore. But it would take only one heavy sea for the ship to break up and have her spars and timbers scattered far and wide. All above water traces of her would disappear. Beneath the surface, coral would gradually colonise the canons lodged in crevices in the reef. The ever shifting sands would bury the remains of the keel until no sign of her would remain.

After dragging for about an hour, during which time there were several false alarms, Harry suggested I got kitted up.

When I was ready he stopped the *Shearwater* and told me to look for ballast and any irregular or unnatural looking shapes. The two old men climbed slowly and stiffly back on board.

My drag partner was strongly built, athletic and well over six feet tall. I put my foot into the loop in the rope and stretched my hand in front of me holding the rope taut against my body. But maintaining the rope in that position was far from easy and I kept rolling over. How had the old men managed this operation with such ease? When I was more or less stabilised in a prone position, my partner, who was an experienced drag man, raised his hand and signalled for the drag to begin.

I held on tight. The rope went as taut as a violin string, and I surged forward in a mass of bubbles. My mask felt as if someone was pushing it onto my face with the heel of their hand. My snorkel tube vibrated in the streaming water and I had to bite the end to prevent my losing the mouthpiece. For the first minute I paid little heed to what was passing beneath me. I concentrated all of my attention and strength on just staying attached to the line.

I was rapidly gaining a new respect for the two old boys who had endured such physical stress for over an hour. I gradually became accustomed to the strain and once I found I could hang on my mood changed to one of exhilaration. I peered into the coral underworld that was moving past my gaze. The visibility was in the region of 100 feet and I swung my gaze from side to side to see the maximum area. When I turned my head fully left I could see my partner gripping the rope with one arm outstretched fully forward. When I looked down I saw gullies of sand intersecting and isolating clumps of coral. Suddenly the sea became deeper and the coral was far away. We had come to the 'drop off'. We had come to the edge of the top of the volcano upon which the islands of Bermuda sit like a coral hat, with the outer reef forming the edge of the upturned brim. From here the sea drops rapidly to a depth of 3,000 feet. This was where the big sharks were reputed to roam.

I looked down into the deep blue water for any sign of their torpedo bodies and recalled that some wit on board had expressed the opinion that trailing two men over the stern of the *Shearwater* was like trailing for sharks with live bait — human live bait. The rope went slack as the *Shearwater* turned. Without a camera I wouldn't even be able to get a picture of my partner being taken by a shark.

All thoughts of sharks vanished when the rope went taut and I was hauled savagely back towards the reef.

I peered into the depths, straining to see any of the tell-tale signs that would indicate a wreck. But all I saw was the occasional flash of silver as a fish attacked a tasty morsel on the reef. As soon as the fish resumed a normal swimming motion it merged with the coral and was much more difficult to detect from above.

During one of my traverses of the reef we passed suddenly into an area where there were numerous nodules of coral. Were these natural or man-made objects covered in coral? Would they think me a fool for stopping the boat in an area that was so obviously not the site of a wreck? In the few seconds I spent debating this possibility with myself we had passed into an area where all of the formations looked completely natural. I decided not to drop off the line and looked across at my partner who was an experienced dragline diver. He must have also seen the nodules. Or had he?

I was perturbed and realised I did not really know what I was looking for.

I recalled a visit I had made to Professor Stirrer at the Marine Biological Station in Bermuda where I had looked at a whole series of aerial photographs taken over the reef on a very calm day. As I studied the three foot by four foot prints I saw a cigar shape amidst the jumble of subsea coral and was told that it was a well-known wreck, about sixty years old.

If the entire area had been surveyed from the air, what

were our chances of locating a new site? Had I passed over a fortune and not known it? I honestly did not know at that moment, although later I was to find out just how subtle the changes in the sea bed are at the site of an ancient wreck.

After we had been in the water for about an hour and a quarter Harry decided it was time to call off the drag. By this time I was feeling chilled and I climbed slowly aboard the *Shearwater,* bent forward clasping the rail with the slow deliberate movements of a frail arthritic old man. My respect for Harry's team grew by the minute.

'Now I'm going to take you to the wreck of the *Eagle,*' said Harry as we hauled in the drag lines and set course for the North-East Breaker.

As we approached, the North-East Breaker was easily visible from the *Shearwater* for in places the coral reef projected a few feet above the sea. The *Shearwater* was soon anchored and within a short time I was falling through clear water to Harry who had plummeted to the bottom like a stone and was sitting patiently on a large sausage-shaped piece of coral in the midst of a patch of sand. As always my ears took twice as long to clear as those of anyone else. And Nancy passed me on the way down.

When en route for the bottom I thought the structure upon which Harry was sitting was a little unusual — long thin strips of coral do not usually grow in the middle of patches of sand. When I landed beside him I realised why. The object upon which he had parked himself was a large cannon completely encrusted in coral.

Jammed in a gully nearby was a large metal object. It was the keel of a modern sailing ship. Even in the days of multiple navigation aids the reef still claimed its victims. I recognised the debris immediately. It was the keel of the vessel, the loss of which Harry had vividly described at the Belmont Hotel.

After a brief inspection of the remains of a once proud yacht, which had not as yet been colonised, we swam through an alley in the coral into a broad gully with a brilliant yellow sandy floor.

The gully was buzzing with activity. The other divers from the *Shearwater* were actively engaged in the serious business of looking for artefacts or treasure. Finned feet projected from clouds in the water as the head-down treasure seekers scooped the sand from crevices in the rocks and let it run through their fingers. I quickly found a likely-looking spot and followed their example. But nothing but sand trickled through my trembling fingers. I was now the victim of treasure fever. Would such a random, unscientific approach lead to a find?

A modicum of commonsense then took hold of me. I was in the company of a master treasure hunter. Why not see how he was searching. I looked around and saw Harry moving a large spherical boulder from a crevice. He looked for all the world like a strongman act in a circus as he planted his feet squarely on either side of the gully and grasped the underside of the boulder in his hands. I watched his back and strong legs straighten as the rock yielded its attachment to the reef. He clasped it to his chest and staggered forward a few paces. He dropped the rock and a cloud of sand swirled up briefly as it landed. The water cleared quickly.

I joined Nancy and Harry as they dug into the freshly uncovered sand with their hands. I picked up a handful of sand and let it fall through my fingers. Nothing remained. I scooped out a small depression and farmed away the lighter sand particles which quickly settled out. The bottom of the hole was filled with pebbles.

A piece of brown pottery was just visible. I pulled it out and gave it to Harry who turned it over in his fingers and handed it back to me. I went back to my hole and dug deeply into it with my fingers until I felt an unusual shape. I pulled out a few more handfuls of pebbles and sand and there in the bottom of the depression was the white bowl of an old clay pipe.

I tucked the piece of pottery under the jacket of my wetsuit and gently removed the pipe from its gravel grave. The yellow and black stones mixed with sand in the depression were of considerable significance and refocused my attention on something that Harry had said before we started dragging. He had instructed me to look for ballast.

Bermuda is made entirely of coral, which is a relatively

soft limestone-like rock. When broken up and ground by the sea it does not form pebbles. Coral breaks down to a coarse white sand.

The pebbles I was looking at were not of Bermudian origin. They had probably been gathered from an English beach in the early 1600s and were part of the ballast of the ill fated *Eagle* that had foundered on the reef in 1659. Ballast is by its nature heavy material and therefore tends to remain at the site of a wreck. It is one of the clues that the wreck detective looks for when he is trying to identify the origin of a sunken vessel. The site of the wreck of the *Eagle* had been worked several times by diving parties but nobody had admitted to finding anything more than general objects relating to the everyday life on board a ship of the period. My clay pipe was of little intrinsic value, but to me it was worth its weight in copper, if not in gold, as a souvenir of a memorable dive. I was very pleased to have it and it satisfied my treasure fever. My ever-burning photography fever, however, raged unabated and when Harry headed back to the *Shearwater*, I digressed from treasure hunting to picture hunting.

I swam along the reef with Nancy until we came to what looked like the branch of a huge coral tree lopped off at the end. It was only when I examined it very closely that I realised I was looking at a cannon completely encrusted with coral. The breech of the gun was fused in a mass of coral that had completely disguised the shape. I would certainly never have noticed it had I passed over it during the drag in the morning. I had grave doubts about my ability to penetrate the disguising cloak of coral that would cover any wreckage that had been on the reef for two or three hundred years. Through the experience gained on seeing the *Eagle* site, however, I felt I might be slightly less useless in any future surveys I might undertake.

My first participation in the treasure trail caused me to wonder if Harry's techniques were unscientific and needlessly time-consuming. But the visit to the *Eagle* site changed my mind. Aerial surveys were likely to reveal only relatively modern wrecks. Towing metal detectors across the reef would be far from easy in an area where the depths and coral varied so dramatically. No, the trained human eye was probably still the best tool, especially if the wreckage was camouflaged with 300 years of coral growth. What better and simpler method of applying the trained human eye than the Harry Cox dragline system?

Our sea journey back to Hamilton was pleasant with those on board the *Shearwater* discussing the day's activities. Harry's young son William berthed the boat with the precision of a practised fisherman. It was time for me to arrange transport of myself and my large bag of diving and photographic equipment back to 'Avocado Lodge' on Corkscrew Hill, where I was staying.

I explained my need to Harry and he said he would take me back. He disappeared to get what I thought would be a car. He reappeared shortly, however, riding a battered Lambretta scooter.

I looked at Harry, whom one could hardly describe as a small man, my pile of luggage and young William. Surely there had been a misunderstanding. We could not all travel by scooter. I offered to find a taxi — but Harry insisted. He was obviously not going to be deterred by such a minor problem as having only a two seater scooter to transport three people and a huge pile of baggage.

Harry sat on the front of the seat and I piled my bag and other luggage on the footrest platform in front of the saddle. By the time I had finished tucking the various pieces into position, the heap of luggage was almost as high as the handlebars.

William sat close behind his father leaving me about six inches of saddle to perch upon but nowhere to rest my feet. I held on to William and William held on to his father. However, sitting astride the saddle trying to keep my feet from touching the ground was a very ungainly leg-aching process. And before we had traversed a few yards of jetty it was clear that I would not be able to sustain the muscular effort until we reached 'Avocado Lodge'.

I decided therefore to relinquish my hold on William and use my hands to hold up my legs by the ankles, at the same time clasping the scooter with my thighs. We wobbled our way to the gates to the jetty and out onto the main street of the Hamilton waterfront. As we picked up speed and proceeded in a straight line the scooter with its unprecedented load became stable and I felt a little more secure on my tiny precarious perch. But my security was shattered a few moments later when a police car drove straight out of a side road directly into our path. Harry braked hard and swerved. I grabbed him to prevent myself from falling off and he in turn held our luggage tightly between his legs to prevent it from spilling onto the road. The incident was over in a few seconds. The police car accelerated away and we regained an even keel and gradually increased our speed to about 25 mph. We reached 'Avocado Lodge' without further incident and I slipped thankfully off my perch.

Mr. Fixit kept my diary full until my last day on Bermuda, 14 November 1973, which I was free to organise myself, and that was the day I persuaded Harry to show me his treasures. He agreed to do so at 4.30 in the afternoon which I calculated would leave me just enough time to catch my plane which was scheduled to depart at 7.30.

The approach to Harry's house was impressive. The drive wound its way between high palm trees before the large white house revealed itself. I arrived exactly on time and was greeted by a pack of barking dogs and a flock of clucking chickens. A knock on the door caused the dogs to become even more frenzied. They rushed hither and thither sending the chickens scurrying in all directions. No-one answered the door. Harry was out. I wandered round the outside of the house and inspected a bronze cannon, with a split breach, that was lying on the ground. Then a taxi came crunching along the drive, but instead of Harry, out stepped a gentleman I had never seen before. He said he was from the *National Geographic* and he had come to see the treasure. Five minutes later another car drove up and deposited another one of Harry's friends who had also come to see the treasure. It was going to be some party.

I looked anxiously at my watch. I couldn't be sure that BOAC would keep Harry Cox Bermuda time. How disappointing it would be if all of the other visitors assembling were to see the treasure whilst I sped off to the airport.

The minutes ticked by. The dusk gathered.

The next car to arrive did not bring Harry. Instead it conveyed his beautiful wife Jessica. I was reminded of the days when I had been a wedding photographer. I would stand at the lych gate of the church as car after car pulled up, deposited its passengers and left, whilst I waited for the star — the bride — to arrive. In this instance, however, it was Harry who was playing the role of the bride. At length the bridal car arrived and out stepped Harry in the now familiar red blazer, yellow socks and Bermuda shorts.

We all bustled into the kitchen whilst Harry fixed one of his superb rum drunks. I was handed a tankard with a sailing ship engraved on it. Inside a mixture of rum, ice and Canada Dry snapped and crackled as the ice from the deep freeze succumbed to the stresses of the warm alcohol. The drink was deceivingly potent and it was not long before any fears I had about missing the aeroplane dissolved in the feeling of personal well-being that invaded me. We were joined in the kitchen by a monkey called Percy. Percy accepted the grape Harry offered and sat on his shoulder turning the grape over in his tiny, delicate, human-like hands before nibbling at it with his front teeth. Both Harry and Percy posed for a picture. Percy subsequently left the kitchen riding on the back of Jake the dog.

Jessica had no interest in her husband's treasure on that day for it was the day Princess Anne married Captain Mark Phillips and she left us to watch the ceremony on television. I stood beside her chair briefly as she excitedly watched the carriages bearing the royal family to Westminster Abbey. The commentator described the clothing and jewels worn by the Queen and her daughter with accuracy, dignity and controlled enthusiasm. But for me the remote black and white cathode ray image of a bejewelled royal occasion could not compete with the prospect of seeing and handling real jewels. So I bade the enthralled Jessica *au revoir* and followed the other guests through to the end of the main room of the house. Befitting the occasion Harry spread a royal blue velvet cloth over a large stool in front of the fireplace. He kicked off his shoes revealing a large hole in the heel of one of his yellow socks.

'This is the eleventh pair Jake (the dog) has ruined,' he said as he sat on the floor, his feet projecting forward in our direction under the table.

On the floor beside him, next to his tankard of rum punch, was an old brown paper bag bearing the symbol of his supermarket 'Miles'. His hand delved into the bag and from it he withdrew an old cigar box and other miscellaneous packages. One by one he unwrapped the parcels and placed their priceless contents upon the royal blue velvet. With drama and sincerity he described the finding of the treasure which consisted not only of gold objects, but included a rare bronze astrolabe. His search for information on the origins and uses of the various pieces had taken him to museums and experts throughout the world. Such was the unique nature of some of the artefacts that their precise use could only be speculated upon. He held us spellbound.

One of the most magnificent pieces was a double link gold chain fifteen and a half feet long.

'Can you imagine the work that must have gone into this?' he questioned. 'Every link is perfect and hand forged.'

I held one of the gold bars in my hand, and I again felt the electric thrill I had when I first touched the gold ring Melanie and I discovered on the sea bed off the island of Gemini.

Two dogs bounded into the room and had a rough and tumble on the floor. One of them, on the losing end of the game, scampered up to the stool and placing his front paws on the table demanded attention from his master. Getting no response he playfully, but deliberately disarranged the pieces before being admonished by a completely unperturbed Harry who was still lost in his wonderment at the fortunes of life that had conspired to make him the possessor of such a unique holding in the stockmarket of history. A large green emerald flashed like a cat's eye.

I suspect that most people would liken the thrill of finding a fortune on the sea bed to winning a gamble with very long odds. But the reality is far more complex than that. To Harry Cox finding the treasure was as painful and beautiful as giving birth to a child. It brought with it many problems as well as pleasures. Amongst them was the responsibility of ownership which extended beyond the obvious security risk. Harry's descendants had been on Bermuda for over 300 years. He felt passionately that the treasure should be kept alive and stay in his beloved homeland. So should he keep it, or should he sell it — and if so to whom? If it was auctioned would it be split up and locked away in sterile bank vaults to accrue value for faceless speculators?

I suppose it would have been possible to put some kind of value in dollars on Harry's treasure. But when I flew out of Bermuda I knew nobody could put a value on the extra items that had been added to my personal treasure chest of diving memories — they were beyond price yet nobody could ever steal them.

6

A Wonderland in the Wilderness

THE RED SEA

The deserts of Arabia have had an incomprehensible yet totally hypnotic appeal for many Europeans since the times of the Crusaders. Before I visited the Negev I often wondered what it would be like to travel on a camel in a caravan across its desiccated mineral wasteland and be greeted by the blue expanse of the Red Sea knowing that it was totally undrinkable. As my imaginary camel train continued on its journey south along the shoreline some of the sun-scorched, wind-burned riders would look down into the sea and wonder what existed in the blue depths. Even today the Bedouin glide along the paths beside the Red Sea on their long-legged camels unaware of the underwater Garden of Eden which is so close by — yet as remote to them as the moon.

Now after many excursions into the clear blue depths of the Red Sea I feel as privileged as one of the first space travellers to have explored a realm I have dubbed 'A Wonderland in the Wilderness.' My journeys to the Red Sea have also given me a slight insight into what it was about Arabia that mesmerised men like T. E. Lawrence. For even without diving as a *raison d'être*, just wandering through a vast sun-baked desert is an experience that touches a deep primeval sense within me.

My opportunity to engage in adventurous desert journeys coupled with diving began in the office of Twickenham Travel in Church Street in Twickenham. There I met Bruce and Hedda Lyons who were looking to expand their business to Israel knowing that Eilat, situated at the northernmost tip of the Red Sea, could provide pallid Brits with some welcome sunshine in the winter months.

The outcome of that meeting was that I was to lead the first major British Diving Safari through the Sinai to a place that has since become the Moslem equivalent of Mecca for divers. It is called Ras Muhammed. Many underwater

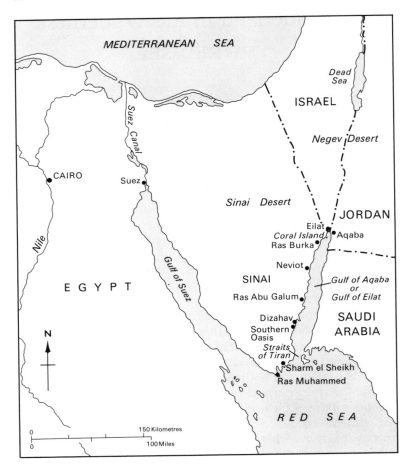

explorers rate it as the greatest dive in the world. Despite its remote location, and the often tiresome and difficult journey to get there, the thousands of devotees who now make the pilgrimage are rewarded with an experience that can be as uplifting to the soul as a visit to a holy shrine.

The event which was to launch an era of diving pilgrimages to Ras Muhammed commenced when twenty-two people from a wide variety of backgrounds with ages from mid-twenties to mid-sixties gathered in the lecture room at the Aquasport Diving Centre in Eilat for a briefing on 5 November 1976. It was obvious from their appearance that the physical fitness of the group was as diverse as their personalities. It is important in such a group to work out compatible diving partners and to identify those who might give assistance in an emergency. I therefore asked each person to recount briefly his or her diving experience. This interesting exercise revealed that they ranged from complete novices to qualified instructors.

The Aquasport Diving Centre in Eilat is beside the beach and the first check-out dives were made simply by walking across the sand and into the sea. Isolated coral outcrops, with the romantic names of Japanese Gardens and Moses Rock Gardens, were the destinations. For many of the group it was their first taste of coral reef diving and after diving only in British waters they could not believe that anything more colourful and exotic could possibly be found. However as later dives were to reveal they could. The further south we travelled the more spectacular the diving became.

I knew this was so from reconnaissance dives made months before the major expedition during which I drove across the Sinai with Bruce Lyons and Soames Sommer-hayes in a Volkswagen Beetle. On that occasion we had taken full tanks of air and had no means of recharging them. Now we planned to do much more diving and to achieve this we needed to be self-sufficient. This entailed taking food supplies and compressors with us, in addition to the weightbelts and other bulky and heavy equipment associated with diving which we would transport in specially-prepared trailers towed behind the Desert jeeps in which the humans would travel.

Willy Halpert, who ran the Aquasport Centre at Eilat, was to be our guide. He had taken on a young law graduate from England as an assistant and he too was to accompany us. Jon Kenfield was his name.

It was arranged that I would drive one of the jeeps and that Jon and Willy would drive the other two with the rest of the party tightly packed into the other seats. As always with such expeditions there were some last-minute difficulties but after frantic 'phone calls, and with the paint still drying on the sides of the untested and heavily-laden trailers, the convoy set off south along a well surfaced road beside the sea. Just how untried both the transport and the drivers were became apparent on the first severe bend when one of the jeeps nearly left the road. The stress was too much for the grossly overladen trailer it was pulling and a few moments later there was a loud bang as one of the tyres burst. As I recall we had a spare tyre for the jeeps but not the trailer. So we had to unhitch the trailer and send one of the jeeps back a few miles into Eilat to get another tyre that hopefully was not a remould.

The incident happened where the road runs alongside a small island topped with the ruins of a Crusader castle. Coral Island, as it was called, sat in the sea as alluring and enticing to the stranded divers as a mermaid to a mariner. So some went for a snorkel whilst others helped me rearrange the weight distribution. Lead weightbelts were stuffed under the seats in the jeeps to lighten the excessive loads in the trailers.

To counteract a possible mutiny by those who had paid good money to come on a trip that had ground so ignominiously to a halt just a few miles from base, the driver of the returning jeep not only carried a spare tyre, he also brought a cardboard box containing twenty-four samples of that twentieth century gastronomic delicacy — the hamburger. These were avidly consumed whilst the wheel was changed and in a short time we were rolling again.

Ras is the Arabic word for headland. Thus Ras Muhammed presumably means Muhammed's headland. I didn't know who, or what, Abu Galum was but his headland was to be our first camp. To get there we left the smooth tarmacadam road and the really adventurous travel across the Sinai began. We passed the Bedouin village of Nuweiba el Museini — a hot windy shanty town of huts made from old packing cases from which women hidden in the black recesses watched us in silence. Young girls tending animals urged goats off the track with sticks to let us pass by. When they had done so they stood still gazing at us, shielding their eyes with their brown arms — their black hair streaming and black dresses billowing in the desert wind.

If you designed a road for the destructive testing of motor vehicles and their drivers you'd be hard put to it to improve upon the trans-Sinai track that led to Ras Abu Galum. At times it was like corrugated iron which caused the jeeps to vibrate like pneumatic drills. This immediately eliminated conversation as it was difficult to control the motion of your lower jaw whilst your head was rattling up and down at the same frequency as the vertebrae in your spine were being separated and reassembled. On other occasions the road was a path through sand as soft as flour. Then everyone got out and shovelled and shoved whilst the four-wheel drive slowly powered the vehicle and its heavy trailer forward. In places the track was covered with boulders the size of small footballs which fired like cannons into the underside of the chassis when clipped by the edges of passing tyres. However the greatest test of nerve of man and strength of vehicle came shortly before we reached our camp site where the road consisted of a ledge cut into the side of a steep rockface. It was just wide enough to take a jeep and one side dropped straight down into the sea — this would not have been too bad if it had not been on a steep incline round a bend and had been made for camels which are not as susceptible as cars to ruts, potholes and loose boulders. A number of the passengers made rapid undignified exits from the back of my jeep when we careered over at an alarming angle towards the sea when the camber of the track tilted us in that direction. Those with some faith in me and more in Allah clenched their chattering teeth into a smile. Slowly we ground round the track — the trailer often leaning in a different direction to that of the jeep. By the time we reached Ras Abu Galum, Jon's jeep was minus its exhaust pipe and mine had shed several unimportant appendages. As we had no tents or ground sheets, setting up camp didn't entail more than telling the group where the shovels and loo rolls were located and making the obvious request that they dug their holes well away from the main camping area. Some of us made, from boulders and bags, little walls the shape and size of coffins around the patch of ground upon which we placed our sleeping bags. These were more for protection from the wind rather than privacy. Other annexed territories were marked merely by piles of bags — the squatters proposing to resort to the use of large plastic bags to exclude the wind and sand from their bedding when they eventually settled down for the night.

The diving at Ras Abu Galum gave us a taste of what was to come further down the coast in terms of the diversity of the corals and fish life. One part of the headland was particularly suitable for our group because it consisted of a very steep sandy beach that continued to dip deep into the sea. It was bounded one side by a rambling coral garden and on the other by a nearly vertical wall.

I had seen many small sea anemones with their attendant yellow clown fish in the Red Sea. On the open reef the anemones themselves were usually sandy coloured. However at Ras Abu Galum, in a small cave at a depth of about fifteen feet I found an anemone that was pale ruby in colour and nearly three feet across. When I approached it, the brave clown fish that had made their home in the anemone rushed out and threatened me. It was an example of a symbiotic relationship in which two very different species live together for the mutual benefit of one another. The brightly-coloured clown fish lure other small fish to the anemone by flitting to and fro in its waving arms and then nestling in them in provocative postures. Those who have wandered through the red-light district of Amsterdam will recognise the technique. By the time those attracted by the decorous dance of the damsels realise their mistake it is too late. The tentacles of the anemone, against which the clown fish brush with gay abandon, contain stinging cells to which the dancers are immune but which are deadly for the luckless passers-by looking for a good time. Poisonous barbs are fired into the newcomers and they are prevented from darting away by threads connecting the warhead to the launching pad. Within minutes the fish is paralysed, encircled by tentacles and then engulfed in the central stomach of the anemone. Lunch or elevenses, the end result of thetechnique is the same. The clown fish picks up the scraps — soboth parties in this act of co-operative underwater warfare aresatisfied. The victim presumably is soon beyond caring.

On the reef the sea anemone looks disarmingly like a flower head with tentacles for petals — but it is classified as an animal. Humans have a thick layer of dead cells on their skins, the epidermis, which protects them from the weapons concealed in the anemone's tentacles. When I touched the anemone with my finger it felt tacky. This was the result of my stretching and breaking the threads attached to the stinging cells which were fitted into my skin but did not penetrate far enough to cause me any sense of pain or discomfort. It did occur to me, however, that a scaled-up version of an anemone would make a good evil adversary in a science fiction story.

Eating seems to be the main pre-occupation of most of the inhabitants of a coral reef. The parrot fish, which I saw in abundance were constantly nibbling with their parrot-like beaks at the stony corals. The white marks where they had chiselled off chunks could be seen very clearly. The nutritional value of rocky corals is very low. The poor parrot fish therefore need to eat prodigious quantities to extract sufficient nutrients to keep body and soul together. As a result of their high-roughage diet they are frequently seen excreting clouds of undigested coral particles in the form of white coral sand. Just sitting quietly on the reef and watching what is going on all around makes one aware of the many activities which keep a bustling coral city in balance.

A fish which makes an essential contribution to the smooth running of the coral metropolis is the cleaner wrasse. He hangs his sign out at certain downtown sections of the reef and his customers queue up for his services like patients in a dentist's waiting room. He is small and his clients are large — often groupers. He commences with a general inspection and then starts picking off parasites from the gill covers and other nooks and crannies — to smarten up the exterior bodywork of his customers. During this period the cleaner wrasse flits around like a feather duster whilst the object of his attention stays impassively still. The customer opens his mouth wide and the cleaner fish disappears inside. To the uninformed observer this may seem a little ungrateful on the part of the spruced-up grouper, to demolish the cleaner wrasses, especially as skilled hard-working staff must be as difficult to come by in a coral city as they are in London. However faith is restored if one keeps watching. For after a few moments the little wrasse wriggles out through the gills cheerfully chomping on some delicious morsel he has removed from the inner labyrinths of the grouper's now gaping maw. When treatment is complete the grouper shakes himself a little and then moves off down the reef like a dandy with a new suit. Before he has gone two coral blocks a new customer will have moved into the 'cleaner station' — which is the term scientists have coined for the section of the reef where a cleaner wrasse operates.

However, even a coral reef is not without its undesirable elements. A parasite-burdened grouper strolling along through the coral city looking for a wash and brush-up after spending a night in one of the less salubrious caves must beware of the villainous con-fish. These cunning fellows are called false cleaner fish, because they look very much like genuine cleaner wrasse. They even hover at openings in the reef and wriggle like the genuine article does when custom is scarce. But when the unsuspecting punter sidles in for treatment he doesn't get what he's looking for. Instead of delicately picking off a parasite the false cleaner takes as big a chunk as his jaws will accommodate in one swift bite out of the side of the grouper. He then disappears like an arrow into a narrow cleft in the coral where the grouper can't get at him.

Just how important genuine cleaner stations are on a reef was demonstrated by a group of submerged scientists who removed all of the cleaner fish from a prescribed section of a reef. After a time all of the big fish disappeared too. Which would seem to show that a coral community is as interdependent as human society and points very clearly to the often unsuspected repercussions that may occur if humans selectively remove a single species.

On one of my dives at Ras Abu Galum I took the oldest member of the party on her first aqualung dive. She was not a strong person and had had a lot of illness. Even so, at sixty-five years of age she wanted to see the undersea world from the inside. She was not strong enough to carry an aqualung plus a weightbelt and walk to the water's edge. So she stood three-quarters submerged on the steep sandy beach whilst we strapped the cumbersome and heavy equipment to her. When we submerged her aqualung cylinder became neutrally buoyant i.e. underwater it was weightless. So with her natural buoyancy compensated for by lead weights we drifted slowly down the slope into the deep blue depths. At first I held her hand. But when I felt she was comfortable I let her go and she finned amongst the shallow water corals peering into the wonderland, her eyes joyously observing the plethora of fishes and coral. It was of course a memorable moment for her. But it was also for me because it proved to me once again that it is the spirit of a human being that is all-important — not the constantly ageing physical body in which it is caged.

Another dive I made at Ras Abu Galum could not have been a greater contrast to the leisurely shallow dive I made with that spirited elderly novice diver. A number of the experienced divers wanted to descend to a depth below the mark which is generally regarded as the maximum depth to which amateur divers should descend using air.

I agreed to lead the group of five knowing that any of us could suffer from nitrogen narcosis or rapture of the deep as it is called. It occurs when the partial pressure of nitrogen in the air being inhaled rises above a certain level which varies from individual to individual. The result is that divers may become totally irresponsible and behave as if they are drunk. In one incident a diver insisted on offering his mouthpiece to a passing fish. The effect however passes, or so the books say, as soon as one rises above one's susceptible depth.

Nitrogen at pressure can also cause another problem — the bends. In this case the effects are not apparent until after the dive, when the nitrogen that has dissolved in the blood at depth reappears as bubbles in the blood. This happens if the ascent is made too rapidly and the dissolved gas is not given sufficient time to be safely expelled via exhalations. Minor bends cause itchiness in the skin and pains in the joints. More serious bends cause paralysis and sometimes death. Bends are avoided by a programmed ascent with decompression stops in shallow water.

In view of these possible hazards the pre-dive briefing for the proposed deep dive was detailed and very specific. We agreed that if any of us saw another member behaving in a foolish manner we would forcefully push him or her back towards the surface until the narcosis passed. We also planned our decompression stops.

As I invariably carry a camera with me when diving I picked up my Nikonos, complete with its flashgun, to record the epic dive. As it turned out that was a mistake.

We set off down the sandy slope keeping close together like a squadron of Spitfires on a dangerous mission. The squadron broke formation however when the weightbelt encircling the narrow waist of the one lady in the group came loose. One of the divers saw her attempting to sort out the problem and went to her rescue. Their struggles raised a cloud of sand. The sight of the two of them, apparently embraced, and disappearing in the sand cloud looked as if they were participating in an underwater dance on a bizarre misty film set. So I took a photograph. The incident was quickly over however, and we continued our descent. I was aware of my responsibility for the safety of the group and was very concerned that I should not narcotise myself. Instead of feeling elated with increasing depth I felt only anxiety. My condition was not changed when we were well past the 150 feet mark. Then suddenly there was a loud retort like a shot being fired. At the same time I felt a thump in my chest. The Perspex housing of my flashgun had imploded under a pressure of over five atmospheres. This I later worked out to be about seventy-five pounds per square inch, which imposed a total load on the plastic box of over half a ton. No wonder it collapsed. However, there was nothing I could do to remedy the situation. The flashgun was a write-off, so I carried the shattered box and its already corroding flashgun down into the depths with me.

At two hundred feet we all checked our depth gauges, and then moved a bit deeper as one of the gauges indicated a slightly shallower depth. We all shook hands. The sea bed was not particularly interesting — indeed, as is usual on coral reefs we had left the more prolific reef life behind us. So after briefly examining a few unspectacular isolated coral heads the squadron headed back towards the surface. We split into pairs. My partner and I did our decompression ferreting around the shallow reef including in our excursion another visit to the cave with the giant anemone.

Because entry and exit to the water was so easy, Ras Abu Galum was an excellent place for a night dive. We had two members of a BBC film unit from Bristol with us. They had joined the expedition to get some material for a new David Attenborough series. On the list of species they wanted to film was the flashlight fish — *photobletheron* — which can only be appreciated at night. This is a remarkable little fish that has a bioluminescent (biologically produced light) patch behind the gills. The light is continuously produced by bacteria but the fish has a cover that conceals it. However, when the cover is flicked back the bioluminescent patch is revealed. During the day it is insignificant and looks like a white patch. But at night its brightness is accentuated a thousand-fold and it appears to glow with the brightness of a torch. In the darkness the fish itself is almost invisible. As we swam over the shallow reef with our underwater lights switched off we were greeted by a display of flashing fairylights that hovered in the inky eerie stillness of the night sea.

The track we had followed to Ras Abu Galum was part of an ancient camel route that hugged the shoreline. It continued further south but was not wide enough to accommodate a vehicle. It was still in use by camels and we had several visits from Bedouin, who would appear round the headland. It took a practised eye to spot them — the camels blending perfectly with the background. More often than not it was their riders wearing a mixture of cast-off western jackets and traditional Arabic clothes who gave their presence away. It was not until I had driven across the Sinai that I realised how superbly adapted camels are to a desert terrain. Their feet, flat and large as plates can support a large weight without sinking into soft sand. Their long legs enable them to pick their way over rocky ground and they move with deceptive speed. I remember watching a camel train covering the ground I had fought to conquer with my desert jeep and its trailer on the final leg of the journey to our campsite. The camels flowed along the undulations like a convoy of cars over a smooth switchback road. Within a few moments they were just a line of ants following the shoreline on the far side of the bay.

I was still pursuing my quest for shark pictures. As the film crew also wanted footage of the same subject I had additional legitimate grounds for setting this as one of the objectives of the expedition. So whilst one of the camels that passed through our camp munched on a piece of rock-hard stale bread, his owner was questioned about where he had seen sharks on his coastal treks. The outcome of a protracted conversation was, 'Ras Muhammed at dawn is the place to see sharks.' Thus Ras Muhammed, already established as the Everest of our expedition assumed even greater significance.

The metaphorical climb from our base camp at Ras Abu Galum to the top of our Everest, Ras Muhammed embraced many more dives at a variety of diving sites. And in many ways it was like climbing a mountain with new and often more spectacular underwater vistas opening before our gaze as we progressed south. Then finally we made it and drove our jeeps right down onto the beach at the very southernmost tip of the Sinai Peninsula.

About a quarter of a mile offshore from the beach were two submerged islands. We discovered that it was possible, if the dive was organised to take advantage of the currents, to circumnavigate both islands underwater on a single tank of air. However, the manner in which the currents run was difficult to pre-determine. It did not seem to be related to the tides and was probably affected by the wind direction. Furthermore the place where we were told we might see sharks was a near-vertical wall that dropped to a depth of more than a thousand feet. Thus there was no way anyone who panicked or got into trouble and sank could be rescued.

They would take a one-way ticket to Davy Jones locker.

By the time we reached Ras Muhammed the divers had sorted themselves into groups whose interests and air consumption were compatible. This always takes some time as there are divers who like to cover as much terrain as possible, and with fins flaying skim across an area like swallows in flight. There are others who prefer to devote themselves to closely examining a single outcrop. The most difficult to pair up is the photographer, because such a diver can get totally engrossed in a single subject and may spend ages waiting for a fish to pop out of a hole. The photographer gets annoyed if his or her partner swoops in and frightens the subject just as it is about to pose perfectly. Having taken, or lost his shot, the photographer then moves on to the next subject. So he traverses the dive site like a grasshopper — and would really prefer not to have a partner at all. As I fall very distinctly into this category I had organised the diving rota such that most of my dives were made with an excellent diver who was to become a very good underwater photographer herself. In addition to the asset of long photogenic hair, another point that was distinctly in her favour was that she was prepared to pose for pictures when requested and would leave me alone when I was obviously in pursuit of a less obliging model and would spend an age holding my breath waiting for the judicious moment to fire the shutter. Amongst the most memorable dives I had with her was one at dawn at Ras Muhammed.

In 1976 the Sinai was occupied by the Israelis whose army patrols would appear at our campsites and then disappear into the desert again. As virtually every able-bodied man in Israel had to spend some time during the year doing military service many of them knew Willy Halpert — our Israeli guide — who himself had frequently to take time out from his diving business for army duty.

Because of the strategic significance of Ras Muhammed camping on the beach at night was prohibited. As the sun set an army patrol appeared and asked us to leave, a request we dutifully complied with and we moved just outside the forbidden area. Looking for somewhere comfortable to lie, I put my sleeping bag on the ground at some distance from the main party where the sand was a little softer. I paid for it later however, when I was woken in the middle of the night by a hyena who had the end of my sleeping bag in its mouth and was shaking it from side to side! I decided the old adage about there being safety in numbers was one worth abiding by and moved my sleeping bag back into the proximity of the group.

On the night before our dive, we re-mobilised our forces and moved back on the forbidden beach as soon as it got dark. Having learned my lesson, I put my sleeping bag next to one of the girls on the not-very-gallant grounds that she would make a more tender meal than I for any wandering hungry hyena. It was also rumoured that she kept her diving knife under her pillow.

When the first crack of pale light opened the eastern sky I opened my eyes. The awakening day on the western shore of the Red Sea is a magical time. A pale cream light gradually intensifies behind the mountains of the far side of the gulf and their silhouettes become darker and stronger. A pink colour then suffuses into the cream light heralding the slow mystical appearance of a sun that rises majestically from behind the mountains. The gargantuan glowing orange spills its blood-red juice onto the sea. The emerging life force of the new day flows along a dancing path of deep red from the shores of far away Saudi Arabia right up to the beach in the Sinai where it is welcomed by the gentle lapping waves. To lie on a beach and experience it fills me with a sense of being totally detached from my body: I am the soft air, the cool water and the eternal earth, and we are all one. By the time the sun has risen above the mountains and is lighting the land with familiar day-time hues I have resumed my existence as a human being and again become part of the living world of defined shapes, distinct sounds, hard and soft textures and sweet and sour tastes.

My rebirth on the morning of 14 November 1976 — the day of our dawn dive — was shorter than usual. As soon as the sun had started its ascent I emerged from my sleeping bag and put on my wetsuit. My aqualung, fully charged and assembled for use, was hauled from its resting place alongside my sleeping bag and heaved onto my back. The straps were tightened. All of my equipment was checked before I finally slung a weightbelt around my waist. My partner went through the same routine. Such was the mutual feeling of our reverence for the wonder of the dawn that the few words that passed between us were as hushed as if we had been in church. We moved towards the water's edge and made our way slowly over the shallow coral to the drop off. A final check was made. I set my underwater compass on a bearing that would take us to the submerged island offshore. The OK signals were exchanged and we launched ourselves into a void the colour of royal blue ink.

We were two capsules journeying slowly, side-by-side, through the inner space of the ocean. Our aqualungs were our life support systems and I navigated with the aid of a compass and the knowledge that up was the way my bubbles went and down was indicated by the direction of the weights on my belt.

The face mask restricts your view to tunnel vision. When swimming forward it is possible to scan what is in an arc ahead by moving the head from side to side. It is also easy to look down. But it is not possible to look directly up without stopping to do so, or swimming upside down. So I kept a careful watch on my depth gauge to make sure that we did not sink too deep, which is very easy to do when all you can see around you is featureless, intensely blue water. I sometimes peered intently into the depths beneath me and thought I saw some dark shapes gliding through the water at the limit of visibility. I had timed our entry into the sea but in the excitement had not noted the moment we left the drop off.

'We should have reached the submerged island by now. If I have made a mistake in my navigation or there is a current we could be swimming directly out to sea. If that is the case the water beneath us is over a thousand feet deep. If we sink here we shall never be found. Should we surface and try to check our position from the land? No. I've tried that in the past and it's almost impossible. We'll keep going for a few more minutes.

'What's that ahead? Are my eyes deceiving me? Keep

going. Yes the colour of the water is changing. It's turning brown. A wall is gradually materialising as we swim towards it. Whoopee! It's the undersea island. With the solid rock as a reference I feel secure again.

'I check the depth — sixty feet. The wall is covered with the most exquisite corals and swarms of tiny fish are flowing along it. The rockface is nearly vertical. In parts it overhangs, in other regions there are ledges.

'We rest on a small ledge and gather our thoughts. Are the sharks we want to see deeper down? Shall we dive deeper or should we stay here? We'll swim on a bit further. The agreed plan is that we will sit quietly and just watch what happens.

'Here's a comfortable ledge. I signal to my partner that we should stop. She understands immediately. We deflate our lifejackets and holding on to the coral with one hand we sit with our backs to the island and look out into the sea that is getting brighter and brighter but is still intensely blue.

'With the rising sun the dawn patrol has begun. A jackfish nearly two feet long, swims up close to inspect us. I follow him with my eyes as he moves away and he takes up station close alongside a gigantic fish called a Napoleon wrasse that is cruising along the reef face with the authority of a Centurion tank. Nothing can tackle him and he knows it. With no apparent movement of his tail he glides slowly along the reef and out of visibility, still very closely escorted by the jackfish.

'I look up and out. A large shoal of barracudas has appeared. They are moving slowly and are forming up like a platoon of soldiers, the sun glinting on their armour. When they are all in line and roughly equi-spaced, an unheard order is given and they march out. Slowly they too disappear. Several large tuna swim swiftly past.

'Meanwhile the reef is coming to life. Fish, like the parrot fish that hide in the deep recesses in the coral during the hours of darkness, are emerging and adding to the ever-increasing activity all around us. Some fish

196

I can recognise — but there are many I can't. I am bewildered and bemused by the sheer brilliance and colour of the spectacle. I feel as if I am sitting in the box of a theatre watching an extraordinary extravaganza set against the royal blue backcloth of the sea. But time is running out and we still haven't seen the star of the show. The needle on the pressure gauge of my air cylinder is creeping towards the red.

'Then he makes his entry from stage left. A magnificent hammerhead shark, ten to twelve feet long is gliding into view. I know without nudging my partner that she has also seen him. He appears with the self-assurance of a warrior who has been made a king because of his prowess on the battlefield. His tail sweeping slowly from side to side propels him through the water with the easy grace of great power. He has clearly seen us but does not change his direction. Nobody could say he is beautiful with his strange hammer head with an eye at each extremity. But he has a presence that sets my blood tingling. For a few very brief moments I look into the eye of a shark as he passes by. He exits stage right and disappears into the wings.

'The show doesn't stop here. But we must go. Very reluctantly I signal to my partner that we should leave, checking our depth and duration to make sure that we are not running into decompression time.

'We continue our journey and completely circumnavigate the island as we slowly rise to the surface. Vista after vista unfolds as we do so. A turtle doesn't notice us until we are close and then he flippers off like a startled rabbit. We see countless fish and pass grottos filled with exotic soft corals. I surface when it becomes difficult to breathe and the air in my cylinder has run out completely. We have been underwater for one hour and ten minutes to a maximum depth of 100 feet. I inflate my lifejacket and look around.

'The sun is shining harshly down out of a pale blue sky. After being in the subdued light and soft horizons of the coral wonderland the cliffs appear stark and on the beach, far away I can see people moving around.

Despite the clarity it all seems a little unreal. My mind is still drifting along the coral wall.

'I take a compass bearing that will bring us back to the beach — and breakfast. I blow the water out of my snorkel tube, put my head down and begin the long swim back to base.'

I have been back to Ras Muhammed many times since that dawn dive. The last time it was on board a luxury yacht — the *Lady Jenny III* — which we moored alongside the island. So not only was I spared the long swim from the beach but I had the ultimate luxury of a hot water shower immediately after the dive. Also a Greek freighter conveniently sank on the site after hitting the submerged island in 1980 so I was able to do a wreck dive on my way back to the *Lady Jenny III*.

Many of the large fish have become very tame and will swim up to a diver expecting to be fed. The sharks, however, are still timid, and will shy away if a diver tries to approach them by swimming vigorously.

The Sinai is now Egyptian territory and the sea around Ras Muhammed is a protected nature reserve, thanks to the efforts of people like those who formed a group called Friends of the Red Sea, with the purpose of preserving this wonderland in the wilderness for future generations to enjoy. I hope they succeed for Ras Muhammed is truly one of the wonders of the underwater world.

7

Sunken Tombs of Truk Lagoon
THE PACIFIC OCEAN

Millions of year ago an enormous volcano erupted in the Pacific Ocean. Just how far-reaching the immediate effects of that cataclysmic upheaval in the earth's crust were, no-one can say. But it would not be unreasonable to suggest that it sent gigantic tidal waves rushing across the Pacific that caused havoc and destruction in their paths. Today the remains of that long-extinct volcano tower from the deep ocean floor like an undersea mountain. The rim of the cone breaks the surface forming a roughly circular chain of low islands enclosing the largest coral lagoon in the world — approximately forty miles in diameter. The maximum depth of the lagoon is about two hundred and forty feet and within it are several islands. Entrance to the lagoon is via channels through the outer reefs. Thus it provides a gigantic natural anchorage in the vast open space of the Eastern Pacific Ocean.

To the Japanese in World War II Truk Lagoon was of vital strategic importance. At the peak of its role as a Japanese military base 40,000 personnel were stationed on the islands in the lagoon. 1,200 buildings, many of them re-inforced concrete, were erected on the island of Dublon which was the main sea-plane and submarine base. Two hundred aircraft were located around the airstrip on the island of Eten. Other islands were used as radar bases. All were heavily protected with anti-aircraft guns and long-range naval and coastal artillery. All of the passes into the 822 square miles of lagoon were mined except for the north and south passes.

The Japanese regarded Truk Lagoon as impregnable. To the allies it was the 'Gibraltar of the Pacific'.

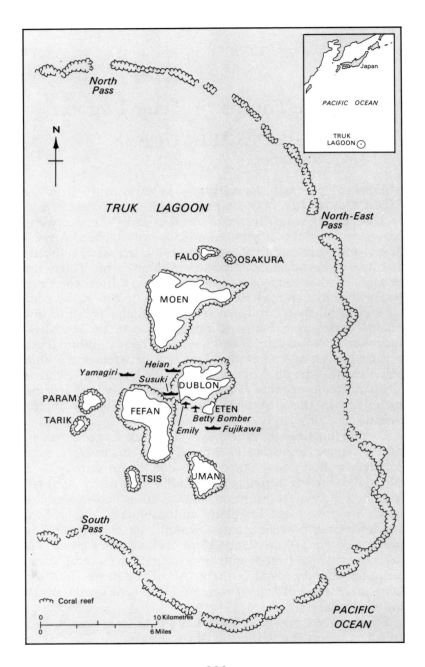

North
Pass

N

TRUK LAGOON

FALO OSAKURA

MOEN

Heian
Yamagiri
Susuki
PARAM
TARIK
FEFAN
Emily
Fujikawa

DUBLON
ETEN
Betty Bomber

TSIS
UMAN

South
Pass

Coral reef

0   10 Kilometres
0   6 Miles

North-East
Pass

Japan

PACIFIC OCEAN

TRUK
LAGOON

PACIFIC
OCEAN

200

However, the myth that Truk was invincible was convincingly shattered in a mighty naval air raid that began at dawn on 17 February 1944 and caught the Japanese by surprise. From aircraft carriers ninety miles away wave upon wave of American fighters and bombers stormed over Truk Lagoon leaving havoc, destruction and death in their wake.

Most of the Japanese defences were directed towards an attack from the sea. And it was the fact that the thirty-six-hour assault came from the air that made it so effective. When the din ceased and the smoke cleared the Japanese counted their losses. More than 60 ships including naval vessels, 17 cargo ships and 6 tankers had been sunk or permanently damaged. 250 aircraft were destroyed.

The Americans had taken their retribution for Pearl Harbour.

So sudden and surprising was the Truk raid that most of the ships, many of them loaded with ammunition and supplies, sank at their anchorage. Collectively they represented the largest fleet of ships sunk at one time in the history of the world. Each sunken vessel was a time capsule in which the clock stopped on a fateful day in February 1944. Had it not been for the development of skin diving as a recreation this sunken fleet would have been unvisited and largely forgotten, which indeed it was until discovered and filmed by the American diver Al Giddings in the early 1970s. When I saw his film I realised that Truk Lagoon had to be the most spectacular wreck diving site in the world, so I immediately set my own sights on diving there, although it was not until 1979 that one of the schemes I devised came to fruition.

I had gone into partnership with Chris Goosen and formed a company called Dobbs Goosen Films. We set up the company with the simple but challenging objective of making a series of underwater films for television of the very best diving area in the world. Chris — a business entrepreneur — would provide the financial resources and technical back-up. I would contribute the stories, act as an underwater cameraman and fulfil various other roles. If you have ever studied the list of credits at the end of a feature film you will certainly realise that Chris and I did not each wear just two hats — we had to wear hordes of them. Making films can be frighteningly expensive. Very few people make money at it at all. Many lose a lot. In the mid-nineteen eighties a very modest documentary film costs about one thousand pounds a minute to produce. It can easily escalate to double or even treble that amount.

From the start Chris insisted that Dobbs Goosen Films should be a financially sound venture. As there was no way our limited financial resources would cover the full costs of getting the film crew to a lagoon in the Eastern Caroline Islands a method had to be found of subsidising the considerable cost of travel. I worked out a way of doing it.

By the time Dobbs Goosen Films came into being I had formed a close relationship with Bruce and Hedda Lyons — the extremely hard-working and enterprising couple who ran Twickenham Travel. I put a proposal to them. I would lead the first major British expedition to Truk Lagoon. They would make all the travel arrangements and between us we would recruit divers who were willing to pay to join an expedition and be filmed exploring the most exotic and exciting wreck diving site in the world. The cost of the trip to our clients would be set so that my expenses would be covered. Twickenham Travel (now Twickers World) would not lose financially but would benefit from the publicity the film created.

Many hours were spent working the proposition through. After a couple of false starts and by offering an extra free trip as a prize at an underwater conference we recruited sufficient people for the expedition to take place.

And so it was that on 30 April 1979 I set out with nineteen other divers on a round-the-world trip. For most of those involved, the expedition was a once-in-a-lifetime adventure in which they had invested a great deal of money. Several of them were wreck fanatics. The group's experience varied greatly as did their ages and their physical fitness. Indeed, it would be difficult to find a greater range of personalities from different backgrounds under any circumstances.

Now, diving is one of those activities which involves the use of quite a lot of heavy equipment. Although it had been arranged in advance that aqualung cylinders and weights would be provided in Truk, all other items such as regulators, knives, fins, cameras etc. had to be taken with us. Even allowing for generous hand baggage it was obvious when we assembled in Terminal 3 at London's Heathrow airport that I would have to do more than a little bit of smooth talking to get us through the check-in desk without bankrupting Dobbs Goosen Films with charges for excess baggage. And I was as bad as everyone else — I had hoped to lose thirteen cases of bulky and extremely heavy filming equipment in the baggage of the rest of the group on the basis that the additional filming equipment represented only about three-quarters of a case per person — which would have been quite all right if everyone else hadn't thought of the same idea too.

My technique under such circumstances is to produce as much confusion as I can at the check-in desk in the hope that in the hustle and bustle bags are labelled and whisked through before the indicator stops moving and the scales register their real weight. I reconcile my conscience to this deceit on the basis that the fat lady behind me in the queue is carrying more extra weight about her person than I plonk on the baggage scales at a mere $10^1/2$ stones of body weight. However, even I had to admit 6 hundredweight of excess baggage would need to be compensated for by more than just one or two exceptionally skinny passengers.

Fortunately Hedda Lyons came to see us off. Having sensed my disquiet, she disappeared behind the scenes. Whilst the cumulative weight of the bags was being added up on the strip of paper two yards long a man sidled up from behind us to the young lady doing the addition. After a few moments of consultation and the perceptible raising of an eyebrow when the final figure was reached he nodded. The check-in clerk smiled, gave me twenty boarding cards and told me our bags were checked through to San Francisco. I heaved a sigh of relief. The first hurdle was over.

Hedda reappeared and before she saw us off into the departure lounge she gave me an envelope addressed 'To whom it may concern'. As subsequent events were to reveal, the contents of that envelope were to be worth more to me than their weight in gold or even platinum, for the start of the trip had been too easy — far too easy.

By flying westwards we gained time. Having left London at 8.30 am we arrived 12^1/$_2$ hours later in San Francisco at a local time of 1.00 pm. The group spent a very pleasant afternoon and evening roaming the city before boarding a plane at 9.00 pm bound for Honolulu. As we had not crossed the international date line we arrived in Honolulu at 11.05 pm on the same day that we had left London. As might be imagined, having had a very early start, we were all exhausted when we eventually arrived at the Holiday Inn at Honolulu airport for an overnight stop. The final leg of the journey to Truk Lagoon was scheduled for departure at 8.15 the next morning. So it seemed that no sooner had I put my head on the pillow than it was time to get up again.

After various delays I eventually managed to assemble my group complete with baggage mountain, in the departure lounge at the airport half-an-hour before departure — which as it happens is just about the right kind of time to introduce the Dobbs confusion factor in order to get the baggage through to the plane as quickly as possible and not devote too much time to weighing in. So I prepared myself for the final assault and put the twenty tickets on the desk.

The clerk picked the tickets up, scrutinised them carefully and went away with them without saying a word. Minutes ticked by before he re-appeared with another official — a distinctly oriental gentleman who addressed me.

'Ah sir,' he said. 'We have ploblem.'

Little does he know, I thought, just how big the problem is.

'You want go Truk, yes?' he asked.

Before I could gather the words for a suitable reply he continued.

'Thees flight does not exeest. Next flight to Truk in four days' time. Fully booked. Velly solly.'

After a few minutes' further chat it became quite clear that there really were no flights out of Honolulu for Truk — and worse still, the next one in four days' time was also fully booked.

If you have ever met a group of typical wreck divers you

will know what they are like; they are physical men. Usually strong and heavily built, they are extremely tough and nothing, absolutely nothing, stops them bringing back from the depths of the sea a souvenir they have chiselled, sawn, wrenched or preferably dynamited from its sub-sea resting place; determination is one of their characteristics. If you add to that the investment of a life's savings, the expectation of diving in tropical waters and of becoming a film star, you will understand the concern with which I received this bombshell. My problem was obviously not going to be resolved in five minutes or even half-an-hour.

I have just mentioned some of the stronger characteristics of wreck divers. I also knew their weaknesses. So I suggested that most of the group should sample the pleasures of Waikiki Beach whilst I tried to negotiate a settlement of the problem. A couple of the more experienced world-wide travellers stayed with me to give support.

It was at this stage that I produced my envelope addressed 'To whom it may concern' which contained a letter from Pan-Am in London explaining who I was, what our objective was and that we should be given every assistance. The letter had a magical effect. Those who read it became concerned and helpful.

After an interminable morning of phone calls to London, telexes and counter telexes the source of the error became apparent. A flight from Honolulu to Truk had indeed existed the previous year, but the service had since been discontinued. However, nobody had told a computer. So it was a computer who had booked us on to a non-existent flight, which conveniently meant that no-one was to blame. It took a further half-day of intensive and exhausting discussions with various officials to reach a solution.

Late that night the re-assembled group, some looking ruddy and smelling of coconut suntan oil, were given the news by their pallid expedition leader. We would overfly Truk to Guam and spend a few hours in the Guam Hilton Hotel before retracing our path to Truk from Guam.

We were thankful to arrive on the island of Moen but not so thankful to be handed, upon arrival, a notice which informed us that Truk was 'dry' and that anyone caught with alcoholic drinks was likely to end up in a very uncomfortable jail. Now another characteristic of most divers, especially wreck divers, is that they like to consume the odd alcoholic beverage. Indeed, some might regard the lack of availability of booze as about the biggest disaster they might encounter, apart from actually not going wreck diving. So despite the possible penalties some bottles of duty free liquor were hastily pushed to the bottom of diving bags in the hopes that they would escape detection and confiscation.

Our first impression of Truk was not relieved by the journey to our hotel which was in a beaten-up truck along a wet, pot-holed road past the depressing shacks that housed the poverty-ridden islanders. It was hot, humid and overcast. There was no sign of the gaiety which I had encountered in other tropical, albeit poor regions I had visited.

The base for our stay on the island of Moen, The Truk Continental Hotel, was a piece of American real estate that could have been transplanted from Florida — an air-conditioned oasis for affluent travellers whose way of life and expectations were so different to those of the majority of the indigenous population that we might have come from a different planet. Indeed once inside its cool interior, where we unpacked and played with our complex cameras, tape recorders, charging units and other electronic gadgetry we were shielded from the islanders who were caught in a poverty trap and sat silent and sullen outside their homes apparently resigned to living at a subsistence level on hand-outs from the American Government.

Although I found the poverty disturbing I put it to the back of my mind. I was in Truk to make a film about shipwrecks, and having come so far that was what I was going to do.

When a battered boat drew up alongside the jetty the next morning I faced the immediate problem of getting aqualung cylinders and lead weight belts allocated and organising the diving programme. When all the gear, including our bulky cameras and lights was on board, the remaining accommodation for the humans was cramped. The engine coughed into life and we chugged out to sea for our first look into a vessel that had been on the sea bed for thirty-five years.

The *Heian Maru* was a submarine tender, 530 feet long with a displacement of 11,614 tons. She lay on her side. Chris and I drifted slowly down towards the uppermost side of the vessel which spread away from us in all directions and disappeared into the mists of the slightly milky water. It was like gently parachuting down onto a huge curved iron field. There were no corals growing out of the smooth surface which was covered with a powdery grey-green film some of which swirled off into the eddies produced by our gently waving fins. Towards the bows we found and filmed the name of the vessel clearly defined in Roman and Japanese letters. The edge of our iron field terminated suddenly and we found ourselves suspended alongside a walkway along the deck of the vessel which was now vertical instead of horizontal. A cargo of periscopes were still secured in their original positions. Much of the projecting exterior metalwork was encrusted with corals which blazed into brilliant hues, especially reds, when the filming lights were switched on. Other parts were less heavily encrusted. I scraped a small wheel with my knife and the bronze revealed gleamed a dull gold. A ship's telegraph stuck out sideways. I held the handle and in my mind I could hear the bell clanging in the engine room as the engineer took his instructions from the bridge. I gave the coral encrusted handle a tug and the entire unit juddered. Clearly the sea was slowly eating into the iron deck plate to which it was attached. Being constructed of brass or bronze the telegraph itself would not corrode but its weight would eventually take it crashing into the depths like a heavy branch falling from a tree.

The underwater visibility was about fifty feet at its maximum, which is not exceptional for tropical waters. However, it was certainly sufficient to give a good impression of the wreck and when we surfaced I was hopeful that the first 100 feet of film we had shot would contain some useable sequences.

Three hours after leaving the water we were dropping back into the sea again onto another wreck — the *Susuki Maru*. It was a relatively shallow dive. One of the davits, which when the vessel sank probably had a lifeboat suspended from it, reached to the surface. The davit provided a new living space for marine life and every part of its surface was colonised by corals and sponges. Different species have a preference for different depths and scientists have spent a long time finding out and defining just what likes to live where. Just sinking slowly down past the richly encrusted davit was like having a marine biology lesson, but instead of seeing the different species drawn out on a page, there they were, neatly occupying their chosen sites. However, not every surface is suitable for corals to set up their homesteads. Some parts of the ship clearly did not have the same desirability in the underwater real estate market. Such a place was the steeply sloping deck of the vessel. As corals are not particularly comfortable for humans to sit upon, the availability of a clear space on a cylindrical object attached to the deck, appeared to me to provide the underwater equivalent to a wayside seat for a weary traveller. So I deflated my lifejacket and landed on it, the base of my metal aqualung cylinder hitting it with a clearly perceptible clunk. I sat there waving to the other divers as they passed by on their tour of this particular exhibit in its giant underwater maritime museum. It was only later when I surfaced that one of the more knowledge-able members of the group pointed out to me that I had been sitting on an unexploded depth charge, which was probably still primed with a pressure-activated detonator. He added a further note of spice to the conversation by pointing out that had I dislodged the depth charge and it had rolled off the near-vertical deck into the depths, the increase in water pressure would have caused it to explode, which in turn would have caused more than a little discomfort to the divers swimming around the wreck. However, later dives were to reveal the expedition could have had an even more spectacular ending. The next day we dived on what for me was the most exciting wreck in Truk Lagoon, the *Fujikawa Maru*. One of the first advantages of the wreck was that it was easy to find due to the masts sticking out of the water. Secondly, it was upright and on an even keel. Thirdly, its cargo was fascinating.

The *Fujikawa Maru* was a submarine tender and aircraft ferry. There were no hatch covers over the holds and the visibility was exceptionally good. There was very little silt on the surface of the vessel which meant that the bane of the underwater photographer's life — silt stirred up by passing divers — was absent outside the holds.

We dropped into the water and drifted down past the two huge king posts like leaves falling beside two huge tree trunks. They were completely covered in the most exquisite growths and I could have spent an entire dive peering into the intricate complexity of this exotic vertical coral garden.

When we reached deck level we shone the beams of our powerful filming lights into the gloomy penumbra of an open hold. Lights that would have seemed dazzlingly bright in a confined space barely seemed to shine at all. It was like pointing a torch beam into the open sky at night. We turned them off to conserve their limited life. Then an apparition appeared before us. One of the divers had found an old gasmask in the hold and had put it over his head. He rose out of the open hold like a ghost. It was an eerie sight. After enjoying the colourful natural beauty of the coral on the king posts it jolted me into the reality that we were entering a man-made vessel that had once been the workplace for living human beings going about their daily duties. Somebody must have stacked the wooden cases containing the rubber masks which were never used. The opening into the hold was like the entrance into a giant tomb. But unlike the tombs in ancient Egypt, which were stacked with items to provide for the incumbent's journey through the next world, the tomb I entered was full of objects produced to remove humans violently from this. Most of those engaged in warfare are so in the hope that although many of their fellows will be killed they themselves will survive. The only exception to this is the Japanese kamikaze pilot who is given complex and expensive training to fly aircraft in order to carry out a single suicide mission.

I sank very slowly onto one of the aircraft used in such missions — a so-called zero fighter. Having swum round it I eased myself into the cockpit. The joystick projected upwards between my legs. I grasped it with my hand. It moved. It was still connected to the various parts that would enable the tiny aircraft to be manoeuvred in the sky. I looked behind me and the tail fin moved. For a brief moment I became the Japanese pilot of a flying machine. I pushed the joystick forward and with the engine screaming plunged down into instant oblivion in a yellow explosion.

The sound of the air gurgling round my facemask from the exhaust valve in the regulator still clenched between my teeth brought me back abruptly into the reality of my unreal world ninety feet down in the warm Pacific Ocean in the cone of a long-extinct volcano. The lights from the cameraman just outside the cockpit were switched on. When the beams illuminated the metal framework of the windscreen in front of me it took on a dimension of extra reality. Where the light splashed across my body the yellow stripes of my wetsuit blazed into colour. Isolated as it was by the pool of light the aircraft was more clearly defined than anything else and took on an even more solid three dimensional appearance as if it was the only thing that existed in the world.

When the lights were switched off all was dark except for a luminous rectangle overhead representing the opening into the hold. As my eyes adapted to the darkness I was aware of the other divers gliding around me and the zero fighter once again became just a small part of the blue-grey cargo of the *Fujikawa Maru*.

Research revealed that the *Fujikawa Maru* was built by Mitsubishi in Nagasaki in 1938. She was 450 feet long and had a displacement of 6,938 tons. She had six cargo holds filled with a variety of equipment. The guns mounted on the bow and stern pointed forwards and backwards respectively into the quiet clear blue sea around them, the trigger handles and sighting mechanisms were still intact. Inside the bridge area were two large tiled backrooms complete with baths. At 110 feet directly aft of the bridge was a gaping hole where she was struck by a torpedo. Numerous hard and soft corals blossomed along the corridors and passageways.

Had the *Fujikawa Maru* come to her last resting place on top of the reef she would have been an ugly rusting iron hulk. But under the sea with her canopy of coral she was being transformed into a colourful wonderland. The ill-fated sailors who went down with her could never have had a more beautiful monument to mark their graves.

The afternoon dive on the second day of our expedition was on a totally different site. We descended fifty feet down to a sandy bottom where an Emily H8K2 flying boat built by Kawanishi was resting upside down. With a range of 4,500 miles the Emily had a reputation for being one of the finest flying boats in her class. She lay on the sea bed like a sleeping whale. It was very difficult not to stir up the silt and with twenty people swimming round her she was soon enveloped in a cloud of suspended particles. In the log I wrote, 'By the end of the dive the upside-down seaplane looked like Piccadilly in the fog. Next time put divers down in two waves.'

I put that recommendation into practice when we located another aircraft the following afternoon. The subject that time was an aircraft called a 'Betty Bomber' by the Americans which we found resting on a sandy bottom in sixty feet of water. She was twin-engined with a wingspan of eighty-two feet and was shot down just after take-off, the impact of the crash distorting the cockpit area. However the rest of the aircraft was in remarkably good condition with no coral on her, just a layer of silt. We entered the aircraft through the tail and swam the entire length of the fuselage until we entered the cockpit. She carried no bombs but we did find a machine-gun amidships which we removed through the gunner's opening in the middle of the fuselage. We raised it to the surface using air from our regulators to fill a lifting bag. Having examined it we returned it to where we had found it.

The expedition to Truk Lagoon continued, as it had started, with its trying moments for the expedition leader, but it had its lighter moments too — provided mainly by an exceptional diver, named Bill Lewis, who enjoyed the apt nickname of Aquaman. He was extremely strong, had a superb physique and took a masochistic delight in physical exercise. He also had an unusual sense of humour which took the form of dressing up and then appearing at unexpected moments. The preparation for these antics must have taken him considerable time and effort, and I hope our appreciation of them made it worthwhile for him.

One day whilst filming on the *Fujikawa Maru* a figure with a silver cloak streaming out behind him in true Superman style flew into frame and then disappeared at great speed into the wreck. On another day, when we were sweating profusely climbing up a hill to film one of the land locations, the bushes parted and out jumped a painted warrior waving a spear. His blood-curdling yells stopped us in our tracks, and for a moment I was convinced he was going to spear one of us. But no, it was Aquaman. Somehow he had managed to get ahead of us. When we had recovered our composure I realised he had provided a moment of hilarity at a time when it was much needed.

The food at the Intercontinental Hotel would probably have been listed as 'indescribable' in a gourmet guide. So you can imagine our delight when one evening a waiter arrived in the middle of a particularly dreary meal immaculately dressed in a white dinner jacket with a napkin over his crooked arm. Moving from table to table he enquired if everyone was enjoying the food and asked if the wine was at the correct temperature. When he reached our table though his cover was blown — it was Aquaman up to another of his pranks!

In addition to being the expedition jester, Bill Lewis became the lighting man of the filming crew. He was an extremely good diver and relished the more dangerous and exciting dives. On one grey day when the sea was rough we dived on a 6,440 ton vessel called the *Yamagiri Maru*. We saw the 140-mm gun on the bow before going deep into the holds. There we found a stack of the largest shells used in World War II. The eighteen-inch live shells were destined for the Command Battleship *Yamoto*. In front of the camera with Bill lighting me with a hand lamp I fanned off the layer of silt with my hand. It rose like dust in an ancient tomb. I had no doubt about the outcome if I had accidentally caused one of them to explode — so I refrained from disturbing them further; with the sea slowly eating into the detonators nobody could be absolutely sure just how stable the shells were. We left the wreck via a gaping hole made by a torpedo in the hull. Even though we were deep in the ocean coming out of the wreck into the blue sea was like emerging from a musty cave into sunlight and fresh air.

By the time we dived the *Yamagiri Maru* the filming team had become a well co-ordinated efficient four-man unit. In addition to Chris Goosen, my partner and Aquaman, another fine physical specimen — Mike Stevens — acted as grips i.e. he carried heavy gear around for us and also acted as assistant lighting man. Despite his considerable physical strength Mike was a softy at heart. He was also a keen photographer and had a passion for manta rays — a twin-horned ray often called a devil fish. His normal complete co-operation and acquiescence to the wishes of the cameraman were overtaken by an inner impulse on the day we visited the outer reef.

It was a blustery grey day and the sea was choppy. Leaving the majority of the group on the big vessel the film crew took to a small boat for the long trip from our island base in the middle of the lagoon to the North-East Pass encircling reef. By the time all of our cylinders, weightbelts, diving equipment and filming gear were stowed on board, the battered vessel was low in the water and water poured in through the decking whenever a wave broke over the bows. Back in the UK such a vessel would not have been granted a licence to cruise on the Thames let alone go to sea.

Well before we reached the reef we could hear the sea breaking on its outer edge. If the sea was rough inside the lagoon what was the mighty Pacific Ocean like outside? We got some idea as we approached a gap in the coral wall that encircled the lagoon. Through the channel marched waves as high as houses that fanned out and lost height until they married with the turbulent sea inside the lagoon.

Close inside the reef was a lee shore with calm water. Here we anchored and prepared to dive. We knew that this was where we would find the large predators. Fish swept along by the strong current coming into the lagoon would be picked off by the sharks who would dart out into the channel, pick off their prey and return to the relatively calm water inside to digest their meal. Our Trukese guide, who was intrepid when it came to diving the wrecks, was terrified of sharks.

I jumped into the sea and was handed the film camera. I called out to the guide to join me and I saw him slide very reluctantly into the sea. I descended and swam well clear before remaining vertical in the water with my back to the boat and the coral wall looking for sharks. After a few moments I had the distinct feeling I was alone. In the distance a shark cruised past. I looked from side to side but could see no sign of the guide. I eventually discovered him just submerged beside the boat ready to make a quick exit. When the rest of the group jumped into the water he summoned up enough courage to move away from the boat, but he stayed as close to me as a pilot fish.

We swam underwater towards the opening in the reef until we could feel the current running. Then we settled in and watched, waiting for the action. It was not long in coming. A curious shark headed towards me. I raised the camera and through the viewfinder watched it get bigger and bigger. We desperately wanted a shark sequence and when I pushed the button, I could hear the film running through the shutter. I felt like a fighter pilot with an enemy aircraft in his sights. But instead of shooting with a gun I was shooting with a camera. I kept the camera running and still the shark came on. When it completely filled the frame, it veered away; I filmed it until it disappeared.

I turned around to see where the others were. I was startled to find myself facemask to facemask with our Trukese guide who had moved as close to my back as he could without touching me, and whose wide-eyed terror shone like a lighthouse beam.

Before we descended I had told everyone to keep their backs to the reef and not swim out towards open water as that would frighten the big fish away and we would not get the film I desperately wanted. When the sharks came by Mike, our muscular grip, did as we requested and took still pictures. However, when a couple of magnificent manta rays came along the reef like two huge condors with wings going in slow motion, Mike could not contain his enthusiasm. He swam as rapidly as he could towards them, clicking his camera as he went. I was furious because the rays did exactly what I expected and veered away from the reef leaving me with only distant images to capture on film. However, I quickly relented when I saw the look of sheer joy, mixed with a little guilt, in Mike's eyes when he returned. He had done what he had dreamed of doing. He had swum with mantas. When the mantas arrived everything else went from his mind and he swam out to greet them. For him they were more memorable than all of the wrecks in the lagoon.

The shark footage I shot added a nice sequence to our final television film which was awarded a gold medal together with an award for the best commercial film at the Brighton Film Festival in 1982 and had the same title as this chapter: The Sunken Tombs of Truk Lagoon.

8

Nature on a Knife-Edge

THE GALAPAGOS ISLANDS, THE PACIFIC OCEAN

The Galapagos Islands were dubbed the Enchanted Islands by the early explorers who visited them. The islands would appear and disappear in the mists as their sailing ships were carried silently and sometimes swiftly past them by complex invisible ocean currents. I also think of them as enchanted islands but for a totally different reason. For me the enchantment is the total lack of fear shown by the prolific wildlife above and below the sea. It is the place where I have had my most enchanting experiences with groups of wild animals. After my first visit I remember saying to my wife, 'If ever I am told I have just a few more weeks to live, one thing I would want to do more than anything else is to go back to Galapagos.'

It was a diving experience towards the end of my third visit to the archipelago that provides the best example of what it is that makes these islands so compelling to a diver like me — who I must admit would readily swap finding treasure on the sea bed for a few moments in harmony with a sealion or a dolphin playing under the sea.

The event in question took place at Punta Albemarle off the island of Isabela on Sunday, 25 April 1982.

At the time I was still feeling high because a few days before I had accompanied in a small open dinghy, a large male killer whale (which I prefer to call an Orca) for several miles as it cruised leisurely close to rocks feeding as it went. It was immensely exciting to anticipate where the Orca would surface and then have him rise majestically close-by with no apparent concern for the dinghy. The Orca dwarfed the dinghy and with the old Seagull outboard engine going flat out I was just able to keep pace with this largest member of the dolphin family. The captain and crew of the sailing yacht, *Encantada*, upon which my party was based were terrified of the Orca and openly expressed their discontent at me for putting myself at risk — and perhaps more importantly — possibly losing a dinghy. However, it was one of the few times when I, as expedition leader, overruled the captain and took full responsibility for my actions and for the only two members of the party who wished to accompany me when the option was put to them. When we

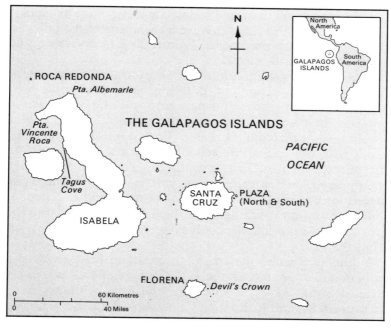

eventually returned safely to the large vessel bubbling with excitement I think some of the members regretted their lack of spirit of adventure. So one afternoon a few days later when I saw dozens of leaping dolphins and a large flock of sea birds diving repeatedly into the sea and said I was going to take a dinghy out to get amongst them I had a greater response to my request for companions. It was one of those occasions when decisions have to be made quickly. Those who said 'yes' grabbed their gear and jumped into the dinghy; those who vacillated stayed on board the base ship.

As we got near to the dolphins and sea birds, a couple of Galapagos penguins who were hurrying along and bobbing up and down on the waves like ducks in the wake of a cruiser on the Thames, suddenly dived. We could see them arrowing through the water and moving much more efficiently than when they were paddling on the surface. As they pursued their prey into the depths the sea around us erupted with silver flashes accompanied by a swishing sound like water being sprayed onto a pond with a hose. It lasted for no more than two seconds and was gone as quickly as it came. But it told me that we were in the midst of a vast shoal of fry that was being bombarded from above and attacked from underneath.

Like a fast-moving convoy of ships travelling purposefully forward a school of dolphins was making its way towards us. Some broke formation to ride the bow wave of our boat that was going as fast as our little Seagull engine would push it through the water. Then our escorts vanished along with the rest of the school — presumably to feed on the unseen shoal of fish beneath us. Then suddenly they re-appeared, half a mile away, still running in the same direction. We didn't go after them because another school of dolphins was approaching us. So we swung in an arc into the area where blue-footed boobies were falling like arrows from the sky.

I quickly donned my mask, snorkel and fins, grabbed a camera and slipped over the side. The water was extremely clear. I swam slowly away from the boat with my head immersed, scanning the view. The surface of the sea, seen from just underneath, looked like a vast silver cloth that was being gently ruffled by the wind. Below, deep blue and flecked with the silver flashes of twisting fishes, the sea appeared as vast and mysterious as a night sky.

Into my vision came the swiftly moving black silhouettes of two sealions that moved with extreme speed and amazing agility. Like swallows feeding on insects in the air the sealions constantly changed direction to pluck their prey from the sea, but such was the speed of their movements I could not see the fish they were snapping up. One after another they surfaced to snatch a breath then zoomed back down again. They seemed to take no notice of me or the other divers who had joined me and they were soon lost to our sight as their hunt took them beyond the limit of our underwater visibility. For a while more sealions came into view and took their place. Then they too disappeared and for a short time the sea beneath was totally empty. Suddenly I became aware of other silhouettes, moving in a different manner — not with the swift agility of the sealions — but equally purposefully. Unlike the sealions the new arivals took a distinct interest in our presence in the water.

Here is how the scene was recorded by the expedition log keeper for the day, Robin Benstead-Smith, who joined us in the water at this stage.

'Slipping into the water I found that the fish had attracted not only many dolphins but also several sealions and hordes of sharks. The latter upstaged even the dolphins. Our splashing about clearly interested them and they circled around us. Black-finned sharks up to ten feet long, Galapagos sharks and one or two white-tipped reef sharks all mingled together. Before long Horace was the only one prepared to mingle with them. Opinions varied about the health of his mind and the immediate future of his body. He had at least a dozen companions. With some trepidation I joined them and was told by Horace to 'go over there so I can take a picture of you with a shark in it' — or was it of a shark with me in it? The sharks began to come very close — within a few feet. One decided Horace's blue fins would look smarter than his own black ones and tried to borrow them. Horace kicked him away and fearing that such impoliteness might be resented we left the water.

'We now split into two groups. One went to do the planned dive by the coast, the other to pick up the rest of our party and continue dolphin, shark and booby watching. The divers were Tom, Ron, Philippe and I. The times in and out tell the story. Tom jumped in, hit an invisible trampoline at six ft and landed back in the panga with the information that there was a reasonably big shark reasonably near by. The other three of us continued undeterred but far from cool. Philippe imitated the lobsters he'd been hunting earlier by huddling in a hole in some rocks; Ron courageously tried to talk the shark out of it, but the shark seemed to be hard of hearing for he kept coming closer to catch what Ron said; myself, I stayed with Ron since there was no room in Philippe's hole and besides I felt that it would take the shark so long to swallow Ron that I'd be able to make my get-away. Finding that no amount of demanding through his demand valve would deter the shark Ron took the first opportunity of returning to the panga. Then there were two. Disguising ourselves as gorgonias we slipped unobtrusively away amongst the many rocks and boulders to look at the many typical fish, corals, invertebrates etc. It was a very pretty spot and our dive was enhanced by the appearance of a total of five turtles, who came very close to us. We returned to the *Encantada*. The other group did not come back until the sun was setting. They were full of stories of dolphins plunging all around the panga, of numerous sharks bravely swimming with Horace, of Albert somehow photographing the scenes underwater with one finger whilst clutching the side of the panga with the other nine and a prehensile snorkel. Horace says that this day was the best diving day he's had in all his 250 years of experience. As this is only my fifth day I feel rather fortunate. I'll leave a few lines here for the comments of the man himself. Meanwhile the crew are steering us on towards James Bay — another eight hours in a long day. They, like the rest of us, are busy digesting lobster as a fine end to a great day at sea.'

Here is my response to his amusing account of some of the day's activities:

Leaping dolphins, cavorting sealions, charming penguins, diving boobies, swirling sharks and small fish swarming like driven snowflakes — all on one snorkel dive. Surely there is nowhere else in the world where such a spectacle can be experienced — but it happened off Punta Albemarle.

Reading my comments in the expedition log for Sunday, 25 April 1982 instantly brings back memories of the other diving events of that special day — on a day that could not be surpassed for adventure and excitement.

It was a day that started early for the captain and crew of the *Encantada*. On the previous night we stayed at Punta Vincente Roca, the tall masts of our sailing yacht dwarfed by the cliffs that towered beside us to a height of 1,000 feet. We were compelled to moor very close to the rock-face because that was the only place where the water was shallow enough to anchor.

Most of the time the sea was calm and innocent wavelets gently lapped the volcanic rocks. But at unpredictable intervals a big swell would suddenly appear. Hissing white foam would rush, mast-high, across the almost vertical rock-face. Then all would be quiet again. The captain was uneasy and spent the night on deck.

At four o'clock in the morning he started the engine and we set off for a tiny island called Roca Redonda in the north-west of the Galapagos Archipelago. It is the top part of a volcano, that is 10,000 feet high and fifteen miles across on the sea floor. But such is the depth of the sea in this region that just the tip of the volcano protrudes above the surface. Herman Melville describes it thus: 'From a broken stair-like base, washed as the steps of a water-palace, by the waves, the tower rose in entablatures of strata to a shaven summit . . . Roca Redonda is 220 feet high, 400 yards long and less than 200 yards across. And as the eaves of any old barn or abbey are alive with swallows, so were all these rocky ledges with unnumbered seafowl . . . I know not where one can better study the natural history of strange seafowl than at Redonda.'

But it was not the seafowl at Redonda which attracted me back to the island. It was the dolphins I had seen and dived with there two years previously, almost to the day. Indeed, after spending eight years devoting much of my time attempting to study wild dolphins in their natural environment it was my experience off Roca Redonda with an entire school of dolphins that stood out as my most memorable group encounter. One aspect which made that first visit so exciting was that our early-morning arrival had been heralded by dolphins quite unexpectedly.

The surface was flat calm and the island materialised out of a pink, misty sea shortly after sunrise. As we drew closer we could see the cap of the island clearly, but its base was lost in low-lying haze that would soon burn off with the rising sun. It was a tranquil ethereal scene that was suddenly transformed by the arrival of a school of dolphins who crowded round our two vessels and escorted us towards our destination jumping joyfully at our bows as they pushed through the sea. The dolphins stayed with us until we were close to the island where everyone got into the water and snorkelled with them. The log keeper, the immensely experienced German diver, Dieter Paulman, concluded the daily log with the following paragraph:

> 'The day of the dolphin was the highlight of the trip! It kept me hours from sleeping. I think we will probably only once in our life have such a wonderful dolphin day!'

As we sailed away at the end of Dieter's 'wonderful dolphin day' I vowed I would return to Roca Redonda to revisit the dolphins.

★   ★   ★

Now, after two years I am on my way back. As the ship hurries forward I wonder if the dolphins will keep our secret rendezvous.

It is 6.30 am and the ship is coming to life. Half-awake, bleary eyed people are wandering on the deck and joining me on the bow. I have stationed myself on top of the heavy jib sail which is rolled up into a ball and stowed, ready for use.

Sitting astride the bowsprit with my legs dangling over

the most forward part of the boat I watch the lonely and magnetic rock of Roca Redonda get closer and closer. I will the dolphins to come and join me as they had done two years previously. But there is no sign of them.

There is a call for breakfast and everyone departs into the saloon leaving me to keep a lonely vigil.

We are about one mile from the island. I spot a recurved fin cutting through the water and heading towards the *Encantada*. A few seconds later the dolphin is riding the bow wave. He is immediately joined by a dozen more. From my perch I look down and watch them gliding effortlessly through the water as they zig-zag back and forth in front of me. They are mostly adult Bottlenose dolphins. The biggest is a fine heavily-built male well over twelve feet in length.

I recognise one of the dolphins from two years previously — a large male with a big remora fish attached just below his dorsal fin. There are also two females in the group. They are smaller and more slender. One of them has a calf which stays with its mother as if joined by elastic.

A feeling of sheer bliss floods through me to my fingertips. The dolphins have come. The dolphins have come.

I will not allow myself to be distracted by taking pictures. Instead I remain perfectly still and let the magic of the dolphins encapsulate me. The glittering patterns of the sun reflected by the waves slipping endlessly by the bow mesmerise me. In my mind I join the dolphins in their luminous blue world. In a dream in which I am fully awake, I speed forward and twirl from side to side caught up in their joyous undersea carnival procession.

After a few moments of utterly selfish pleasure I try to communicate my feelings to the increasing number of dolphins accumulating round the bows of the *Encantada* (which means enchanted in English). Our vessel could never have been given a more appropriate name.

Having silently thanked the dolphins for keeping the appointment I made with them I leave the bow and put my head through an open window in the saloon.

'They are here,' I say quietly.

There is a clatter as knives and forks are dropped onto

plates and everyone scrambles on deck. Cameras click and shouts of 'Wow', 'Look there,' 'Here's one,' 'This one's got a baby,' roll across the water towards the pinnacle of rock looming up in front of us. The dolphins leave us when we get very close to the rock. It is as if we have passed a boundary line over which they do not want to pass. As they are total masters of the situation we swing the *Encantada* into the zone in which they are playing and they immediately join us again.

Breakfast is totally forgotten. An opportunity to swim with a host of dolphins is not to be missed. We don't trouble to put on our wetsuits. Fins, masks and snorkels are all we need. The captain slows down and the dolphins move off. Although we are of interest to them they have their own games to play which can and do take immediate priority. So the captain watches which way the group is swimming and swings the *Encantada* round to intercept them. As we close we jump overboard into the deep blue sea.

I immediately get the electric tingle that comes with being in very deep clear water. It is totally different to the sensation I get in coastal waters. How much of it is psychosomatic i.e. it comes with *knowing* that there is a mile of water underneath me, or how much of it is an instinctive feeling that comes from my ancestral forebears, I know not. But I feel it and enjoy the thrill of a high-wire act with no safety net. If I fall from the surface of the sea here it could take hours for my body to reach the sea bed.

I remain balanced on the silver surface of the sea and peer into turquoise blue space beneath.

The space is full of sound. High pitched it comes into my head and rolls around inside like an echo in the canyons of my mind. The dolphins are talking to one another. I can hear their conversation but I can't understand it. They are all around me, talking, talking, talking. Are they really trying to talk to me, or are their whistles just the expression of joy of free spirits enjoying being alive in a sun-filled ocean?

A very rotund member of my group is crossing my path intently peering ahead looking for the source of the sound he can hear but not knowing that a dolphin with a cheeky expression is following three feet behind his fins. I laugh into my snorkel tube. I feel sure the dolphin knows the human can't see him and is enjoying the joke.

The fat man has stopped swimming. He looks at me and points ahead. Coming up towards us from the depths is a large shark. It cruises past us both and the dolphin swims off apparently totally unconcerned. More sharks appear. I can see the baby dolphin with his mother.

The sound of the dolphins has gone. So have the dolphins. The sharks are cruising silently into and out of my view. I look up. The *Encantada* is cruising nearby. I shout to the captain. 'Where are the dolphins?' He looks around and points to a place several hundred yards away. The dolphins have moved off. It's time for breakfast.

★   ★   ★

The expedition programme included two dives a day plus at least one shore excursion.

By the time we reached Roca Redonda everyone in the group had become familiar with a very flexible routine worked around meal times which were also flexible. The pre-breakfast swim with the dolphins was a bonus. So when our breakfast had settled preparations for the scheduled dive went ahead smoothly.

When everyone was kitted-up and lined-up along the gunwale the captain took the yacht very close in to the near vertical wall of the island. With the boat rolling in the swell the divers jumped overboard one after another in quick succession. As soon as the last one was in the water the boat, which was just a few feet from the cliffs, moved away to lay off at a safe distance.

The water was very cold and clear. As soon as we entered the sea many of the numerous sealions, that had been resting on ledges at the foot of the cliffs, plopped into the water too. They escorted us throughout the dive. Usually they travelled at speed, twisting and turning with consummate ease, periodically shooting to the surface to snatch a quick breath before returning with equal velocity. Occasionally, however, they would stop and watch us with a mixture of amusement and curiosity.

There were a vast number of different species of fish in the water, including a large shoal of barracuda. We entered the water above a shelf of rock, which gave me a static reference. By looking at the way it was moving past I was aware that we were being carried along by the current — which is not possible to tell in open water. Like snowflakes in the wind the divers around me slowly descended, drifting down diagonally past the rock wall of the island. On the ledge I stopped and examined a stream of bubbles that continuously emerged from a crack. We were diving on the top of a volcano and I wondered what activity below, past or present, the leaking gas indicated.

Amongst the many species of fish we saw were golden hogfish. These are endemic to the Galapagos Islands, i.e. they occur nowhere else in the world and are unusual insomuch as every fish has a very distinctive colour pattern made up of large blotches of colour that vary from white through yellow to golden brown to black. Thus it is possible to identify easily a single specimen, which would make a study of the day to day life of individuals relatively easy. What benefit the fish derives from being totally different to his companions, in contrast to most species whose members are very similar to one another, nobody knows.

When I looked up to draw the attention of the other divers to my discovery of the gas stream I was greeted by the sight of the fat man flying over my head holding onto the carapace of a turtle. I am not sure what the turtle made of the situation but his passenger was clearly enjoying a lot of fun from his ride and it was certainly an amusing sight for the other human spectators. The sealions seemed to enjoy it too. When he let go of the turtle it swam off looking as if its dignity had been ruffled — that is as much as a turtle can ever look indignant. However, the turtle's curiosity soon overcame its disquiet for a few moments later it was again circling round — but keeping out of hand's reach.

We drifted through more curtains of fish but never went below fifty feet. After half an hour in the water the cold Humboldt Current that flows along the west coast of South America towards the equator was getting the better of my thin wetsuit and I felt distinctly chilly and was happy to surface. I put a hand vertically in the air — the signal that I was OK and needed to be picked up. Within a few moments one of the small wooden tenders (called pangas) from the *Encantada* was alongside me. I deftly unbuckled my weight belt and aqualung harness as the Ecuadorian boatman leaned over the side and lifted my heavy gear swiftly and efficiently into the panga. Seconds later I hauled myself over the gunwale and flopped onto the gear piled on the duckboards like a landed fish.

During the time we had been under water the wind had risen — as the captain predicted it would — and a big swell was swishing up the exposed cliffs of the Roca Redonda. I never ceased to admire the expert way the boatmen handled the pangas picking up divers who surfaced within a few yards of the cliff face in a swell that rose up the rocks and was often shredded into a seething white froth as it fell to meet the next assaulting wave.

As soon as everyone was on board the captain hoisted the sails. The *Encantada* responded immediately, heeling over and slicing through the white waves like a spirited horse. The dolphins who had been playing in the white-capped waves and riding them like surfriders, came to join us in a glorious farewell dance. They zig-zagged around us surfacing in front and alongside the speeding red hull of the *Encantada*.

When we were about three miles from the island the dolphins all veered off and we watched them disappear into the distance like a troupe of entertainers who performed just for the fun of it. As we got closer to the island of Isabela I could smell the scent of the vegetation in the warm air as I sat on the deck, mesmerised by the flow of the sea past our hull and luxuriating in the sensuous warmth of the tropical sun on my body.

Again I marvelled at how privileged I was to have such experiences. And as I have already recounted there were even more to come because it was later that afternoon that we snorkelled into the area where the boobies were feeding.

At one time the Galapagos archipelago was the haunt of pirates and buccaneers and Tagus Cove, on Isabela, was one of the places they frequented. I saw Tagus Cove on my first visit to the islands when I was on board a vessel called *The Sulidae*. She was a Baltic trader, built at the beginning of the century and later converted for cruising. Accommodation in the cargo holds was cramped, but she was a vessel of great character. The oak on oak planking of the hull was as sound as the day she was built. When under sail she had that special feel below decks that you get when surrounded by gently creaking wood that doesn't exist in steel-hulled ships which are noisier. However, I was on deck beside the bowsprit when I sailed into Tagus Cove for the first time. The sea was sparkling, and as we rounded the high rocky headland a sandy beach opened to view with absolutely no sign of human presence. The sun shone down from a sky of unbroken azure blue. I felt as if I was sailing into a film set. Those on board were a motley, happy, sunburned but sophisticated bunch who had found paradise and knew it. Their cameras clicked to record the adventure and some dreamed of the pirates' gold that was reputedly hidden nearby. But for me my accumulated memories of Tagus Cove (I have been there three times) and the underwater life I discovered there are worth more than any bars of gold I might have dug up.

The underwater visibility is not exceptionally good, and the underwater scenery is certainly not as spectacular as I have seen elsewhere, but the Cove does have a large number of endemic species which contribute to its unique character and give it its special place in my personal album of memories.

On my first visit I discovered a very delicate coral in beautiful shades of orange and yellow that was as vulnerable as a large chrysanthemum flower near the end of its life as a bloom. It hung in profusion under an archway. Accidentally brushing against it with my aqualung cylinder I unfortunately caused some of the coral strands to break off and cascade into the depths like petals falling from a flower. Being unable to identify it I christened it 'chrysanthemum coral'. In a cave nearby were growths, white as swan's down, hanging from the roof like miniature stalactites.

On my second visit I was in the company of my erstwhile partner Chris Goosen to make a film for our TV series

'Wonders of the Underwater World'. I had been exploring and filming the headland under water and had just swum to the extremity. I was scanning the milky blue wall of sea beyond for sharks, when I saw a large black disc suspended in the water in front of me. I pulled the viewfinder of my cine camera up to my eye and swam very slowly towards it, holding my breath. As I got closer, with fewer suspended particles to obscure the image, I could see it more clearly.

It was a magnificent ocean sun fish — which grow to weigh as much as a ton but still retain their disc shape. When I could hold my breath no longer I exhaled and inhaled. All the time I approached, the *Mola mola,* as sun fish are called, had been aware of my presence and was nervously standing its ground. But when my bubbles rattled out of my regulator it clearly thought discretion was the better part of valour, turned its insignificant tail towards me and swam gently into the obscuring haze— its fading silhouette seemingly as high and no wider than a lamp-post.

On the same evening one of the German members of my party called my attention to a small strange fish under the boat and held a light over it in order that I could film it. Such was the extraordinary appearance of the fish that on my third visit in May 1982 I organised a night dive in Tagus Cove specifically to see it again.

The beams from our underwater lamps prodded the darkness, exposing the night life on the sandy sea bed. Instead of the monotonous flat dun-coloured vista of the daytime the beams cast intense shadows causing the objects illuminated to stand out starkly in the velvety blackness of the surrounding sea. Concentric puffer fish, another endemic species, mesmerised by the lights, had the comic expression of whistling schoolboys in fancy dress and allowed us to approach as close as we liked. Our beams also picked out numerous specimens of the strange fish we had come to search for which had the common name of Galapagos Batfish. The Latin name *(Ogocephalus darwini)* reveals that they were first described by Darwin and I wonder if they contributed in some way to the development of his revolutionary theory of evolution which took clear shape in his mind for the first time in the Galapagos Islands when he came to the astounding conclusion that all of the different finches on the islands were derived from a common stock that had diversified through the process of evolution to new, distinctly different, species.

It is thought that life on land started with creatures crawling out of the sea. Well, the Galapagos Batfish looks as if it has gone the other way and is a land animal that is half-way adapted to living under water. It is nearly all head and shoulders with a tapering tail that enables it to swim sluggishly through the water. It props its head up on its pectoral fins and has an almost froglike posture in the water using another set of fins, that look more like legs, to hop over the sea bed. It has a horny protrusion jutting from its forehead, large unblinking eyes and the bright red mouth of a clown. The ones we saw squatted on the sea bed, looking upwards and forwards with their comic faces. They didn't move unless we disturbed them when they would swim in an ungainly manner for a few feet before dropping back to the sea bed again — apparently exhausted from the exertion. We easily caught a couple of specimens and took them to the surface for the benefit of non-divers on board who examined the four-inch long biological curiosities before returning them to the sea.

My memories of the Galapagos Islands are bountiful, exciting and exotic but it is the sealions who really dominate my overall recollections and impression because we met them on virtually every dive. Of the many encounters I had with sealions there were two locations which I recall as being exceptional.

One of them was at a location aptly called The Devil's Crown (Corona del Diablo) off the island of Floreana. It is the cone of a very small volcano and consists of a ring of jagged rocks surrounding a small shallow lagoon the depth of water in which varies according to the tide. Access to the central pool is easy via gaps in the encircling rocks, but there are also underwater tunnels through which it is dangerous and exciting to swim. It is an ideal place to snorkel and under the right conditions is a good place to take novices. Each time I have visited The Devil's Crown the sealions have performed a beautiful underwater ballet, in which I mingled with the performers. The stage, which is the central coral-covered bowl of the crown, is also the home of numerous reef fishes whose gentle flowing movements and colour add to the atmosphere of the setting. The undersea tunnels are the wings from which the sealions appear in a spontaneous show that is all the more charming because it is unstructured — the artistes responding according to the appreciation of the audience. Of all the creatures in the sea none can surpass the sinuous flowing motion of the sealions whose passage through the water creates curve upon curve that leave a delicate tracery of images in the mind. Sometimes in the middle of a frenzied performance all of the sealions leave and one is left, feeling slightly saddened that the show is over. Then, without announcement the ballet troupe reappear, perhaps one at a time, or even as a *corps de ballet*, to twirl and whirl in another spectacular display in which they seem to occupy the entire enclosure, often swimming at great speed, crossing and recrossing one another's paths. Up, down, in, out, this way, that way, behind you, in front of you, beside you, above you, below you, bulls, cows and cubs all interwoven in a transient tapestry of flowing lines executed with a sense of sheer uninhibited joy. Attempting to chase after them only seems to increase their determination to demonstrate their total mastery of their aquatic environment.

The other place where I have enjoyed the company of hordes of sealions was off the tiny island of South Plaza which is located a short distance to the east of the large island of Santa Cruz and is separated by a channel from another small island called North Plaza.

The channel provides a very convenient mooring for a large vessel and it is a short journey by panga to a jetty on South Plaza which has a high population of land iguanas and is dotted with opuntia cactuses upon which the iguanas can feed. A trail leads quickly to the southern cliffs where delicate swallow-tailed gulls congregate and, like all the birds on Galapagos, are unafraid of humans and can be approached closely.

Further east along the cliffs is an area which is occupied by young male sealions, not yet able to defend a territory.

Standing proud of the surrounding terrain are a number of flat-topped rocks upon which the huge old bulls disport themselves. It is as if nature has provided seats for the older statesmen of the sealion colony of South Plaza. The tops of the rocks have been worn down to a fine polish by generations of large old bulls presumably dreaming of their past glories. The reigning champions in the mating stakes are to be found closer to the water's edge near the jetty where they can keep a close eye on their harem who in turn can keep a watch on their offspring who congregate in a small area of sea off the stone jetty. Here the young sealions sport endlessly in the water. Ever since my first visit I have thought of it as being like a school playground which is continuously occupied by energetic juvenile sealions whose play involves the continuous charging around that goes on in every infant or junior school I have visited at playtime.

The water is no more than ten feet deep and to swim into this zone under water wearing an aqualung is an experience beyond compare. The water is black with curious whirling sealion cubs whose inquisitive gentle nature is instantly revealed by their large liquid eyes when they momentarily hover in front of you and peer into your facemask with their beautiful faces just inches away. Just as in a children's playground the atmosphere in the sealions' underwater play area is charged with pent-up juvenile energy being released in vigorous but non-competitive play. A small piece of seaweed can instantly become a source of immense amusement as one after another of the baby sealions takes it in his or her mouth and charges through the water with it hotly pursued by ten other youngsters who take it in turns to snatch it in their mouths when it is released and then hurtle off with it in another direction.

For a television sequence I took a small plastic ring attached to a length of tape into the water and filmed their response. It provided an opportunity for them to play a game of dare. Several of them plucked up courage and took the ring in their mouths and tried to swim away with it. But I held onto the tape and after a few very gentle tugs they let it go. It was the sensitivity with which they attempted to play with it that impressed me most. They made no attempt to snatch it forcefully away from me. I was very happy to quietly withdraw taking my toy with me and leaving them to play with a piece of gorgonian coral that was suddenly produced by one of the troupe. The twig of coral was passed from one sealion to another without resistance.

On my last visit to the island of South Plaza one of the members of the group left a facemask on the back seat of the panga we had used to ferry us ashore. The little wooden dinghy was left tied to the jetty. As we climbed up the path we saw a young sealion jump into the panga and remove the facemask, flopping back into the sea with a new toy to the obvious delight of his fellows. The owner of the mask thought that would be the last he would see of it and continued on his tour of the island.

A couple of hours later when we were ferried back to our mother ship, the *Encantada,* we had an escort of young sealions who frolicked alongside jumping like porpoises. Most of them would not venture beyond the limits of their play area and left us as soon as we passed over the boundary line. But a few of the older and more bold ones remained until we were back on the yacht. They swam round the *Encantada* inviting us to jump in and play with them, which we did immediately we discovered that they were passing the missing facemask from one to another. Although they could outswim us with consummate ease they allowed us to join in the game and we recovered the mask not wishing to contaminate their natural world with one of our machine-made possessions.

My visits to the Galapagos Islands have had a profound influence on me and have put me in a moral dilemma because I realise that by publicising them and exposing the wonderful life I discovered there I shall encourage many more people to visit them. The resultant over exposure could lead to the destruction of the very thing I most cherish about the archipelago: that feeling of being with a few fellow pioneers, or better still being alone and coming very close to some of my fellow creatures who are unafraid of me and do not regard my presence as a threat.

One thing that is clear in my mind, however, is that the Galapagos Islands provide a supreme example of how wild creatures and humans can coexist. I defy anybody to go there and not come back with a greater respect and concern for all wildlife. So I have come to terms with myself with the argument that the more people who are made aware of the need to preserve wildlife and wild places the more hope there is that the wonders I have seen and enjoyed around the Galapagos Islands and elsewhere will survive to be experienced by others.

9

Shipwrecked

THE PHILIPPINES; THE SOUTH CHINA SEA

When I first started diving in the 1950s I could not afford a full set of diving equipment and therefore slowly built it up — making most of it myself. A snorkel tube, for instance, was made from a piece of rigid polythene tubing. When two of the more affluent members of the diving club produced dry suits and then expounded on the luxury of being warm when immersed in cold water, and it was apparent from my male peers that they did not regard such cosseting as being sissy, I bent my mind to achieving the same end without the same expenditure.

Purchase, for a nominal sum, of an ex-World War II Davis submarine escape suit did not provide the answer. In principle it was supposed to exclude water and should therefore have qualified as a so-called dry suit. In practice it seemed to suck in the surrounding environment to such an extent that when I emerged from the Thames after its first field trial I could barely stand for the weight of brown river water trapped inside. Then I read in a foreign magazine about a new development that was revolutionising the business of keeping divers warm underwater. It was called a wetsuit. On the basis of the information I gleaned, and a photograph of a male model wearing one, I set about making a copy of the French design which had the trendy, suitably masculine-sounding tag of 'Tarzan'.

My first 'Tarzan' wetsuit was made from a patchwork sheet of oddments of natural sponge rubber. I was the first to admit that the finished product lacked the chic *haute couture* appearance of its Parisian counterpart. However, I was convinced of its efficiency as an insulator the first time I put it on because by the time I had inserted myself into the second skin made of smelly rubber I was running with perspiration.

Having confirmed, in my lounge at home, the soundness

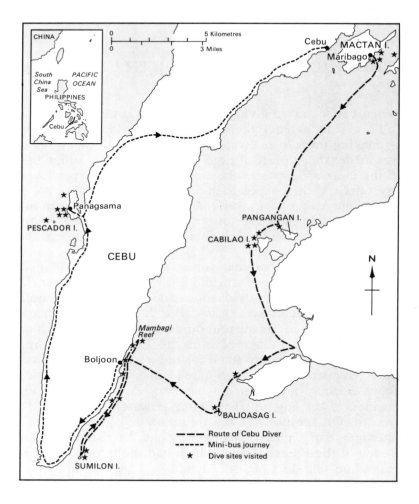

of this breakthrough in diver comfort I couldn't wait to get to the swimming pool to expound on the principle to my more affluent — but less well-read fellow divers.

At last I stood by the pool, my squashed red face beaded

with sweat, proudly beaming out of a circular hole in the hood at an openly sceptical audience who clearly lacked the sensitivity to appreciate the full majesty of such an historic moment as the unveiling of the first wetsuit in Britain.

I was keen not to protract the pre-wetting ceremony too long for two reasons. Firstly, because I was becoming overwhelmed by the nauseating smell of the rubber solution I had used to make a last-minute repair to the suit which had split when I struggled into it. Secondly, I was close to expiring from overheating.

So with the minimum of delay I proudly jumped into the pool with uninhibited bravura.

My moment of glory was short-lived however. Before I had swum a few yards the thing started to fall apart. By the time I was halfway along the length of the pool my home-made wetsuit had disintegrated completely and pieces of black rubber of all sizes were zig-zagging down towards the white tiles on the bottom of the pool. Fortunately I had put on some swimming trunks under the wetsuit. I self-consciously swam down and picked up the chunks of waterlogged sponge, before returning quickly to the changing rooms with as much dignity as I could muster whilst being bombarded by a fusillade of stinging comments fired at me by the assembled spectators who were falling into the pool with laughter.

Next day — back at the drawing board — I discovered my mistake. I should not have used sheet rubber in which all the holes were inter-connected and which therefore soaked up water like a proper sponge. Instead, I should have utilised a new synthetic sponge neoprene rubber which did not absorb water because all the trapped nitrogen bubbles were isolated from one another. I eventually managed to obtain some sheets of sponge neoprene. My Mark II Tarzan wetsuit, which I tested in the privacy of the bath at home before venturing into public in it, proved to be the breakthrough I had prophesied and enabled me to expand my diving capabilities to limits which would have been impossible without it.

Things changed rapidly in the 1960s. We saw the birth of an age of widespread affluence which was heralded by the

Beatles and could possibly best be described by Prime Minister Harold Macmillan's expression, 'You've never had it so good'. Now, in the 1980s many things which were once regarded as the sole prerogative of a privileged minority such as ownership of a refrigerator and a television, holidays abroad, houses with central heating and even a full set of diving equipment have become a normal expectation for many people of Britain — especially the young. Despite the woes of high unemployment and the iniquity of a poverty-stricken minority the majority of British people today are enjoying a higher standard of living than ever before.

This fact came home to me very forcefully when I looked back to an underwater expedition I led to the Philippines in 1981 which brought me into close contact with people, many of whom were still on the lowest rung of the ladder of affluence and for most of whom ownership of the ultimate status symbol — a car — was still an impossible dream.

The expedition to the Philippines came about as a result of my two friends Bruce and Hedda Lyons of Twickenham Travel, whose business expansion plans were based on finding new destinations for the ever-increasing number of British divers who were travelling abroad. 'Where would divers want to go after they have visited the Mediterranean, the Red Sea and the Caribbean?' was the question asked.

We agreed, with long-distance air fares becoming relatively cheap, that the Philippines was one obvious choice. However, before such a location could be offered as a destination where clients could be assured of good diving, it needed to be researched.

Previous experience had taught us that the proprietors of some hotels and some diving operators were inclined to let literary licence override the facts when it came to describing the amenities they had to offer. When a group of divers fly half-way round the world for a diving holiday only to find that the compressor, essential for filling aqualungs, isn't working or hasn't even been delivered, it leaves the tour operator sitting in a very hot seat indeed. So when Twickenham Travel advertised for paying customers to come with me on a pioneering trip to the Philippines I was pleased that the three who eventually joined it were Esna and Martin Kaufman and John Cockerill — all of whom had been on previous expeditions with me and knew what to expect. However, I am certain they didn't bargain for the adventures into which we were all eventually to be plunged. For John Cockerill the adventures began when his wife decided to drive along a ditch instead of the slippery road whilst ferrying her husband to Gatwick airport on Saturday, 11 April 1981 for the thirty-two-hour flight to Manila.

From Manila we took an eleven-hour onward flight to Cebu where we were met by Stuart and Antoinette Gould who were based at the Dive Inn and ran Cebu Diving Tours. Their modest brochure described what Cebu Diving Tours had to offer as: A PHOTOGRAPHER'S DREAM. A SPORTSMAN'S PARADISE. AN EXPERIENCE NEVER TO BE FORGOTTEN. I can now personally vouch for the fact that none of their claims, especially the last one, contravenes the Trade Descriptions Act.

Our first dive was at Maribago on the island of Mactan which was connected to Cebu city via a bridge. We travelled there in a powered tricycle more ornately decorated than a fairground switchback car and just as perilous and exciting to ride. The minute we fell out of the vehicle at our destination we were besieged by vendors of all ages trying to sell us shells and souvenirs. However, we were anxious to have our first look at the place where the shells came from — the sea bed in Cebu Strait.

After a short swim over a shallow bottom we arrived at a surprisingly spectacular drop-off on which I saw many new and some familiar species of fish and coral.

Our feelings after that first dive are best summed up by John Cockerill's entry in the log which reads as follows: 'First dive in the afternoon — weather sunny and warm, viz good, coral and marine life as interesting as in the Red Sea. Philippine people very considerate and most helpful. I am sure this will be a great diving holiday.' Esna added the laconic note 'I agree.'

To put us further into a holiday mood that night we were taken on a tour of the noisy, neon-lit nightspots with which Cebu abounds, and ended up at Reflections 77 on Osmena

Boulevard where beautiful girls stripped in front of a mixed audience. We moved on when John Cockerill's glasses steamed up, not staying to see if one of us had won the raffle with his entrance ticket. We had, after all, come to find out what the Philippines had to offer as a diving holiday location. The amenities offered in the Philippines for those seeking sporting holidays of a different kind were already widely known.

The next morning we joined the vessel which we were told would be our base for the next two weeks. At first sight it was impressively large with an overall length of seventy-two feet; two large outriggers and a superstructure that extended over the canoe hull which had a maximum width of only five feet. Inside the superstructure were a wheelhouse, cabins with a total of six bunks, a galley, a loo and an Indec Pecker 15 hp diesel engine. Stu regretted that he would be unable to accompany us because of business commitments and left us in the hands of Feliciano who was to act as skipper, plus a crew of three young Filipinos.

The cabins and bunk space were soon allocated, the engine was started, and after a three-hour journey with a following wind we threw the anchor overboard at Panganan Island. At 4.00 pm we jumped into the sea for our second dive in the Philippines. An hour later we returned to the boat — delighted with our underwater journeys round a headland rich in colourful corals, with an underwater visibility of about seventy feet.

As soon as we had recovered the anchor was hauled inboard and we set sail for the Island of Cabilao where we planned to spend the night. Martin identified it as the correct location by the five-second flash of the lighthouse. We anchored close to the lighthouse on the edge of a deep drop-off close to the headland. Having consulted the chart this was the area where I predicted we would find the most spectacular underwater life — including sharks.

Whilst supper was being prepared Martin and Esna decided they would go for a night dive. They were a husband and wife team of considerable experience and both were keen underwater photographers. The sea was calm, warm and clear. John and I watched their yellow lights sweeping the shallow water corals beneath the boat. They moved to the edge of the drop-off, their lights briefly silhouetting the fantastic shapes of the corals along the top of the wall. Then they disappeared from view. Thirty-five minutes later they were back alongside the boat handing up their lights and cameras before removing their diving equipment whilst treading water. They were delighted with their dive and during the meal recounted how beautiful the underwater scenery was with many spectacular large crinoid starfish whose feathery arms closed up into a basket shape when their light fell upon them. During the day these beautiful basket stars, as they are often called, hide in dark crevices or on the underside of coral. They come out at night to feed. The two divers also reported the presence of lots of long-spined and pencil sea urchins. These are also night feeders that browse on the corals and rocks scraping off algae and other growths with their bony mouths. At night they move silently and slowly across the reef with the aid of numerous retractable tube feet and their spines. During the day they move into holes with their spines projecting towards the opening to defend themselves against the parrot fish who can only attack them from the underside. During the hours of darkness the parrot fish tuck themselves into caves and holes in the reef to sleep, making way on the reef for the night shift of more primitive forms of marine life.

It had been an interesting day and by 10.00 o'clock we were all tired and decided to retire to our respective bunks. We had put out only one anchor when we first arrived at Cabilao and when I climbed into my bunk I left the captain to put out the other one. After reading a brief part of *The Brendan Voyage* by Tim Severin I balanced the book on top of the cork lifejacket attached to the cabin wall above my head and quickly drifted into an untroubled slumber. So too did the rest of my group. However, I had been wrong to assume that our vessel was skippered by a captain with the qualities and qualifications we take so much for granted in our organised, disciplined and regulated way of life in the West.

At about 1.00 am Martin heard Esna say, 'We're afloat.'

'Of course we are, we're on a boat aren't we?' he mumbled in a half-conscious reply as he prepared to resume his sleep.

'No!' exclaimed Esna shaking her husband into wakefulness. 'We're afloat and the boat's sinking.'

At this point Martin could feel the water swirling around him. The boat was sinking rapidly, stern first.

The Kaufmans' cabin was astern of the cabin in which John and I were sleeping and the passageway through to the wheelhouse was between our bunks. It was very dark in the cabins and by the time Martin and Esna had felt their way through the door into my cabin the water was already nearly bunk high. I awoke when they scrambled past into the wheelhouse and thence out onto the foredeck. John followed quickly behind them. I grabbed the handle of the bag, like a large briefcase, which contained my papers and money and which was floating in the water alongside me. I also plucked the copy of '*The Brendan Voyage*' I had been reading from on top of the lifejacket. And leaving the lifejacket still attached to the wall I ducked out of the doorway just as it submerged. I scrambled up the inclined door through the wheelhouse to the foredeck where the others had assembled and had woken the captain and crew who had been asleep on the roof of my cabin.

Buoyant items that had been lying on the deck started to float and drift away.

'Quick,' I shouted. 'Grab anything that is floating and shove it into the wheelhouse for buoyancy.'

The boat stopped sinking. The stern was on the sea bed and the foredeck remained poking out of the water with seven people clinging to it. We were right on the edge of the drop-off where the sharks patrolled at night looking for a late-night supper. The crew were convinced they would not see another sunrise. I have to admit that unlike them I did not find the situation at all terrifying. It was serious but at the same time extremely amusing. If the worst came to the worst I knew we could all swim ashore.

It was a bright clear tropical night. Apart from our voices there was not a sound. The full moon shone down. The lighthouse rhythmically flicked its beam over our heads.

I parked my bag and book on a small part of the cabin roof

that had not submerged and was considering how best to resolve our problem when a solution literally floated into view. A native fisherman in a dugout canoe with one outrigger was paddling out from the beach for a night's fishing. From the way in which he was going it looked as if he would pass right past us without taking any notice of us at all. 'Perhaps he is just being polite and doesn't want to embarrass us because of our predicament' I thought. So I called out to him. He paddled over and rested the front of his tiny hollowed-out log against the bow of our sinking ship. With one of the crew acting as interpreter I asked for his help. He agreed to ferry us ashore. The crew almost fell over themselves in their attempts to get into his canoe and thereby to safety on the island.

The maximum load he could take without swamping his tiny canoe was two persons. So under the light of a tropical moon we watched him paddle away to the palm tree fringed beach with two of the young Filipino crew on board.

Our bags of diving equipment had been stowed on the foredeck. We located them and took out our underwater torches. Martin wanted to recover a suitcase which was still in his cabin. So taking a torch and a facemask he ducked into the cabin knowing that there was an air space in the roof, which had still not filled completely. He found the case, pushed it through the window opening and we hauled it up onto the roof. The bag containing John Cockerill's valuables was also recovered in a similar manner.

The cooking on board was done on an open fire and the galley was next to Martin and Esna's cabin. As the vessel sank the charcoal from the fire floated and mixed with the cooking and other oil that also floated upwards and was trapped under the cabin roof. Martin had to submerge through this black oil slick several times and when he eventually returned triumphant to the foredeck he looked as if he had just auditioned for an underwater version of The Black & White Minstrel Show.

When our boatman returned with his dugout canoe I decided a full salvage operation could be carried out. This would not only save lots of valuable equipment but would lessen the likelihood of the vessel sinking beyond recovery.

So instead of taking two people the boatman ferried one person and as much baggage as his boat would carry each time he paddled back to shore.

In this way we managed to get all of the diving equipment, plus the compressor, which needed a special trip all of its own, onto dry land.

I was the last to leave and when I reached the beach I looked around for the others who had all disappeared. I was wondering if they were all right when they reappeared with the head-man of the tiny village who said we could spend what was left of the night in a partially completed thatched building with a raised wooden floor. During our stay on the island John Cockerill was to become quite friendly with this helpful, English-speaking man.

Cocks crowed throughout our first night on Cabilao as we slept fitfully on mattresses rescued from the boat. When daylight broke at about five o'clock we stirred and were soon assessing the damage. Looking out from the land I spotted the bows of our boat, still just afloat, on a flat-calm, Cambridge-blue, sunlit sea. Around us in higgledy-piggledy confusion were the piles of diving equipment and the personal baggage we had salvaged from the boat.

I was lucky. The bulk of my most important possessions, including my passport, which were in the bag I had retrieved when I clambered out of the cabin as it flooded, were not sodden. The same was not true of Martin and Esna's accoutrements which were well and truly waterlogged. As the sun came up we spread out our valuables to dry. Passports, travellers' cheques, films and books gradually dried out under the scorching sun. So too did the clothes we hung out on an improvised washing line slung between two palm trees.

A few early risers from the village strolled down and stood silently watching us with unabashed curiosity. Then the word spread and we were soon encircled by the entire population of the tiny village many of whom squatted on their haunches. What they said about the display which included Esna's underwear and a neat row of packets of condoms I could not understand. But from the expressions on their faces and their giggles they obviously enjoyed the

244

unexpected and novel source of early morning entertainment. Amongst the items displayed were lots of 100 peso notes (about £6) which although not excessively valuable to us represented a fortune to our spectators. Yet the throng of obviously very poor people around us never came close enough to filch anything and we never doubted for one moment their absolute honesty. Indeed, when we put into a heap all of the items such as tape recorders, cameras and electrical goods which were damaged beyond repair nobody took as much as a cardboard film box without asking our permission — despite the fact that we tried to make it clear that we wished to throw them away.

Surrounded by happy, smiling, honest, very poor people who made us welcome, who enjoyed simple pleasure and did not resent our affluence, made us all realise how much we in the West had lost as well as gained in our scramble up the mountain of materialism.

The Filipino crew borrowed food and utensils and cooked breakfast on an open driftwood fire on the beach. Over breakfast I confirmed the conclusion we had already come to concerning the reason why our boat had sunk. The crew only put out one anchor, and during the night the boat had swung on the anchor until the hull came to rest against an extra high coral head which the Filipinos called a 'bommie'. The gentle movements of the boat caused the coral to rub a hole in the hull, through which the water entered slowly filling the bilges. There was no keel or ballast and the weight of the heavy engine at the back caused the stern to submerge first. Once the water came over the side the boat filled and started to sink quickly, stern first. It was at this stage that Esna and Martin woke up.

However, establishing the cause of our plight was not as important as resolving it. And that meant salvaging the boat.

As well as being happy-go-lucky the Filipinos are diligent and intelligent. As we sorted out our baggage a couple of them were attempting to resuscitate the half-drowned compressor which we used to charge our aqualung cylinders with air. Just as we finished our breakfast the early morning peace was disturbed by some coughs and splutters, then the

245

continuous roar of a petrol engine running at fast throttle.

Our compressor was running — all of our diving gear was on shore which meant that even if the boat sank completely we could salvage it provided it didn't go down beyond the drop-off where the water was about 1,000 feet deep. So recovery of the boat became our next priority.

After surveying the situation from the land and then snorkelling out to the boat we agreed that the best way to do it would be to raise the anchor and pull the stricken vessel as close to shore as possible at high water. When the tide receded it would leave the boat on the beach where she could be emptied and patched up before the tide came in and floated her off. Once afloat again she could be dried out and we could start work on the boat engine.

Feliciano, the young skipper, said we could leave it to him and his crew to enlist the necessary labour from the fishermen. He said he had already sent a boat back to Cebu city to report our plight.

Being marooned on a tropical island with beautiful, friendly natives, diving equipment, a compressor plus a supply of fuel is about as close as you can get to most divers' dreams of paradise, especially as our reconnaissance snorkels over the edge of the drop-off had revealed enticing vistas of spectacular beauty with extremely good underwater visibility. So we abandoned all concern for the tape recorders plus Nikon and Minolta cameras that had been flooded. Relieved of the burden to make a comprehensive above-water record of our adventure we decided to enjoy the diving and use only our underwater cameras which had been salvaged without damage and with which we could take above-water pictures anyway.

At 3.00 pm John and I put on full diving equipment and snorkelled out on the surface from the village on the beach. The drop-off could easily be seen from the shore because the colour of the sea changed sharply from turquoise to deep blue. Under water the change was even more dramatic. One minute we were moving slowly over a sandy bottom with outcrops of coral — then suddenly before us was a wall of deep blue sea as devoid of features as a cloudless Californian sky. Immediately beneath us was a near vertical wall sprouting an immense variety of coral and swarming with tiny fish.

We turned to the left at the drop-off and followed its line until we reached a small underwater headland, all of the time travelling on the surface to conserve our air. Then it was time to dive. So we switched from snorkel to aqualung, deflated our lifejackets and let our weight carry us very gently down, as smoothly as a slow moving lift, into an underwater Garden of Eden. On our downward journey we passed glowing outcrops of soft gorgonian corals that radiated colour. In places the wall was overhung and suspended under the roofs of the caves branched sponges hung like upside-down candelabra.

Growing out from the wall with their arms outstretched to catch the food that drifted in the slow current along the reef were giant fan corals eight feet in width. We stopped descending at 150 feet and trimmed our buoyancy. We then swam slowly back up the reef in a diagonal line passing more wonders on the way. These included a giant pitcher sponge which stood out from the rocks like a huge chalice and was big enough for a man to sit inside. We ended our dive back at the top of the drop-off where we decompressed amidst the fishes and anemones that seemed even more brightly coloured after our sojourn in the spectacular but less colourful depths. Here we watched a lion fish, with its splendid feather-like fins, drifting freely and without concern amongst the coral in the knowledge that the ends of its spines were poisonous and we, and any other possible predators on the reed, would be well advised not to interfere with it. At 4.00 pm we surfaced and fifteen minutes later Martin and Esna were following in our fin tracks — but such was the richness of the reef they saw many things we hadn't and vice versa.

During the late afternoon an outrigger with an engine arrived at the beach. It was Stu Gould's Filipino brother-in-law, Ned, who had come to take us back to Cebu city where hotel accommodation had been reserved for us until such time as the dive boat could be made serviceable again. To help offset any aggression on our part he brought with him an ice box full of cans of cold beer. We unanimously decided to accept his beer and rejected his offer of a return trip to Cebu city.

Most Filipinos seemed to play the guitar and Ned was no exception. That night he stayed on the island with us and after supper serenaded us with Beatles' songs as we sat round the driftwood fire over which the evening meal had been cooked. We made our beds on the beach and eventually went to sleep beside a tropical sea under a tropical moon.

Here is what I wrote in the expedition log the following morning:

> 'What a magnificent feeling it is to go to bed in the open with the stars and the moon for company and a gently swishing sea to add its own note to the silence. A slight breeze occasionally moves the still air. The moon slowly sinks and at 4.00 am it is gone and the air is cooler. By 5.00 am light starts to fill the sky and a red dawn breaks over a breathless sea. I'm glad we did not go back to Cebu city to a hotel.'

The next day another outrigger arrived from Cebu to provide us with transport to continue our proposed odyssey. On board were an engineer and a spare compressor. On the day following its arrival we left the island of Cabilao but not before we had two more superb aqualung dives. One of them, at what we dubbed Lighthouse Point, John rated in the log as one of his ten best dives in the world. We saw sting rays, huge organ pipe sponges and pitcher sponges. On swimming through a hole in the reef we found ourselves finning along a coral terrace which was the home of a large crocodile fish. Very dainty striped fish called Moorish Idols, that had long pennants trailing from the tips of their dorsal fins, paraded past us as if they were in a carnival procession. And growing out of the rockface just like a tree on the land was a magnificent black coral. It would have fetched a high price on the coral market but we left it unmolested, hopefully to grow for another 100 years. On the way back across the reef table I saw the greatest variety of anemones and clown fish I have seen anywhere in the world.

The boat that sank — the *Cebu Diver* — was soon back in

commission again and we transferred back to it. For the next ten days we used it as a base — sometimes we slept on board and sometimes on the beach. Stu Gould's Filipino wife Antoinette seemed to have relatives everywhere and some nights we spent with Filipino families sleeping on the slatted bamboo floors of thatched houses raised on stilts, underneath which pigs grunted, dogs howled and cocks crowed. We found the Filipinos to be absolutely delightful company; they were noisy and loved western music and many spoke English. When we made it clear that the tinned food which had been provided specifically for our consumption was definitely not to our liking the cans remained unopened and we ate only Filipino food which was as exotic, spicy, varied and delicious as the people.

It transpired that the young skipper, Feliciano and the crew were all related to Antoinette Gould in some way and they adopted us into their family.

We spent the night of Saturday, 18 April 1981 at Boljoon on the eastern side of the island of Cebu in the house of one of our newly-acquired relatives called Tessa. We were aroused at 3.00 am by the noise from a radio set at maximum output and coming down through the wide cracks in the floorboards over our heads. It was Easter Sunday and by 4.00 am we had joined the crowds in the dark unmade streets for the Easter Festival in which a statue of Jesus and a statue of the Virgin Mary were paraded around the town in separate tightly packed candlelit processions. The two jostling groups met at the entrance to the church where a service was conducted for a packed standing congregation many of whom stayed outside. Our boat was moored just off the beach outside the church and we sat on one of the outriggers at five o'clock listening to the service and watching the sunrise before returning to our hosts who treated us to a special breakfast of sweet rice pudding wrapped in leaves. By seven o'clock we were back on board again and the boat was soon under way for a dive at Mambagi Reef.

There were many highlights on our journey round paradise. One of them was being surrounded by a school of dolphins who stayed with the boat joyously weaving between the hull and the outriggers. Then they disappeared as quickly as they had come. Another was a dive at Balioasag Island. There we watched fishermen who had gathered in small boats to fish for sharks. We didn't see them land any sharks and saw none ourselves whilst diving.

However, one of the dives which I would put in my world's top ten list took place off the tiny island of Pescador which we visited in a small outrigger canoe from the village of Moalboal on the western side of Cebu Island. It was one of those dives where everything went right. We were all very experienced divers in a harmonious group. We used the current to carry us on an underwater journey during which we circumnavigated the entire island and came up beside the boat where we started. It was dive number eighteen on the expedition and by the time we made it we were all co-ordinated. We dived in a foursome and as soon as we left the surface found ourselves being swept along like this-tledown on the wind. Probably because of the current the soft corals were all fully open to take advantage of the food being carried through their outstretched brilliantly coloured arms. The visibility was in the region of 100 feet and this enabled us to appreciate what for me was the most exotic and colourful display of soft coral I had ever seen, set in stunningly spectacular caves and overhangs in the submerged rock wall of the island. We descended to a maximum depth of about 100 feet always flowing with the current which left us with little opportunity to take pictures, but ferried us effortlessly past one scenic wonder after another like passengers on an open-topped bus on a mystery tour. Much of the time we were in the subdued blue light of deep water, but as the tour came to an end we rose into the pale bright blue sea that covered the sunlight-dappled hard corals that grew in profusion in the shallows.

The small outrigger was moored near an overhang in the soft coral rock of the island. We used up the last of our air under the boat taking pictures of a striped sea snake — a species none of us had seen before.

We left Cebu for a flight to Manila on Monday, 27 April 1981. On that same day one of the headlines in the Philippines Daily Express read 'BLIZZARDS SWEEP

UK: SNOW PILES UP.' Underneath it stated: 'London, April 26 — The worst April blizzards this century swept across the British Isles to pile snow drifts up to six feet in some parts on Saturday, causing widespread misery to humans, widespread death to newborn lambs and the destruction of early vegetable crops.

And the weathermen see no respite.'

The last words written on the same day in the expedition log were: 'We have not seen a drop of rain in our entire stay. The weather has been perfect — not even any strong winds to make the sea rough. The people have been fabulous. And we all have an adventure to tell.'

We did indeed have an adventure to tell. A few days later I was driving across the Pennines in thick snow to give a lecture in a remote village in the North York Moors near to where a man caught in the blizzard had lost his life in the snow.

★   ★   ★

But I was lucky, a few days later I escaped to fly to Australia where I dived on the Great Barrier Reef. We went out in a thirty-foot power boat and spent the night anchored on the reef eighty miles off shore. In my cabin I could hear the anchor chaffing on the coral — but could not be certain it wasn't the side of the boat rubbing against a coral head. I openly admit that I was nervous and hardly slept, getting up several times to check that our mooring was safe. When we sank off the island of Cabilao in the Philippines I could see the shore and knew I could swim to safety if I had to. However, even with my phenomenal luck, I wasn't certain I could make it back to the continent of Australia across eighty miles of shark-infested seas.

There is an amusing postscript to my diving adventures in the Philippines which makes an appropriate end to this book. John Cockerill, as I have said, had been on several of my expeditions but he rated the trip to the Philippines as the best holiday he had ever had. So much so that the following year he decided to return with his own party, with the particular intention of returning to Cabilao to dive the

Lighthouse Reef which he rated as one of the best dives in the world. So he contacted Stu Gould of Cebu Divers and duly returned to Cabilao aboard the same outrigger that had been patched up after its encounter with the bommie a year before.

As I have already mentioned John had become friendly with the headman on the island and on his return John re-introduced himself, then went off for a dive.

The group decided to sleep on the outrigger that night and as before went to sleep in their bunks whilst the crew slept on the roof. At 2.00 am John woke up to the sound of gurgling water. He floated off his bunk as the water rose quickly in the cabin.

'Oh no, not again!' he cried.

Having been through the routine one year previously, he knew the boat wouldn't sink completely so he assembled the passengers and crew on the foredeck. This time, however, there was no passing fisherman in a dugout canoe to give assistance.

So John volunteered to swim ashore and get help.

Having snorkelled across the reputedly shark-infested lagoon John took off his fins, walked up the beach and found his way to the headman's thatched house. He rattled the door. There was no reply. So he rattled harder. Eventually a bleary-eyed Filipino appeared who recognised him.

'Hallo, John,' he mumbled in half-awake surprise. 'What do you want at this ungodly hour?'

'You're not going to believe this,' said John, 'but . . .'